The Writing Occurs as Song

The Writing Occurs as Song

a Kelvin Corcoran Reader

Edited by
Andy Brown

Shearsman Books

Published in the United Kingdom in 2014 by
Shearsman Books Ltd
50 Westons Hill Drive
Emersons Green
BRISTOL
BS16 7DF

Shearsman Books Ltd Registered Office
30–31 St. James Place, Mangotsfield, Bristol BS16 9JB
(this address not for correspondence)

ISBN 978-1-84861-320-1
First Edition

CONTENTS

PART 3
APPROACHES

INTRODUCTION

This book offers a critical overview of the work of the British poet Kelvin Corcoran who, over nearly 30 years, has established a reputation as one of the most significant innovative British lyric poets; 'a giant of the middle generation' as Andrew Duncan has described him, placed between the radical poetics of the '60s and '70s and subsequent generations (Duncan *Heresy* 146). With the publication of 14 individual collections of poetry – including a *New and Selected Poems* in 2004 and a new and selected Greek Poems, *For the Greek Spring*, in 2013 – Corcoran has, according to Don Paterson in a review in *The Observer* 'allied a strikingly individual intelligence to a genuinely musical sensibility.' It is the widespread recognition of his critical intelligence and lyric precision that signals Corcoran as a leading inheritor of the British modernist tradition. It is also this critical appreciation from both mainstream *and* independent critics (Paterson *and* Duncan), alongside the selection of *Helen Mania* as the Poetry Book Society Choice in 2005, that perhaps marks Corcoran's work as an exemplar of a trend in British lyric poetry over the past 20 years: what I have identified in two earlier books as the 'Binary Myth' and what other writers and commentators have been identifying for some time as 'cusp' poetry, on the border of varying traditions. If this, perhaps, helps to *place* Corcoran somewhere on the map of contemporary poetry, then paradoxically none of it matters greatly to him. What seems to solely matter is the writing, reading and lived experience of poetry.

The critical essays collected here examine Corcoran's poetry from the publication of his first book, *Robin Hood in the Dark Ages* (1985), to *Words Through A Hole…* (2011). These essays were in preparation whilst *For the Greek Spring* (2013) was being published, and so mostly do not cover that book, although many of the poems in *Greek Spring* were published in earlier collections and are therefore referenced to those books. The contributors of these new essays represent a range of writing and academic backgrounds and demonstrate how varying critical approaches may illuminate a single oeuvre. The range of their approaches covers issues of place, identity and environment; the prose poem and ekphrasis; medicine; language and subjectivity; material conditions, postcolonialism and politics; Greece and England; myth and family myth; modernisms, and postmodern poetry and poetics, as well as the influences and traditions within which Corcoran's work is placed.

The essays are arranged around three conversations I held with Kelvin in 2012 and 2013. Each conversation is accompanied by a number of critical essays and a more 'personal reflection' from someone familiar with both Kelvin Corcoran the poet and Kelvin the man. Conversation one opens up questions of the myths and traditions behind Kelvin's poems, specifically those of (what he has sometimes called) 'Eng-a-Land' and his more recent focus on Greece. Themes from the conversation are developed in critical essays by David Herd on displacement and 'going to town'; Ian Davidson on place in *The Red and Yellow Book,* and Jos Smith on the historical politics of the pastoral in relation to contemporary settings, Greece and the politics of place. The Greek poems are discussed extensively by Peter Riley and the personal reflection of Part One comes from Lee Harwood who charts some key developments, pleasures and themes across Corcoran's oeuvre.

Conversation two moves on to examine poetic traditions, voice, song and the lyric, and is followed by critical essays from John Hall on song; Scott Thurston on the poetics and linguistic concerns of *Lyric Lyric,* and Simon Smith on the Late Modernist Lyric. The personal reflections from Kat Peddie in this section takes the form of a letter to Kelvin, focussing on the poet's lyric voice. The third and final section of the book – 'Approaches' – opens up other aspects of Kelvin's poetry. My own essay examines recurrent medical themes in Corcoran's 'autopathography' – the medical poems of illness and recovery. Zoe Brigley Thompson writes on the ekphrastic sequences *Your Thinking Tracts or Nations* and *Roger Hilton's Sugar,* while Martin Anderson's essay extends some of the concerns raised there into a wider political discussion of empire and trade. Finally, Luke Kennard examines the techniques and approaches to a specific aspect of Corcoran's work: the poems written in prose. The final conversation accordingly ranges through these varied aspects, alongside a final personal reflection from Alicia Stubbersfield, a poet who taught with Kelvin for several years. The book concludes with new poems from one of Kelvin's current projects, *Glenn Gould and Everything,* and an up-to-date bibliography of his works.

§

A study of Kelvin Corcoran's poetry might usefully begin with his first significant encounters with poetry, at the University of Essex, where he studied English from 1975 to 1978, and where fellow poets Ian Davidson and John Muckle were also studying. He was tutored by Douglas Oliver for a year, reading books from other writers who had taught there: Ed Dorn, Ted Berrigan, Alice Notley, Tom Raworth and Robert Lowell. He also studied practical criticism under Ralph Hawkins, in whose classes he was introduced to the work of Louis Zukofsky, George Oppen, Charles Olson, Frank O'Hara, John Ashbery, Andrew Crozier, Peter Riley, J.H. Prynne and others. 'Ralph Hawkins was generous,' Corcoran has said. 'My first copy of Olson's *Maximus Poems* was a photocopy, like a tree's worth! That was a discovery of considerable excitement, it was completely empowering. We were obliged to talk about the poems and I thought, *I won't be quiet*' (personal conversation). Around this time he also heard Basil Bunting reading, aged 75, an experience he describes as 'overpowering' and which 'lit up the world for me' (Allen & Duncan *Talking* 92). In a previous interview with Kelvin Corcoran, Andrew Duncan has raised the question about the existence of an 'Essex School' of poets, including Ralph Hawkins, Ian Davidson and Corcoran himself. Kelvin's reply dismisses the school as non-existent. Yet it was clearly an environment which helped the young poet discover his craft, and several of this volume's contributors raise it in their essays – Ian Davidson himself contributes an essay examining place in the early work of *The Red and Yellow Book* (1986).

Kelvin Corcoran went on to become an English teacher himself, at the same time beginning an MA at Warwick University. Alicia Stubbersfield's personal reflection towards the end of this book reflects on that period of Corcoran's working life and how it might have informed his poetry. Discussing the MA, Corcoran has said, 'I don't know how I thought I would do it. I started an MA, but I didn't finish it. I was going to write about Peter Riley, but stopped, because of various family crises, which had to come first; having to deal with my mother's death and my father's alcoholism at the same time, which kept my hands quite full' (personal conversation) – subjects that crop up again and again throughout his books. After leaving academia he carried on teaching and building a career, writing poetry, and having a family. Around this time (1985), Robert Vas Dias published Corcoran's first book, *Robin Hood in the Dark Ages*, and thereafter writing poetry became his main focus. Corcoran has described this first publication as 'not a book, it's a collection of poems arranged in sections' (*Talking* 93). Such 'arrangements' have remained important throughout his work, resisting the contemporary predilection for the short, stand-alone lyric poem – Corcoran's ambitions, whilst respecting the individual poem, have always seemed bigger, 'linking the last poem in one book to the first in the next' as if 'I had the idea I was writing one long poem' (96).

Existing critical essays on Corcoran's poetry are few. Andrew Duncan has included commentaries on Corcoran in his books, and David Kennedy has recently published on the ekphrastic poems, alongside varied reviews and articles that have appeared in magazines and websites. Andrew Duncan argues that Corcoran's poetic technique is based on 'dialectical switches' (*Heresy* 147), identifying a process in which 'a poem starts out with shared stories, 'myths' about England, and then jumps to similar myths about South Korea. The juxtaposition reveals a superordinate category – allowing thoughts about the nature of culture' (147). Whilst it is true that Corcoran's work is certainly dialectical – something he alludes to more than once in the conversations here – it is also true that many other forms of poetry (even ones that Duncan might identify as far more mainstream) similarly allow for 'thoughts about the nature of culture'. So what is it about Corcoran's work that is different?

Corcoran clearly uses temporal, spatial and contextual 'jump cuts' to bring different time frames, locations and subjects, into close proximity. Duncan describes this as obviously similar to 'a director cutting between different cameras' (*Heresy* 150), although Corcoran's work is far less visually representational than film. In his essay here, Luke Kennard extends the 'director' analogy in a discussion of Corcoran's prose poems, examining how these works are more like films of the interior world of the mind and language; films that are free to move with the rapid parallelism of myth. And it is to this word 'myth' that we will often find ourselves returning: from personal, local and family myths, to those of nations and whole cultures; an encompassing classicism made possible by Modernism, but reinvented by Corcoran with the cooler possibilities of the postmodern.

Alongside the innovations offered by post/modernist technique, Corcoran's other major contribution to the resources of the late modernist lyric resides in what he finds in the politics of the personal. Duncan has noted that despite the avant-garde surface, 'much of Corcoran's poetry is extremely emotional, and the accumulation of evidence of the outside world just involves us more firmly in his emotions about politics, love, and family tragedy' (*Failure* 276). Such arguments clearly place Corcoran in the 'innovative tradition' of British poetry, but with those words 'extremely emotional' and 'love and family tragedy' also highlight a tendency of the lyric poem towards personal expression, domestic realism and post 1950s 'confession'. With this traditional lyric subject matter underlying much of the work, is Corcoran really a lyric innovator? Even Duncan says that 'It is hard to point to any feature of Corcoran's style which was not developed in the Sixties' (277).

In his essay, Ian Davidson argues that a poet who only asks the reader to share in feelings of loss, or only to understand the maternal role in the poems, for example, is hardly adding to the resources of the lyric; a point that Corcoran himself makes in our first conversation. But Davidson detects greater complexities in Corcoran's technique that complicate and deepen the lyric. Furthermore, Corcoran's poems clearly follow on from the work of poets such as Tom Raworth and Lee Harwood, who also developed techniques from post-war American poets. Given what Corcoran has said about his education in these poets' work at Essex University, the influences of style and technique are not surprising. Yet the apparent dispassion of paratactic collage, with all its possibilities of postmodern irony is, perhaps, paradoxical when read alongside the clearly personal and overtly emotional. Corcoran is unafraid to let the paradox stand.

Corcoran's second publication, for example, *The Red and Yellow Book* (1986), was written, according to the author, when he was 'overwhelmed by my grief when my mother died' (Allen & Duncan 93). Corcoran describes his own technique in these early works as one in which 'I collage away quite happily with the domestic, the intense personal grief, Heidegger' (94). There is a distanced, collaged coolness tempering the work, but also an emotional directness, bringing the two together 'quite happily'. It is this even-handed approach that leads to Corcoran agreeing with Peter Riley's assertion that 'in poetry, the most intimate, the utterly personal is the most common, the most shared experience. I agree' (97), a theme to which he returns in the conversations of this book.

It is, perhaps, this interesting paradox in his work that accounts for Corcoran's real innovation, and which has elicited comments such as this from Ken Edwards: 'He collages domestic English and found language in these lyric poems, and he does it with tenderness, wit, sharp political awareness and quick-burning energy' (in *City Limits*, and used as a blurb on *The Red and Yellow Book*). If we are used to equating descriptors such as 'sharp', 'politically aware' and 'energetic' with 'innovative' lyric poetry, then perhaps we are not so much so with 'tender'; an adjective more often than not associated with traditional lyricism. Lee Harwood himself picks up on the 'tenderness' in Corcoran's work, noting again this fascinating personal/political question:

> His poems – dense, intense, filled with sharp fast thought – expose the horror, the 'swinish morality' of this world, its fraud and pretence, and the cruel greed of its rulers. The outrage is only lightened by the small acts and visions of tenderness in our lives. (Lee Harwood, cover blurb on *TCL*, Pig Press 1989)

In his personal reflection here, Lee Harwood revisits this dust-jacket blurb and finds it still pertinent: there is of course no reason why the coolness of postmodern technique, and the emotion of personal expression should not coexist in a poem. Lee Harwood himself, and now Kelvin Corcoran, are perhaps two of the best-known exponents of this in the contemporary British lyric poem.

A key to understanding how these tensions might coexist in Corcoran's work may lie in his use and understanding of myth. In discussing his extensive use of myths, Corcoran identifies the broader relevance of ancient myth to contemporary situations and problems:

> Imagine that the classical edifice of mythology is no such thing but an overlaying and retelling of competing localised myths and songs, arising out of a sort of civic pride, giving back meaning to the specific group. The ancient landscape overlays the modern and I see the mythology as local and useful and not detached from the everyday. (Allen & Duncan 95)

He goes on to say that 'I think [myth] is also a sort of code which tells us exactly what is happening in the present Oil Wars for instance' (95). For Corcoran 'Troy was a trade war for shipping routes and wheat, a newly self-styled western power against the east with Helen's abduction as a tabloid excuse for action' (96). There is much to unpick here, from mythic and socio-political structures, to critiques of empire, and the role of the quotidian in both poetry and politics. These themes are afforded appropriate discussion at length in several of the essays here, notably in

Martin Anderson's piece on empire and trade and Peter Riley's reading of the Greek poems. For Corcoran, these things are all of a piece: the ancient *is* modern; the personal and local *is* political; story and language *are* the ways in which we understand and communicate ourselves, from the individual to the civic to the national, crossing borders and times; the mythic, historic and political worlds *are* what we think with.

§

On a personal note, I first came to Kelvin's work through the Paladin anthology *the new british poetry* (1988) and, around the same time, a reading he gave at the Subvoicive poetry reading series run by Gilbert Adair in the upstairs room of a London pub. Walking home with another poet that night, I remember waxing lyrical about Corcoran as some kind of postmodern troubadour: politically astute but lyrically tender, engaged in alternative writing processes I was just getting to grips with. Above all, he struck me as songful. Since then I have followed everything he has written: there are few poets who possess not only a consummate lyric technique, but a pertinent and persuasive outlook in which politics, history, poetry, music and the personal give the fullest picture of a life lived through poetry as though it was meant; as if it really mattered; a profound fusion of technical facility with a committed world view.

Over a decade later, when I was directing the Arvon Foundation centre at Totleigh Barton, I invited Kelvin to tutor a writing course for a week with Lee Harwood and a dedicated group of student writers from Tonbridge. Despite the drama of the whole team coming down with the afflictions of an unidentified water-borne bug (washed into the water supply via a careless farmer's effluvia), I remember this as the beginnings of a friendship that has further cemented my fascination with the poems. On the course, Kelvin avoided all the usual creative writing advice of 'Show-Don't-Tell' and 'Writing from the Senses', and went straight for the lyric jugular: he played the students a recording of Basil Bunting reading *Briggflatts* and asked them to listen intently and then to sketch out a diagram of the musical dynamics of the poetry. It was an embodiment of Kelvin's own technique – the lived and working proof that *The Writing Occurs As Song*. This book is borne out of these contexts: a friendship, a long standing admiration of this poet's extraordinary oeuvre, and a conviction that Kelvin Corcoran's poetry is amongst the most significant, innovative lyric poetry of our time.

Andy Brown

WORKS CITED

Allen, Tim, and Duncan, Andrew. *Don't Start Me Talking: Interviews with Contemporary Poets.* Cambridge: Salt Publishing. 2006.
Allnutt, Gillian; D'Aguiar, Fred; Edwards, Ken and Roberts, Michele. eds. *the new british poetry.* London: Paladin. 1988.
Duncan, Andrew. *The Failure of Conservatism in Modern British Poetry.* Cambridge: Salt Publishing. 2003.
_____. *The Council of Heresy: A Primer of Poetry in a Balkanised Terrain.* Exeter: Shearsman Books. 2009.

PART I

ENG-A-LAND, GREECE AND EMPIRE

'There is obviously a distinct history of English poetry about Greece and classical matters, which you don't want to completely ignore.'
—Kelvin Corcoran

FIRST CONVERSATION

AB: *Kelvin, if we could, I'd like to begin with the English stories in your work and, later, the Greek. Your first book follows a historical rebel, Robin Hood, also relating to political events in present day England. There's also a notion of English politics in some of your later work. How do you think of the English story in your poetry?*

KC: In *Robin Hood*, I was assuming a mode of outrage at the then Tory government shenanigans, I imagine, the political use made of the Falklands war and the social divisiveness being engineered in the UK. Shouting at the television was a major engagement during that decade, which of course did no good. That's the context. I suppose it's the same sort of approach in some ways, though the experience of Greece comes later. History and history. If I can use examples, there's what I think of as a very English moment in the waiting-room queue in a recent poem, 'Hearing Mishearing Doug Oliver'. A good deal of that is about the public provision of care, and it's positive; in this case it's medical care and the memories and history that evokes, yet again. That earlier poem, when Thatcher is in town and I'm in the garden with the girls when they were toddlers, 'a jerky grey midget walks her goons'. That's pretty much the earlier mode. More recently it's no cheerier, in 'Season Below Ground'; that's my English landscape – motorways at night, the settlements to the sides, discarded by progress. But that's not the whole story. I think my attempts to write various accounts of the history of English poetry, or particular poets writing in English, or a theory of the ballad, no matter how jokingly, is about England, it draws that material into it.

AB: *You mean poems like 'From Where Song Comes'?*

KC: Well remotely in that poem, but even there it's where the singers end up, singing outside shops on the streets. But in the other poems in that part of *Hotel Shadow*, it's apparent I think. 'Sing Campion Song' might be a different sort of answer to your question. In the first place, Campion's lyrics, read or sung, are beautiful things. I suppose one contrast between these recent examples and the earlier writing is a different and expansive view of poetry and its possibilities, a recognition that history and politics are already in there, and to think you have to impose such material or awareness is a sort of gratuitous sentimentality which could end in sloganising, in an anti-poetry. Poetry already carries that history within itself, I think. It's already in a dialogue. What's the line at the end of that poem we talked about earlier in the Campion set, the one about old learning and money?

AB: *Here it is, 'If songs make us free we already have them all, / called conflict of interest in the history of the English jig.'*

KC: Yes that's it, that's what I'm trying to say here.

AB: *Clearly some of your reading of Greece is Romantic, whereas your reading of England (Eng-a-land as you often used to have it) can be coarser, perhaps, and that goes beyond a simple critique of it being Anglo-Saxon rather than Classical?*

KC: Well the two places are more entangled in the poetry than might be suggested in the question. Perhaps we're talking about earlier forms of tourism, which didn't just begin with the gentleman's grand tour. I don't know about 'Romantic'. Enraptured, perhaps? Romantic? What, after Shelley, Coleridge? Neither of whom set foot in Greece. Of course the only boat Coleridge had been on board before writing 'The Rime of the Ancient Mariner' was the Chepstow ferry. So maybe I've been wasting my time all along. Coleridge nearly went to Greece from Malta on a strategic expedition with Captain Leake to the Black Sea, securing supplies. Also, courtesy of Richard Holmes, Coleridge was certainly writing reports on the disposition of French forces around the Mediterranean, intelligence reports I suppose. Byron did of course go there, raised money for the cause, dressed up fancifully and died of a fever for the Greek revolution, but he's a special case as in most things. There was even support for making him the king of Greece once it was liberated. Arguably he's not a Romantic anyway; a wit and a wag rather, at his best in *Don Juan* – I agree with that view of the poetry I think.

AB: *But you are certainly concerned with the Romantic poets as part of a background to what you write?*

KC: Yes, I am, that's the case. I remember when I first started going to

Greece you would see telephone cards with pictures of Byron on them, and it was known and still is – it must be taught somewhere – that this foreigner, Lordy Viron, was a friend of Greece. The whole business of the relationship between Northern European gentlemen, scholars, antique thieves and Hellenophiles, is an interesting background; you don't want to be ignorant of that sort of history in somebody else's country.

I read somewhere that the grand tour was diverted to Greece because of the Napoleonic Wars in the North – it was safer – although of course Byron did involve himself in war in a possibly theatrical way. However, I think these figures are all rather more enmeshed in worldly matters than the term Romantic might imply. According to Ian Gilmour, it might be the case that when Byron went to Epirus he, unknowingly, was being used by the British authorities as a piece of sexual bait to keep Ali Pasha, the boss of the region, happily in the British cause against Napoleon. That's a curious story. I don't imagine Byron needed much persuading to enjoy the various pleasures on offer in Ali Pasha's court, but it seems he didn't know he was there to sweeten the Pasha's allegiance. But every age reinvents or forgets its Byron. His promotion of the Philhellenic cause, itself based on Romantic assumptions, is something else.

AB: *So you began to admit these stories as a context for your own poems in Greece?*

KC: There is obviously a distinct history of English poetry about Greece and classical matters, which you don't want to completely ignore. My reading of it has been quite literal I suppose; I took it literally. I don't mean the Renaissance mechanism of nymphs and shepherds, but the real import of classicism from then onwards. Ha, oh well, that's my debt; I thought I was just having a holiday. But there it is from the beginning of English poetry in all its forms, variously engaged with classicism through to the Romantics, and to the Philhellenism when modern Greece came to exist after the revolution against the Ottoman Empire. Shelley wrote 'Hellas' during the revolution without going there: 'We are all Greeks' he famously says in the preface, espousing Philhellenism and 'the double continuity' – the idea that contemporary revolutionary Greeks are the inheritors of the virtues of ancient Greeks, and that all Europe owes Greece its cultural origins. Well that second argument itself continues, subject to much re-examination from the likes of Martin Bernal. Any reading of Greece now is, of course, tested by what has happened because of the financial crisis from 2008 onwards; the immiseration most Greeks are facing, which, although not unprecedented, is some distance from ideas about imported classical forms and frames of reference.

AB: *One could argue a similar thing about sectors of the British public being poorer now, lied to by a ruling class, or at least by bankers who pulled a fast one. And an earlier poem in* TCL *(1989) ends with the phrase 'the corruption absolute, normal'?*

KC: Yes you could say that, but there is a marked difference of degree between the UK and Greece, as far as I can see. If you consider unemployment rates, figures on homelessness and the removal of business to neighbouring countries – Albania and Bulgaria for example. Teachers in Athens are taking food into school to feed their students and I've read that there's a marked rise in parents giving up their children to orphanages and other institutions because they cannot feed them. Whilst at the same time in the UK, there is a projected rise in childhood poverty because of welfare changes instigated by the present government. The similarity between Greece and the UK is, of course, that those suffering the crisis are not those who caused it and they will not be the ones to profit by it.

AB: *When you're in Greece do you have a sense that those ancient myths, stories and songs are still part of an everyday culture?*

KC: If it's part of daily life, then that mythology is still in the air: there's an awareness of it in place names, for example, and in the perception of what happened here a long time ago, as well as in the practices of the Orthodox Church. It's the nearness of the mythological intelligence, I think. It's like a different form of television. It's shared. A key aspect for me in this is not so much a poet's enraptured glances off the surface of a culture, but what might be a surprising continuity...

AB: *Can you give me an example of that 'surprising continuity'?*

KC: Yes, it's not that Romantic notion that modern Greeks are the same as ancient Greeks, and you know what, they're the cultural grandparents of us all. What I mean is how the details of pre-Olympian myth and ritual seem to articulate experiences that we now count as our most intimately lived and commonly shared. That's my assumption. I also like being in the climate and physical conditions in which these things happened, as perhaps in the poem 'Apokriatika' and differently, perhaps more dramatically in poems like 'My Journey to Euripides.' Clearly in the 'Apokriatika' example I'm taking the Lent rituals back to older folklore, but that's not the point really – it's the surprising and emotional revelations the process offers; the roots of it still live in us it seems.

Jane Harrison is also partly behind this for me. I don't know if professionals in the field still read her, but I think she is remarkable. If nothing else, just imagine that masculine, scholarly Edwardian world out of which she was writing. However, read professionally or not, she counts in this; examples as in *Themis*, and what she makes of the Hymn of the Kouretes about the infant Zeus, and the ideas of the sacred, at origin, as nothing but the social, the communal. So Apollo too was originally, maybe, the boy from the village whose parents were both still alive, and he led the procession through the village carrying the green stick during the springtime. In this version then, the mythology of Apollo perhaps, suggestively, comes out of just that practice. That's really interesting, that the sacred is nothing other than that; in this case the well-chosen boy from the village. So, as I've said before, when my friend Yannis says, "Ah, but what Homer says is wrong; what we say around here is…", well, then I listen.

AB: *You mean the different version behind your poem 'Helen Mania'?*

KC: Yes, that alerted me to the diverse, localised, multiplicity of myth opposed to the remote, the monolithic. This led to the notion that the great edifice of classicism (manufactured by German and British nineteenth-century scholars, and espoused by the Philhellenes as the glorious adolescence of Europe) is no such thing. Instead it's a mixture of endlessly various accounts and practices given with a particular local colour and civic pride, a sort of local, autochthonic television if you like.

AB: *Like in the long poem 'News of Aristomenes'?*

KC: Exactly. That is where the 'Ah but what we say around here...' comes in. As a preface to that poem, I admit that my usual source, Yannis, knows zilch about Aristomenes. But it's certainly the case that Greek friends in response to casual questions will dig out books and translate for you, or tell you what they know about Aristomenes, for example, or a different version of the story of Helen and Paris. Pausanias, second century A.D., is still a very good guide to what you might find out if you root around. That's a different issue to the Romantic notion of classical continuity.

AB: *Of course. It strikes me that the collective – both the social and the family – is important here. Your poem, 'The Actual Poem About My Father' relates to what you've called elsewhere 'the impossible archaeology of the family'. That idea of unearthing story, its archaeology, and what stories we tell ourselves as 'families' are very important to you?*

KC: That's partly what I mean by the two places becoming entangled in the poetry. There might be an English version of something I've experienced in Greece. I grew up as everyone does in a particular set of circumstances. My version was a big family, poor and with a mother who died young because of my father's alcoholism. It's there scattered around in several poems and in that poem you mention. Yes, it's important to me, it might be a feature of becoming middle aged, but also because it turns out to be about more than just the personal, biographical history. The family archaeology unloads issues of class, political history, war from an English context I think, though it's not unusual for this to be prompted by a Greek occasion.

AB: *Do you think that the sense of singing such family songs is similar to the Greek singing of myths and songs, in that the Greek myths too are an 'archaeology' of the collective family?*

KC: Yes and no. What sense can be made of human behaviour in the distant past tells us how like those people we are and how unlike them we are. An example for your question would be the poem 'Apokriatika'. We're travelling across Greece on Clean Monday, the Monday before Lent, with all the rituals associated with that. It's mixed up with memories of things my mother used to say, and other family stories, and I realised these things several decades afterwards. In Greece, for me, my own family memory is provoked by that atmosphere, reading a little and being in front of all that myth and the ritual that accompanies those myths. They have absolute emotional value still; it's a language. It's also perhaps a transformation of those experiences. I think in poems like 'Apokriatika', the childhood memories appear in the middle of these quite other moments, simple moments of enjoyment of the communal experience. They're not depicted as any sort of crisis, the memory is clarified. We were talking earlier about that curious metaphor in Kerényi…

AB: *The metaphor of 'beads strung along a thread', in which the beads represent 'festival time' and the thread represents 'linear time'?*

KC: That's the one. But I've gone back through his book, *Dionysus Archetypal Image of Indestructible Life*, and I seem to have made up some of this! He uses that nice metaphor of the beads and the thread to distinguish two different Greek words for life, Zoë / ζωή and Bios / βίος. The first indicates the life of all living creatures, and is unlimited – life in general. That's the thread 'upon which every individual bios is strung like a bead.' The second term designates a specified life as characterised differently from other lives, the root of the word – biography.

Another resonance of the term Zoë / ζωή is 'the time of being'. This is a continuous time of being in the individualised life Bios / βίος as long as that particular life endures, the bead hangs on the thread. And this is where I've made something up, or simply can't find the reference. I've read the thread and beads image in my memory as drawing a distinction between different, but related, experiences of time: the linear and the event, the awareness of a past and possible future, and the act of the present moment. The bead, as the individualised event of ritual, the various mysteries that accompany myth in ancient Greek religion, can be seen to allow some insight into the unlimited and continuous experience. Perhaps I've confused this with reading about the seasonal rituals and the year-daemon elsewhere, propitiation reaching out to a future based on what was learnt in the past – that the harvest comes in and the animals mate, including the human ones – so you can carry on and have something to eat.

AB: *So is this a useful metaphor for you, for what poetry is, or does? For example in relation to the expansive sequence versus the stand-alone lyric* *poem: the threaded beads versus the single bead?*

KC: Well, in my misunderstanding and appropriation of the image, it's the difference between the individual bead and the thread it hangs upon, I guess. But to pursue it, thinking of Spicer's ideas on the discrete, one poem and the serial poem, or book, is perhaps becoming dubious; we're certainly stretching the poor metaphor.

It's not Kerényi's fault. My misunderstanding of it has allowed me to think about the ambiguous experience of different kinds of time, and in as much as poetry is a medium working through time, sustained or brief, with its own internal temporal dynamics, then yes, I suppose my botched memory of the metaphor does say something about different types of poetry, the extended or expansive with its plural ways, and the isolated or discrete. With or without the exhausted metaphor, this second type of poem, as Spicer said, doesn't really exist, it can't. So, yes, you could take the metaphor like that, but it's all nothing unless the song rings true in the very moment, in the vocal line, and it might be far from an obvious prosody how that can be made to happen.

AB: *Extending the idea of the personal and the collective story, you've talked about the ways in which myths overlay contemporary stories and history, and that they tell us something about what is going on in current trade wars and oil wars for example?*

KC: I think they do, yes. The past is always present and it's obvious in a different way for me in Greece than in the UK. Modernism in poetry is obsessed with antiquity. Bunting states the Poundian line very directly, simply: 'To appreciate present conditions / collate them with those of antiquity.' So it's not unusual to think of the Trojan War as a trade war, as a way of protecting or claiming resources, and the connection to recent wars in the Middle East is apparent in that sense.

AB: *This has been a feature in your work at least from* Backward Turning Sea *and onwards? I was thinking of a poem like 'Over the Calm, Clear Shining Water'?*

KC: Yes, that's in there. 'From the Hen-Roost' pursues that sort of speculation. It also involves a notion of the ways in which what we take to be family or personal history is really part of (and entangled in) the complex and repeated patterns, with added variations, of imperial history. It's interested me for some time; it's hardly a unique concern obviously. When I used to teach post-colonial literature to A-level students, I used to ask them to go and track back some family history that shows involvement in the history of the British Empire. After some talk to grandparents and digging out old photographs and family stories, none of the students came back empty handed. Grandparents, or even older relatives (who had either come from or served in former parts of the empire), well, both normally, they *were* the story. It involved all the students, and what they were reading became less remote.

If we go back to the poem you mention, 'Over the Calm...', I suppose that's a different kind of answer to your question – there's no extended family archive business going on there – but the past and the present *are* involved with one another in the poem. The title is a translation of a line from an anonymous Greek lyric. As epigraph, the stanza is so astonishing, it prompted the rest of the poem; it reached out and made the rest of the poem. But also the setting in Greece speaks for itself, and it's absolutely to my advantage, for instance, that the molluscs which were the source of the purple dye for imperial Roman robes, lie off the coast of Cape Matapan, just down the coast, and they were used up, all gone, the end, even for Rome. It's instructive isn't it? Writing those poems, and some of the longer pieces in recent books, seems for me to involve catching up the apparently remote but significant past. Do you think the texts and translations collected by Pritchard in *The Ancient Near East* have always sounded so contemporary?

AB: *Certainly. We were also discussing earlier that poetry, story and myth provide collective values and meanings, perhaps a scope, a world view – even if that power has dissipated somewhat in Western culture – but there's the potential power in poetry to tell that story; to protest about its failings?*

KC: Historically, obviously, it has. If the poetry isn't about something, then why bother? Having said that, there is poetry around that seems to set out to deny it's about anything, apart from the impossibility of being about anything. So, rather than that type of dysfunctional product, you want poetry to be about something and to answer something in you and in others. It would certainly be ambitious to dream of collective value in the context you mention.

I've been re-reading William Carlos Williams – he wasn't shy of saying a thing or two which might play here: 'It is difficult / to get the news from poems / yet men die miserably every day / for lack / of what is found there.' There's recognition of collective value and the worth of poetry in one. What other sort of value is there? What, idiosyncrasy? But, as for poetry as protest, that next step, I don't know. The impulse to object, to protest, is clearly not the same as having an impact on the thing you're objecting to – I wish I wish I wish; Tinkerbelle thinking, which of course won't stop the whole inclination. But poetry as protest? It's a popgun. Full spectrum dominance, or whatever the current version of that doctrine is now, versus a popgun; a poem against the suited or robed executives of Houston and Riyadh? Do you think a poem ever changed anything?

AB: *Well, according to Auden, poetry makes nothing happen...*

KC: Right. Thinking of Shelley and those great political poems of 1819, 'The Mask of Anarchy', 'Song to the Men of England' and others; it's exultant, stirring, emphatic poetry which, with hindsight, at best reflected the way democratic thinking was going, articulated a version of the radical zeitgeist. Did they change anything? Were they even read at the time? They should have been, from every available platform, but I don't imagine they were. Shelley was in Italy during these events and those poems weren't published until, what? 'The Mask of Anarchy' in 1832, long after the Peterloo massacre; 'Song to the Men of England' in 1839. So their value, their impact, even then, is historical, and yet they are still contemporary, still speak to us. That nobody's listening, and certainly not those in power, doesn't stop you wanting to object. Every thought calls out. Ridiculously, I've written poems addressed to George W. Bush as *imperator*. It's ok, I know he didn't read them, he certainly didn't reply so far. Do you think he's taken to reading poetry now? I still go on about such matters, evidently. So, I don't know. Thank you for asking the protest question, I can't answer it, that's my answer.

'ANOTHER LANGUAGE LIKE OURS': KELVIN CORCORAN'S LYRIC DISPLACEMENTS

DAVID HERD

'Going to town'

For poets writing in the middle of the twentieth century, it was a matter of some importance to identify the act of composition with the parameters of a given socio-political space. This was not new, hardly, in itself, peculiar to twentieth-century poetry; one could readily name (and therefore doesn't need to) any number of pre-twentieth-century poets for whom such an identification was necessary. There is, though, a substantive sense in which from, say, 1946, to, say, 1970, the act of writing poetry was especially closely connected to the fabric of a given socio-political environment. 1946 was the year William Carlos Williams published the first volume of *Paterson*; it was in 1970, with the death of Charles Olson, that the production of *The Maximus Poems* came to a stop. Between times one could mention the example of Frank O'Hara, or, more locally to Kelvin Corcoran, the case of Roy Fisher. It is part of the specific gravity, in other words, of mid-twentieth-century poetry that the city, as idea and reality, was integral to the act of composition. This, I would suggest, is the backdrop to Corcoran's early poem 'Going to Town':

> The first lights of town, the fixed stars
> on the fovea shine the arc of arrival
> the neighbourhood dislocation shock absorbed
> each day; go forward, kouroi diastole a charge
> in the blood light to both sides
> and I'll be over by eight
> (*Robin Hood* 9)

Such is the 'neighbourhood dislocation' here that one cannot in any straightforward sense place the speaker: we know that he'll be over by eight, but where he is going (amid all the interruptions) the poem declines to make clear. What is clear is that whatever or wherever this place is, its status is critical to the act of writing. It is, as the poem says,

a compositional device and the place
is all around you, unlike the market
up or down, the financial world tonight
but no change, the ports stay closed. (9)

'Going to Town' is from Corcoran's first collection, *Robin Hood in the Dark Ages*, published in 1985. What the book's title announced was a concern with displacement. What does it mean, we are immediately invited to wonder, to displace a figure as familiar to us as Robin Hood? Such displacement goes to the heart of Corcoran's poetics, and not least to the issue of his sense of sociopolitical space. The lines quoted are significant in this regard. What they present is a young poet already writing consciously in a modernist tradition for which identification with such a space is critical to the act of inscription. Whatever else Corcoran's town is, it is, as the poem insists (and as one could equally say of Williams' Paterson, Olson's Gloucester or Fisher's Birmingham) 'a compositional device'. The difference lies in the nature of the space itself; Corcoran, that is to say, in the act of writing, goes to 'town' instead of to 'city'. This is partly a Midlands thing. Where I grew up in the Midlands, 'going to town' was a major event, the word 'town' standing in for any number of geopolitical environments, from village to city and all points in between. If you were going to town, broadly speaking, you were going out, about to have fun, ready to let your hair down. In the context of Corcoran's poetry, however, it means more than this; is more than an instance of a poet inhabiting the vernacular. For Corcoran, this is to say, the recurring reference to the category of 'town' constitutes a significant departure, an aesthetic shift.

To appreciate what's at stake in that decision, it is helpful to consider the definitions. 'Town' is easy enough. As the *Concise Oxford English Dictionary* has it, a town is 'A built up area with a name, defined boundaries, and local government, that is larger than a village and generally smaller than a city.' Etymologically it comes from the Old English *tûn*, meaning 'enclosed piece of land, homestead, village', hence the suffix –'ton', as in Wolverhampton, Drakes Broughton, or Boston. 'City' is a more complex term, or rather, a term with complications. In the UK it is 'a large town, in particular a town created a city by charter and typically containing a cathedral.' In North America, on the other hand, as the dictionary records, it is 'a municipal centre incorporated by a state or province.' Etymologically the word is richer than the word 'town', which goes back directly, and without any real accretion of connation, to the Old English monosyllable that points to a minimally defined human settlement. City, of course, routes through the old French *cité*, and back to the Latin *civitas*, from *civis* meaning citizen. Historically, in other words, there is a politics to the city; a politics of accreditation which constitutes citizenship, or what one can call belonging.

That this politics matters in the context of a discussion of twentieth-century poetry is clear from the example of Olson. Thus, for all that Gloucester, Massachusetts has the bearing of a fishing town, it is critical to Olson that it is in fact (in the American sense of incorporation) a city. Olson is not a Latinist (as he makes clear in 'The Kingfishers') and so the network of terms around the civic are not central to his rhetorical scheme. Instead (although he is no Greek either) he settles on the idea of the *polis*, in which term the question of belonging – the politics of accreditation – is, in fact, more pronounced. If this were an essay about Olson, or about the mid-twentieth-century city poet, it would at this point start to explore the question of civic membership by pointing to the practice of open-field composition. Olson, that is, in his primary formal gesture, outreaches the exclusions of the *polis*, even as he draws them into view. My point, though, instead, is that as he inherits that tradition, Kelvin Corcoran declines the connotations of the city by reverting to the much less politically fraught geopolitical context of the town. Again this could be a Midlands thing; it would have been difficult for a West Midlands poet starting out in the 1980s, with the example of Roy Fisher behind him, to make the city his zone. Again also, though, it is more than that, because Corcoran knows exactly what he is doing when, from that early poem right through until his sixth collection *Lyric Lyric* (the period of his development this essay is concerned with) he repeatedly goes to town. Consider, for instance, the following lines from his 1990 collection *The Next Wave* in which we are:

> Inside the non-human scale
> rising before the sun
> cars drive away,
> air tubes blue street
> semantic drift pervades
> towns displaced under heat.
> (*Next Wave* 30)

There he is again, going to town, and in this case linking the idea with the quality of displacement. Perhaps the best instance of 'going to town', though, is the opening poem of *Qiryat Sepher*, from the section titled 'Ready to Go':

> after all the twentieth century and you
> touch down on a street in a town;
> it possessed the rest of my life,
> slave labour then freed prisoners
> in rubble of house and garden
> stumble to balalaika and speech
>
> under a late and civil sky
> close but never a natural colour
> a common jigsaw of window views
> an actor walk by in an unfixed suit,
> oh stuff my mouth with kisses
> your athletic limbs and lazy heartbeat
>   (*Qiryat Sepher* no page numbers)

There are several things one might mention here, elements this essay will come back to. One might mention, for instance, the historical sweep of the opening line, the immediate effect of which is to claim the tradition of modernist poetics (the poem nodding, as it goes, to O'Hara's great early poem of modernist inheritance, 'Memorial Day 1950'). One might notice the 'unfixed suit', the category of the 'unfixed' being critical to Corcoran's work. One might observe the implied background of political and social exclusion sketched in by the line 'slave labour then freed prisoners'. What the poem establishes, in a large sense, however, is the overarching significance of 'going to town', where the phrase implies both a settling on (and in) a specific kind of geopolitical environment, but where it also implies (in the colloquial sense) doing something with great enthusiasm or abandonment. What Corcoran presents us with, in other words, is a writing which declines certain historically inscribed limits. It is a poetry, as I want to suggest, of lyric displacement.

GEOGRAPHIES

As the opening statement of Corcoran's third book, the poem from 'Ready to Go' constitutes a deft and highly accomplished re-assertion of themes and issues that had defined his first two collections. Already with this poem Corcoran presents what one might think of as a signature brevity, phrases hung together in airy, Miró-like structures. This is not, principally, a poetry of development but a poetry of juxtaposition in which the fragment, clutched from its implied context, is used to fashion unforeseen units of sense. The significance of the category 'town' in such a structure is that it is conceptually un-determined by the issues of identity and belonging that are historically integral to the category of the city. In this late-twentieth-century statement of poetic departure, in other words, the largely unspecified town-scape is critical to the poem's act of thought.

The background to such an unspecified townscape – that environment, as the poem has it, that the twentieth century comes inevitably to touch down on – is what one might term an unsettled geography. Here again the contrast would be with Olson, for whom attention to the realities of a given geography is core to poetic practice. How the locality of Gloucester is actually configured is of critical importance to the design of Olson's epic poem. Corcoran's poetry can similarly be thought to emerge from a sense of the geographic, the form of the writing deriving equally from its engagement with questions of space. Where Corcoran differs is in his refusal to present a pre-existing arrangement or set of contours. What we find ourselves repeatedly passing through in Corcoran's poetry is a series of abruptly displaced environments. Geography, that is to say, in Corcoran's work, is not a pre-text for poetic dwelling (to use the Heideggerean term) but a pre-condition for expressions of motion.

The poem from 'Ready to Go' establishes the technical basis of such a sense of motion. Thus if the principle of the poem is juxtaposition not development, the basic operation of the juxtaposition is a shift of scale. In the opening stanza we pass from a totalising evocation of the twentieth century to an arrival in a given (though unspecified) town; from an image of an individual life to an abstract articulation of human labour; to stumble finally from the apparent specifics of garden and rubble on to the abstractions of 'balalaika and speech'. The second stanza performs a similar set of oscillations, Corcoran's line shifting from the distance of the 'late and civil sky' to the relative proximity of a jigsaw of windows, and from the momentary stability of the appearance of a given human actor in an environment to the outrageous intimacy and interruption of a hungering mouth. One way to think about such a poetry might be to say that as we read it we don't know where we are, that its characteristic shifts and deviations leave us bereft of any sense of place. But this is not quite the phenomenological effect, not quite the way things present themselves in Corcoran's work. What the writing offers instead is a geography in which all the scales of human perspective might at any point be adverted to; in which a range of possible view points, from the socially abstract to the uncomfortably intimate, are constantly available as means of imagining bodies in space.

The untitled opening poem of *Lyric Lyric* presents a development of this mode:

> The helicopter cuts cold air,
> I work in London but live here
> shredding light on frigid grass
> my animals eat and grow:
> shattered in an obscure tongue
> lyrical ballads endure.
>
> Fog rolling over square fields,
> I go the straight song
> straight music drives me,
> it lacks only notes, words;
> the compact town's design
> fixes real business spread.
>
> Paired down to working parts,
> breeze blocks and depletion
> scabbed across the land:
> the human meaning
> out of the dark dream
> breathing immediate words.
>   (*Lyric* 3)

The key markers of this poem can be said to be geographical, even, perhaps, in a text-book sense: we are given London as a point of orientation, are told where the animals feed, we are shown 'fog rolling over square fields' and are given glimpses of an industrially scarred land. It is a poem, in other words, which thinks in terms of human presentations of space. What it explicitly declines is the predominance of any one such presentation. No vantage point, not even the commanding vantage of the helicopter in the opening line, is accorded the kind of authority of perspective which the mid-twentieth-century city poem took to be a prerequisite of utterance. Of the poets mentioned, it is Olson who most clearly fixes the authoritative point of view, *The Maximus Poems* being a sustained intervention in the life of the city of Gloucester by Olson's eponymous narrator. 'Maximus' provides the angle of vision from which the poem's commentary clearly proceeds. But if Olson's narrative persona is unusual in the degree to which it overbears on his poem, it is nonetheless the case that in Williams, O'Hara and Fisher, the commentary is uttered from a clearly articulated perspective. In each case the comings and goings of the city are overseen by a singular poetic presence or point of view. For Olson himself, such singularity of view was so central to the construction of the poem that he worked it up into a theory, his Black Mountain seminar series eventually published as *The Special View of History* being a statement of the unavoidability of the situated view. In fact Olson's title is a little misleading. Grounded as his thinking was in the development and realities of a given place, what his theory equally amounted to was a special view of geography. To think poetically, according to Olson, was to think through the subjective framework accorded by a given place.

It is precisely such framing that the untitled opening poem of *Lyric Lyric* declines to accept. What Corcoran offers instead is a way of registering space that resists the governance of a prevailing view. Thus, while geography is plainly crucial to the poetry's thought, while the writing still presents itself in terms of geography's markers, Corcoran actively refuses an image of the relation between people and landscape which fixes a person to a given site. What he provides, instead, is an image of the relation between person and environment informed first and foremost by the quality of movement. And as the poetry moves so the landscape swims in and out of view, sometimes surveyed by a helicopter, sometimes obscured by fog rolling though fields. It's not that we don't know where we are when we read Corcoran's poetry, it's that we are always having to think again about how any such sense of location is framed. It is a poetry in which the reader's sense of geography is not encouraged to settle, but is adjusted rather, through a series of startling juxtapositions, to an ongoing impression of re-location.

BORDERS

A writer not mentioned so far, in connection with Kelvin Corcoran's emergent poetic of the 1980s and 1990s, is John Ashbery. To set Ashbery alongside Olson and O'Hara in this context is to propose a substantive debt to the New American Poetry. This is not, I think, a misapprehension. Corcoran's writing bears clear traces of his American reading; it is integral, I want to suggest, to his understanding of lyric displacement. To underscore the point, or rather, to indicate that the point was underscored, consider by way of illustration the author page of *The Next Wave*, the opening sentences of which tell us: 'Kelvin Corcoran was born in 1956 near Evesham in Worcestershire. He gained a B.A. in English at the University of Essex in 1978. He worked as a nursing auxiliary and assistant museum caretaker and has been a teacher since 1980.' (*Next Wave* 55) Evesham in Worcestershire is interestingly situated. It is 18 miles south of Redditch and a little further south east of Bromsgrove, both newly developed postwar feeder towns for the industrial West Midlands. It is as near again, however, to Worcester and only a few miles north of Cheltenham. The closest it comes to a literary association (excluding Stratford) is probably Adlestrop. Evesham, in other words, is pretty much at the heart of middle England, a corner of Worcestershire that will be forever Elgar. Largely for this reason, one might suppose, the photograph above the author statement shows a young Kelvin Corcoran wearing a Jerry Lee Lewis t-shirt. The dislocations of text and image are consequently numerous. It matters, of course, that Corcoran's degree was from Essex, the English department where Ed Dorn taught at the invitation of Donald Davie. One might notice also that the line of biography – nursing auxiliary, caretaker – recalls the kind of biographical statement that introduced Don Allen's New American poets to their readers; as people, in other words, with lives like the reader's own. Corcoran, the statement tells us, is the kind of person who holds down a job and goes to town. It is a presentation in a tradition of author images that goes all the way back to Whitman's artfully casual photograph on the fly-leaf of the first edition of *Song of Myself*. The t-shirt, as the logo below the image of a piano keyboard reports, is from Jerry Lee Lewis' most recent European tour.

It is a matter of enduring interest that for some British poets of the postwar period, the most influential aesthetic models were to be found in the US. The larger cultural and economic reasons for this have been well documented. At the level of individual biography, what the New American poetry offered British poets was a form of poetic radicalism that constituted, among other things, an escape from the connotations of class. That Ashbery became part of the American mix for Corcoran is apparent from his poetry's geographies, from the shifts of scale and perspective that provide the basic technical framework of his work. Where Corcoran differs among British readers of Ashbery, however, is in the purpose he puts him to. What Ashbery permits, in other words, in Corcoran, is a significantly politicised mode of displacement.

One way to read Corcoran's early poetry is as a refraction of the effects of Thatcherism. Graduating in 1978, and so coming on to the labour market just as the Conservatives came to power following the winter of discontent, Corcoran's development as a poet coincides precisely with the emergence of Thatcherite politics. What he offers, among other things, is a report on a landscape accelerating towards industrial ruin. As if to recall Olson among the remains of the Maya, Corcoran reads the hieroglyphs of his father's generation's work life, interpreting the increasingly alien industrial acronyms, the left-overs of full employment: MEB, ICI. One reads Thatcherite feedback also in Corcoran's report on the towns, the townscapes of the 1980s being among the most significant battlegrounds of that politically divided period. Faced with an antagonistic political centre, town hall representatives struggled to defend local services and infrastructures and so, among a range of oppositional strategies, the insistence on civic autonomy became a form of political response. It was a matter of some consequence in the 1980s, how one represented the cities and the towns.

Against the background of this deeply fraught socio-economic landscape, the larger question, and one to which poetry in the Modernist tradition was well equipped to speak, was how, in defending social gains and positions, to avoid recourse to statements of atavism. It was a question which emerged from various social quarters and for all political actors. Thus just as industrial decline could induce forms of class nostalgia, and as political centralization could prompt oppositional assertions of regional identity, so for the Thatcherite government one possible response to these oppositional forces was the super-atavism of national identity. Such resistance as people were articulating locally was to be soothed away (so it was hoped) by appeals to shared national inheritance. Whether against enemies from within (the NUM, Liverpool City Council) or without (the Argentine government, European Union administrators) the government of the moment wrapped itself in the flag.

One repeatedly finds the trace of this, the refracted version, in Corcoran's fragmented appropriation of the English lyric tradition. Just as Robin Hood is displaced on to the dark ages, so in 'A Political Poem' (from that first volume), Corcoran writes through snatches of Blake:

> In town I wear a huge cowboy hat,
> my mother laughs behind me
> the wind in our faces
> seven births five children
> and poverty, she arrives
> at love, my hat flaps its wings
> my wife and my mother hold on
> laughing as we go home
> (*Robin Hood* 30)

Deeply invested in the possibilities of lyric as he is, Blake is a most important resource for Corcoran. At no point in his poetry, however, are we presented with the Blakean vision in its entirety, whole and intact. What we are offered is not a re-vision of Albion, but a contemporary poetics within which Blake is one form of verbal charge. What results is a poetry which carries a sure sense of history, but for which no historical moment or episode is held to be exemplary.

What one finds, rather, in Corcoran's poetry of the '80s and '90s is a necessarily complex, political radicalism. That the writing is oppositional is clear from its socio-economic markers. This is a poetry deeply troubled by the impact on individual lives of historical decline and short-term recession, a writing in which the poor are never magicked away. It is also, however, a poetry which refuses, in the face of economic rupture, to settle for easy solidarities. Above all what Corcoran declines is a default to pre-existing cultural identity. Consider the following, untitled lines from *The Next Wave*:

Deep waves form in mid-ocean,
the stuff is in my mouth,
riding the tube scattered farmers
bear the living work
arranged in Asia Minor,
trouble makers and migrants
toil all day, read all night,
transparent speech and trade
reclaim the perfect body.

The idea was simple;
banish feeling to the borders,
fall sky flapping, back lit,
civic contact bitten down to sense
tariffs and national traits seal it,
heretics singing all night duty.
                (*Next Wave* 22)

In its declaratory address ('The idea was simple'), and in its shifting, liminal geography ('banish feeling to the borders,/ fall sky flapping, back lit'), this is a poem which is unthinkable without Ashbery. The example of Ashbery, that is to say, makes the poem's structure of thought possible. By the same token, this is not a poem that one could possibly mistake for Ashbery, its context and purpose too acutely political. What one finds in Corcoran's early work is a poetry deeply engaged with the real politics of its moment, a poetry which transforms the Ashberyan gesture of deferral by writing it into the British context. Above all, then, what Corcoran gains from Ashbery is a readiness to transgress and outreach borders, to deny the foreclosures of identity on which exclusions are found. If it is not possible in any simple way to paraphrase the forgoing lines, what is clear is that the border, and the banishments of the border, are where the politics happens. The focus of the lines are the 'trouble makers and migrants', attention to which is coupled with a desire for the perfect body. The poem is having none of it, though, which is why the migrants in question are toiling and reading.

Corcoran is not under any illusion that complex poetry in the Modernist tradition can intervene directly in conflicted political affairs. As the untitled poem just quoted goes on to report:

> She said to her companion
> – it's too stupid for words,
> what happened to the forward man
> pressing through the crowds,
> just one poem would do – no chance.
>   (ibid)

Just one poem will never do, and nor will the image of the forward man, addressing the crowds from his advanced position. Neither, however, does this invalidate the complex aesthetic task Corcoran's poetry has set itself. Thus as a short and again untitled prose poem from *Lyric Lyric* has it:

> Do you think I'm trying to make this difficult?
> You are not watching the disintegration of anything,
> where the first push went opening sound reduced
> to the scabby politics of acquaintance. Stuff it. The
> ripped voice makes us free.
>   (*Lyric* 20)

'The scabby politics of acquaintance' is a densely polemical phrase, suggesting various images of allegiance from the claims of national identity to the antagonisms of the picket line. To resist all such forms of acquaintance is to court the charge of disintegration, as if the only thing the poetry can achieve is further social and cultural breakdown. But the poem stands its ground as the phrase 'The ripped voice makes us free' announces something like the underlying claim of Corcoran's poetics. The ripped voice is the displaced voice, the voice torn from context. It was through such a voice that Corcoran engaged the British politics of the 1980s.

COMPOSITION

I noted earlier that in Corcoran's early poem 'Going to Town', the town in question, which remained unspecified, was attributed the status 'of compositional device'. I want now to come back to that phrase, to the question of 'composition'. As a way of accounting for the relation between a poetry and a socio-political space, 'compositional device' is a very suggestive description. New York could sometimes be a 'compositional device' for O'Hara in a quite literal sense, his 'I do this, I do that' poems partly taking their form from the layout of mid- to lower-Manhattan. Similarly in Olson, the evolving historical organisation of Gloucester quite frequently informs the design of *The Maximus Poems*. 'Maximus to Gloucester, Letter 11', for instance, orients itself around the monumental rock on Main Street, inscribed as that is with the record of an early encounter between European settlers and Massachusetts' native American population. In both cases, however, the question of 'composition' is also more than formal, more than a matter of the way a given space informs the shape of the poem. What matters to both poets also is the city's constituency. This is apparent in a casual way in O'Hara, in the fact that, in 'A step away from them', for instance, 'There are several Puerto/ Ricans on the avenue today, which/ makes it beautiful and warm'. Olson, being more theoretical in disposition, more inclined to the grand historical claim, makes such a socio-political sense of composition the central theme of his epic. The central question for the *polis* is: who should be accorded membership of the city? Who should be granted the rights of citizenship such membership entails? Gloucester is a 'compositional device' because, as city, it raises Olson's guiding question: how can the poet help determine what and who such a social space might be thought to contain?

Kelvin Corcoran's town differs from the cities to which O'Hara and Olson addressed themselves, in the primary sense that while he may have actual towns in mind, Evesham, say, or Cheltenham, perhaps, the term functions equally as a figure of speech. It is precisely not a fixed space, with a fixed set of conventions or regulations governing mobility, but is an imaginary (as opposed, perhaps, to an imagined) space. It is a compositional device in that precisely what it necessitates, line by line, is composition, where the composition, the make-up of the poem, is governed by an impulse to displacement. Or to phrase the point according to one of Corcoran's preferred terms, his is fundamentally a poetry of the 'unfixed'.

We've seen the 'unfixed' already, in the untitled opening poem of *Qiryat Sepher*:

> under a late and civil sky
> close but never a natural colour
> a common jigsaw of window views
> an actor walks by in an unfixed suit

The adjective 'unfixed' raises various questions of agency. Is it that the actor hasn't 'fixed' his or her suit, or that the poet, in presenting the actor's movement, has declined to attribute definition to his or her clothing? Or is it rather a quality of the 'suit' itself, being an article of dress not fixed (which is to say not determined) by its circumstance. The suit, that is to suggest, has nothing to do with the situation in which it is being worn; as an expression of identity it is displaced.

The adjective frequently comes back. In the eighth poem of *Lyric Lyric* (the absence of titles, and therefore the uncertainty of designation, being very much to the point), the speaker, following an epigraph from Jack Spicer, remarks:

> I took advice, travelled north
> and jumped into the ocean off Cape Wrath,
> ocean is an expected word I think,
> a vast body of water sloshing about;
> endless, deep and cold,
> giant stacks aloft spinning the unfixed sky.
>   (*Lyric* 10)

Similarly, in that volume's fifth poem, this time an untitled prose piece, we find that:

> The tunnel down is steady, the trees overhead let fall
> unfixed statements. If I have run carefully, watching
> my tread along the dark stream, then all things will
> settle into all things and I should arrive at absolute
> normal breathing the air of a new speech. Look at the
> sea, its immense rolling indifference, I love it.
>   (*Lyric* 7)

This is quite grandly aspirational, a statement, perhaps, of the poet's strongest yearning, where the key phrases would seem to be 'unfixed statements' and 'all things will settle into all things'. To take Corcoran at his word, what he can be thought to present is a poetry of settlement and the unfixed, a poetry in which the unfixed are permitted to settle. Such a poetry, as he proposes it here, would have the 'air of a new speech'. It is a significant ambition and one which takes us back to composition.

Consider, from *Qiryat Sepher*, the poem 'I dreamt my house a film', which opens on a note of elegy to O'Hara:

> I dreamt my house a film,
> Frank O'Hara got clubbed to the sand,
> sweet tough and dead
> his upturned body lay in the surf

Following this opening image of metamorphosis – the house become a film, O'Hara clubbed to death – the poem gives way, through a series of variations, to the figure of St. Gregory, pictured in the act of composition:

> St. Gregory composes a world
> an ivory book cover carved in light
>
> We three scribes work in the crypt
> balance the floating crown and palace
> on bent and empty heads
> see it all with blank eyes.

The first two lines here refer the reader to a tenth-century, carved ivory book cover, now held at the Kunsthistorisches Museum in Vienna. In the carving, St. Gregory is depicted at his writing table; the grandeur of his papal palace looms in the background, while squashed below him – and apparently holding him up – three scribes are presented, presumably copying his words out. Gregory appears this way, and figures in Corcoran's poem, because in the history of composition, not least in the history of the composition of Britain, he has unrivalled status. He has the distinction of being the earliest Pope whose correspondence has survived. He gave his name, when he standardized European plainchant, to the liturgical performance known as the Gregorian Chant. In 597 AD, in his single most significant gesture, he commissioned St. Augustine to establish the Christian Church in England. As much as any figure might be said to, St. Gregory can be thought to have composed a world, to have brought a world into being by his thought and writing.

The point of Corcoran's reference is not to invite a comparison with St. Gregory, but rather, as with the image of O'Hara, to indicate an exemplary figure in the history of composition. If there is a comparison, in fact, it is perhaps with the scribes, whose function, as the speaker states, is to 'balance the floating crown and palace' and 'who see it all with blank eyes'. This blank-eyed look (recalling, as it does, the 'indifference of the sea' that the speaker of the prose poem claimed to love) can be said to be integral to Corcoran's idea of composition. What he proposes, I would like to suggest, is poetry as a form of composition in which the unfixed can settle, a setting which can accommodate the displaced. Corcoran ties this aspiration to the idea of the town because to do so is to link an aesthetic objective to the tradition of civic thought. It matters also, though, that the town exists as figure of speech because as such it permits the poetry's compositions to take their own, undetermined forms. Corcoran's writing is not fixed by a given socio-political setting, but instead as writing, as act of composition, aims at a form of expression in which 'all things might settle into all things'.

'ANOTHER LANGUAGE LIKE OURS'

In contemplating the shift marked by Kelvin Corcoran's early poetry, away from a poetics grounded in actual cityscapes, and towards an image of a socio-political space, the town, which is in fact of figure of speech, this essay points to a further displacement. Whereas in Olson (following Williams) and even in O'Hara, the question of belonging, of social accreditation, is shaped by the conventions of actual settings, in Corcoran that question is displaced on to the writing itself. The image of St. Gregory in his scriptorium helps us to see that. Writing in a British context, but in full awareness of a tradition of American civic poetry, Corcoran insisted on the poem itself as the site of composition, as the setting in which issues of identity and acquaintance should be addressed and proposed. In doing so, as I have suggested, he hardly lost sight of the very real divisions of the period during which he emerged as a writer. However, in declining to make any given setting his 'compositional device', he enabled the act of composition itself, the act of writing, to be the basis for his contribution to the politics of the time. Which means that, in conclusion, it is necessary to say something about Corcoran's language itself, about how, in his poems, he performs this socio-political gesture.

The opening of the poem 'Tocharian The I-E Enclave', from *Lyric Lyric*, provides a way of thinking this through:

> They say there is, along the silk route,
> a life away, another language like ours,
> used by people unlike us
> (*Lyric* 17)

The Tocharians were a people who inhabited medieval oasis city-states at the northern edge of the Tarim basin, the area we now know as the Chinese province of Xinjiang. They were a migratory people, moving originally from Eastern Siberia and settling eventually in Northern India. Their language, preserved in manuscripts dating from the sixth-eighth centuries AD, was subsequently superseded by Turkic languages. Historically, then, what the poem points to is a series of displacements, displacements it echoes by its phrasing, 'another language like ours,/ used by people unlike us'. What such a language would be like is the question not just of this poem, but of Corcoran's poetry generally. Or, to state the question as a proposition: what Corcoran's poetry proposes, what it sets out to inscribe, is a language which is, demonstrably, like ours but one which nonetheless (and as a principle of its composition) accommodates unlikeness.

Later in the same section of *Lyric Lyric* Corcoran articulates this aspiration in terms of English itself:

> Can you hear that chainsaw
> and the dog my letter sent
> slicing through the window,
> a screen without surface
>
> Absorbs the sight, the sea
> surrounding this island
> from where I talk
> the politics all around
>
> I know the bays
> where no Eng-a-lish is spoken,
> just the sea, Frances,
> and your journey's tending.
> (ibid)

This is a lovely lyric, 'tending', as the prose poem quoted earlier tended, towards the indifference of the sea. As such, what it registers is the condition of speaking from an island; that island from where the poet talks and where there is 'politics all around'. The lyric's key term is the one Corcoran hyphenates, 'Eng-a-lish', the extra syllable giving the word what one might call its tribal form. 'Eng-a-lish', the poem implies, is spoken by those who identify closely with the place, the speaker by contrast, gesturing towards bays where no such language is spoken.

Corcoran's early poetry is not 'Eng-a-lish' poetry, not a poetry based on a given connection between place and language. What he writes instead is a language which is 'like ours', but one in which elements which are 'unlike' one another provide the work with its basic dynamic. It is a poetry of displacement in which the unfixed, beautifully, provides the governing principle – lyric poetry spoken in a ripped voice.

Between Red and Yellow:
The Red and Yellow Book (1986)

Ian Davidson

Kelvin Corcoran's *The Red and Yellow Book* has thirty pages of poetry between its red and yellow covers.[1] Others in this collection of essays will speak of Corcoran's more recent work and of his poems from his time spent in Greece. I want to explore an earlier and different kind of movement than his recent travels. It is more localised in his childhood hometown of Evesham and in interior domestic scenes. The movement is often more metaphorical and symbolic, between red and yellow and the orange they produce and in the movement between life and death as he charts a period of terminal illness scattered throughout the poems; a death in which the patient is also alive in the poems. Despite the intensely personal nature of much of the material, these poems, as I will demonstrate, are never narrow, or focused exclusively on the emotion within the consciousness of the writer. They are also always located in the motions of capitalism, of the drive to work (and the drive to work) and of the movements of finance and labour, as Margaret Thatcher and Ronald Reagan set about the deregulation of global capital in the 1980s, a process that had one culmination in the credit collapse of 2007.

I am identifying and describing movement and the human practice of mobility in the poems, but that is a starting point rather than a conclusion. Through describing movement I want to try and find out something of the nature of the thing that moves and the nature of the spaces that are moved through, as well as the nature of the movement itself. I also want to examine the human practices of mobility in the poem, of the mobility of the speaking voice and the relative immobility of the mother in life, before her stillness in death.

Movement, particularly in a trajectory from one point to another, causes change, not only in the object that moves, but in the thing it moves towards. Movement changes the points between which the movement has taken place; in Lefebvrian terms movements produce the space they move through, rather than space being a kind of Newtonian absolute, or empty space, that serves as a container for the movement, or a pre-existing grid on which movement can be charted. The movement also reveals something of the material nature of the moving object. In

Marxist and economic terms it might reveal something of the object's material value; in physical terms it might reveal something of the matter of which it is made and, in affective terms, it might reveal why something matters, its import. Movement in a trajectory results in friction, and the movement towards the stillness of death, as the breathing stops or the heart gives its last beat, is a process of degradation of the human body. *The Red and Yellow Book* keeps these different matters and materialities in play, as it explores the ways that the mobility and immobility of the figures in the book enact different practices of movement for different reasons, and begins to examine ways in which mobility practices are predicated on cultures of gender and class.

My explorations of movement and mobility are therefore taking place on the shifting ground that is the point at which any movement is taking place. There is no stability; there are no empirical certainties on which any analysis can be grounded. Red is already bleeding into orange in its link to yellow, at the same time as it asserts its redness. Things in movement become themselves, or at least one of their selves, but they also become more movement. It may be as big an error to try and pin things down in order to examine them as it is to simply assert the metaphysical idea of movement without examining its specific practices. If one set of ideas of movement, those from classical philosophy, are influenced by observation of the planets, then it combines the eternal harmonic hum of a body spinning around itself and the streak of a meteorite across the sky, burning itself up.

Red and yellow function, therefore, not as binaries, but in a dialectical relationship that ensures constant movement between and within the terms and dynamic shifts of perspective, context and interpretation. There are other relationships within the poems that work in a similar way; the voice of the mother moves into silence and the quick become dead. The domestic interior of the home and the public life of the streets and the road and its traffic are frequently counter posed. Much of the material is highly personal, but is also firmly located within a political and social public context of Britain in the late 1980s and the time of the Thatcherite Conservative party. The voices and the bodies that make them are never free of the historical circumstances they produce, or are produced by.

This is not a book, however, that wears its heart on its sleeve, despite the affective raw simplicity of some of its contents. In the first poem, it is only in the title – 'Not that voice' – that the personal, lyrical style and the narrative of the parents' relationship and the mother's death that is to dominate the book are evident. There are other, more ambivalent clues. The narrator of the poem has 'my head in your lap' and says 'I mean to save your life' (1), but the rest of the poem is a series of images that have only an imperfect fit, demonstrated by the 'catachresis' of the final stanza.[2] The connections in the poem seem outside of normal logic; it is the 'trees and grass [that] come up for air' and the sun's afterimage is in the form of blackberries. *Dante's* is a removal firm as well as an Italian poet and the underwater duck is full of water, not air. Despite the concrete nature of the imagery, its movement is between these terms: the things that don't fit together and the friction they create. The movement reveals something of their material (that the duck is a plastic carrier of water) and something of the space it moves through, or in (the water that surrounds it). It is also the movement of capital, within a system of capitalism that depends on movement of money, goods and people to keep itself going. In the second poem, 'Power, Lust and Striving', those economic and material relations are more evident. The fleet is 'bobbing off-shore', while 'the ports are blocked with French farmers' (2). Movement and mobility are implicated not only in the abstractions of the dialectic, but in the physical world where trade becomes impossible because of the lack of movement of the fleet. The narrator of the poem is at odds with the situation, threatened by a house that rocks in the wind, only able to wait, immobile and listen to time pass as 'the bomb of spring is ticking' (2). The house is the symbol of permanency, not because of its four walls and the nature of its construction (this is no Bachelardian bourgeois space), but because of the diurnal round of activities of its inhabitants. The mother is the centre of the house, on the move in her domestic world, with a constancy that suggests harmony rather than the discord of the trajectory, but whose illness is ticking away, running down the clock. The father is always encountered outside the house, in the street or the pub, appearing occasionally in the theatre of the hospital to act out the concerned husband, trying to take control, but without effect.

In such ways, Corcoran stitches together the poems in the book, introducing an idea or concept in one context and then, later in the book, returning to it in order to shift around or clarify the meaning. The 'bomb of spring' becomes the heart of the dying mother, ticking away; spring becomes not the moment of renewal, but an ending of a life. It also, still, contains within itself a moment of rebirth and house and town, private and public, become implicated in a seasonal change that is also a change in personal circumstances.

The third poem in the book, 'Keep', over six sections on six pages, brings the speaking self – the voice referred to in previous poems – into direct conflict with the material conditions of its existence, albeit through the abstraction of money (3-8). This time it is the town that is ticking, waiting for tourists and the spring, or perhaps it is 'ticking over', taking in the money for the 'doll figures' as 'guilts eased.' The 'guilt' (gilt) links the voice of the speaking self to the money on Wall Street; the doll figures that sell are representations of the human form, but also financial 'figures' that are fabricated, with the 'bigger than expected sugar and lemon granules' that he 'sells' to the sleeping figure. The 'guilt' links 'sleep and money', through a performance in which the voice is steady, commanding 'sleep and sleep for England.' A female figure in the poem, exhibits more vulnerability and, less sure of its mobility, wants 'a clean bra and knickers in case I fall'.

The poem develops its own meta-fiction, in which the speaking subject is in possession of the red and yellow book of the title. It is as if the book is being read before it is written, imagined into existence as sufficient for its difficult task. Like the next section, in which the speaking subject expresses relief at reaching 'the fifth line, made it ok', the poetry is in tension between an emotion that is always threatening to go out of control, and a language and form that must contain it (5). The book has agency. It is 'strong / can slay its enemies', like the way the ticking bomb of the previous poems becomes 'spring [that] rips through the world' before 'you breathe out', an action that releases tension as well as accompanies speech. The smashed glass of the poem's first line is only 'a petrol glass', but the cause of the accident, the husband and father, follows the speaking subject through his life, to the point where 'he spoke in my mouth'. The loss of voice is in part the fear of losing the voice of the dying mother, but also of hearing the father's voice in his own, as the family idiolect moves between generations. The mother meanwhile, in her absorption of the father's voice, 'shrank to nothing in a white bed', and her silent immobility is in contrast to the movement of the everyday world where 'You should know voices when you hear them; / sparrows, dogs, post vans and neighbours' (7). The diurnal movement, the harmonic hum of domestic every day where 'I hear cooking' has ceased to function, the planet home no longer spins around itself but has launched itself into the next life.

After her death we are left 'in the angry dark' and in a time in which 'the house fades'. Her actions are now in the past tense: 'she sang to herself / she made cakes / in the kitchen' (19). The click of the jigsaw pieces described (pieces that 'fit together so well') becomes a radical unpredictability and 'something uncertain' in a 'partial jungle of just red' (8). The 'face that fits my face / gone, my name unmade' (19). The red and yellow, the boundaries of the book and the terms that sustain its movement, become fixed in a single colour. This shifting of the focus of intensity of light and voice, becomes a pattern of the poem as the voice relives the moment of death, appearing through the real and imagined everyday landscapes.

In the next poem all that is left is hope that has to contend with knowledge, the medical certainty of death while there is still life, albeit one that exists 'in a myth of light / of diamorphine' (9). It is a life that is now lived out in a parched world without liquid; the last spoken word becomes 'drink'. The everyday world continues to move against the stillness of the human form that is no longer alive; a form that has not only lost its voice, but caused the suffering others to lose their voices through pain and sadness. Morning (and mourning) is located in the 'petroled ways' and a girl that rides 'her bike along the path' (11). The talking is over, the palm against palm that kept his movements restricted has gone now and, for the living, it is 'one / breath / another' and the 'argument of this book', a self reflexive process of writing that reduces movement to 'just faces, just writing'.

Yet the stillness of death, the immobility of the interred human body, is agonisingly reflected in the bodies of the mourners. The effect on the sister is expressed through her body: 'twisting round / crying in me, twisting me round / when it rains' (15). It is a violent internal wrench in contrast to the ill figure that, before death, had sat 'by the window in an easy chair / spectral grey and thin as light / her eyes fixed alive on her grandchildren' (16). It was a figure that was waiting to die and whose only movement was her breathing; a movement that would stop a few poems later as the scene of death is revisited in prose paragraphs and a movement that would similarly stop with 'the last pulse in her neck' (20). But the stillness of the body and the silence of her voice releases the language for the next two major sequences that complete the book: four poems all called 'the sound at the end of waiting' (22-5) and four poems called 'from the red and yellow book' (26-9).

The 'sound at the end of waiting' is the recovery of the lost voice, of the narrator and the dead mother. The figure moves through its daily routine on the way to work in a car; the car stuck in 'jammed layers of separate intentions'. The very nature of the city itself has changed and its base layers and rich values described as 'lead and gold' and 'solid as carbon'. These elements are held within 'shining air', experienced through a windscreen upon which 'wipers fused across the slab of day'. Time and space become fused; the ticking spring may have ended. The millennium moment that is the passing over from life to death has been replaced by the churning continuation of an everyday life within which surfaces are stripped back to reveal what really matters and a memory that is always threatening to disrupt those surfaces. In a syntactic break the poem enters 'just no time' and the past breaks into the present through the 'ashes'. Automobility is reduced through the traffic jammed in the 'councillor's piratised bus route', another reference to the privatisation of public services that was characteristic of the economic policy of the 1980s. Within this economic and social context the body's response to the pain of memory is to 'breathe out', even though the 'brutality of facts' will still 'open bright in your face'. What finally stops, however, is neither the passage of time, nor the spatial relationships, but the ability to move. In a moment 'it all breaks down'; a phrase that describes emotional breakdown as well as the physical. It becomes 'like Muybridge', where motion can also be a series of frozen monochrome frames: 'traffic and trees stuck in grey and white'.[3] The poem's narrator may be alive and mobile, on the way to work, but the world itself can be transformed through grief, a grief that finds its representation in the stalled mobility of a world that must be moving, a real physical world geared into itself. But time marches on, with one morning imposed on another like the stills of a film that constructs the apparent realities of passing through time and space.

The poem suggests a place where language has broken down, but one that is also beyond language, where faces become themselves and where it isn't a picture, but the face behind the picture. It is a process of reorientation, in which the lyric voice must reconstruct a world that has lost its centre. The tension that exists and that constructs the new space of the poems is the house, now only exists in memory and the roads that he has to travel. The poem tries on a variety of other voices, notably that of Frank O'Hara, but always returns to a sense of loss that is unutterable, except in the circular patterns of everyday life and the details that make that up.

Driving becomes a way out of the house and a way into the world, but is also a way of letting the outside world in. In the third poem of the 'waiting' sequence, 'ice snakes up the road across the country' and the poem ends with a memory of those moments when the world seemed complete.

> I stared from the back-step, it was exactly like this,
> she piled up the ironing, sang to herself
> looked at me and care was in the world. (24)

The automobility of the narrator is both a gain and a loss; it is a way to escape but, also, means leaving things behind. The immobility of the mother figure and her location within the house is a process in which she produces the domestic space and is produced by it. The gender politics are as much like those of Carolyn Cassady in *Off the Road*, in which she remains immobile in the house while Neal Cassady drives the length and breadth of America. Or they are like those of Diane di Prima in *Recollections of My Life as a Woman* who remembers her mother on the doorstep of her house, looking out but staying in. The effect of the death is a loss of the containment of the domestic space. Like di Prima's fractured childhood, in which the walls become too thin to contain what they should hold in, Corcoran is caught between inner and outer and in a situation where,

> the sky hits your head, it's so cold
> a door slams in your chest
> shock settles like breath in the garden. (25)

It is also a loss of continuity, in which future time becomes an empty space he tries to fill with driving. The imperfect fit of the earlier poems has cracked wide open and he is unsure of 'what do I do tomorrow'. The car itself becomes fluid and impermanent, and 'can not hold that shape', turning into a rubber car; all he can do is observe 'others jigsaw talk', the closed perfect fit previously discovered in the jigsaw pictures of the six cubes (25). The perfect fit of home and the perfect fit of the voices that make up that home are replaced by a movement back and forth, between the private world of the house and the private grief within the body and the public world of work.

Such ideas are commonplace and Corcoran is adding nothing to the understanding of lyric poetry if all he is asking the reader to do is share his feelings of loss and understand the function and role of the maternal figure. But the simplicity of the narrative is troubled in two ways. The first is, again, commonplace and a stock figure in such tales: the drunk father who cannot cope with the grief and is left as a figure gesturing wildly from the sidelines. His voice only disrupts the perfect fit of mother and son, unable to engage in conversation with them. We finally see him at the hospital, 'drunk and talking about euthanasia'. The second way the narrative is troubled is more complex and more disturbing: it is located in a three way relationship between the poem as an object made of language (the object of objectivist poetry), the function of language as a system of signification with internal structural relations and the ways that language is in a relationship with an external world. These, again, are commonplace concerns of late modernist poetry, but are given increased significance by the death of the mother as subject of the book (if so crude a reduction is allowed) and the ways that the collection of poems constructs its own meta-fiction of itself as a book, thereby increasing its responsibility to make sense of itself as subject and object.

The last four poems, or the last four pages of poetry, are all entitled 'from the Red and Yellow Book', a self-reflexive act that suggests a completion or a return to a theme, or that the voice of *The Red and Yellow Book* has finally emerged from the poems that preceded it. They do have something of the quality of revelation, and the 'book' something of the quality of an Urtext, as it continues to explore the relationships between the public life of world and mobility and the private domestic life worlds that continue to turn in an apparent harmony until the change that is cataclysmic and irreversible. The loved one, the domestic female centre, is two figures – mother and lover – and the poems chart a gradual shift from one to the other. The first poem 'from the Red and Yellow Book' begins:

> the house fronts flip over
> subterranean rivers surface in
> public fountains of gods and tortured horses
> brown and rabid near the rapist's car park

the grand sweep of the municipal offices –
see the hand moving, its trick
the truth has made us free (26)

The walls of the house no longer act as a border between public and private. They are 'flipped'; a term that describes their opening up like the side of a box that the four walls construct. In addition – and ironically – the term 'flipping' is now common in the UK to describe the rapid purchase and sale of houses for profit, making evident what was already inherent in the commodification of private housing in the thirty-five years since this poem was written. The discourse of home becomes overwritten by a historical materialism that reclassifies houses as property. It is a sudden and careless movement, like flipping burgers, those other symbols of global capitalism. The contemporary concern, however, might have been more about the sale of public housing to private individuals (a policy introduced by the UK Conservative government in the 1980s), which brought the possibility of home ownership to working class people; an idea that would connect the 'flip' of the first line to the 'municipal offices' of the fifth.

There is, of course, a more obvious symbolic and psychoanalytical reading. The death of the mother means that the interior of the house is no longer a private place of family life, of which the mother was centre, but which is now open to public view. The interior life is flooded by the 'subterranean rivers' that are not only the subconscious, but also the link between the private house and the 'public fountains'. The private flows into the public, not only along the roads, the 'April Streets and cars' of the second poem, but through the exposed dialectic that thought and feeling can bring together. The only cure is time, the 'hand moving' and a sense of connection through 'telekinesis and country music'. The poems chart a process of searching out meaning in a world that often seems to deny that possibility. From the broader perspectives of Western culture the poem returns to the simple facts of a human body and its condition:

I must wash my hair
I must be happy
            the first
dictionary had only four words
I will tell you what they are
You will live a better life (27)

The search for the four words can go back to the second line of the extract, 'I must be happy', but, despite the initial capitalisation of the last line that suggests a fresh start, the poem fails to deliver the punch line. The examination of origins, however, is now over. In the first two lines he admits defeat, but allows in victory, permitting them both to coexist in the gesture of 'open your hands, let them go'. Spring, the ticking bomb of the opening poems, has arrived, as have 'the level streets of a life before us'. The poem acknowledges that there is 'no going back to that world' and, particularly within a book of 'words before meanings', to the 'verbal substance of the last lines'. Rather than searching through the past for a single cause, the poem becomes multiple; it is not the single house that is the childhood home, but 'all the houses that are lived in'. It might be that this performance of everyday life is only a script over the material, as in Philip K. Dick's novel *Time Out of Joint*, in which material objects disappear to be replaced by a label. But Corcoran's vision is more complex, involving movement back and forth between language that is non-representational (and only its own material) and those things that language might suggest, and the ways that material can exist beyond language:

> happy actors on their blocks
> write sky on a banner above the street,
> they pretend everything is O.K.
> a street in the sky, the real sky
> in blue capitals, the language of delivery (28)

Language, therefore, can be a method of delivery beyond loss, but cannot replace the visual experience or the real thing. The poems chart a gradual process of, in the words of Lee Harwood, living outside oneself; of a movement from internal personal loss to finding a place in the external world.

Ideas of movement and tracing practices of mobility have informed my reading of the book. They support a dialectical reading of the binary in the title, suggesting an orange that never quite appears and draw out the implications of the notion of an imperfect fit between public and private, the home and the road to work, the living and the dead. On a more meta-fictional or theoretical level, the imperfect fit is between language and reality. In an imperfect fit (a notion further developed by Allen Fisher in recent work), there is always movement, a process of trying to get into place and a wearing away of the rough edges. In the process we find out much of the everyday material of the world and nature of language that the body can no longer hold. If the poem concerns itself with everyday life, then it is one that is suffused with ideas of mobility and immobility, in which the lyric voice claims 'I'm sure my ribs don't fit / when I turn, like this, they don't fit' (6).

The principal relationship described in the book – that between mother and son – explores some of the ways that this too is a relationship that demonstrates different ideas of movement and practices of mobility. The mother figure is associated with the house, and to leave it is the cause of some anxiety. I noted previously that in the poem 'Keep' she stresses the need to wear 'a clean bra and knickers in case I fall', as if to leave the house is to expose herself to risk and to a public gaze. By way of contrast the husband's mobility is demonstrated through his absence. Rather than being an initial part of any scene, he enters from an outside that is unknown. For the mother however, her illness only exacerbates her inability to move, and she 'shrank to nothing in a white bed' where she takes 'one / breath / another'. But it is breathing that takes place under 'the dark roof' that 'rests / on the white walls.' The house, like the body, is incapable of movement; it is another body at rest until, towards the end of the poem, public and private intermingle. Descriptions of her during illness also emphasise her immobility. She sits 'by the window in an easy chair', or, 'she sat in her chair, legs propped, never asleep'. When she dies, she takes the house with her: 'in the angry dark / her house fades', leaving the internal environment open to public inspection.

The female figure in the poem is, in some ways, a mother figure that is both specific in terms of the detailed relationship to the lyric voice in the poem, but also general in terms of her 'motherly' attributes. She is in a physical and symbolic relationship to the house that limits her mobility. The poems in the 'book' might be elegiac and an elegy for the lost mother that charts the process of her dying. They also function as a kind of memoir, making permanent the memory of the mother without a voice of her own and as a memoir locating the text more firmly within the context of women writing about the lives of women. The memoir is a form that, as Anne Waldman says in her foreword to *Women of the Beat Generation*, is the 'strongest literary genre by the women of the so-called Beat generation' and produces writing that 'is testament to the lives of these women'.[4] Corcoran's writing partly does that, providing a testimony to the grief of the lyric poet and to the life of the mother as lived through her relationship to the house and family, but not outside it. That he never gets far beyond a grief for a loss of the certainties of childhood, or achieves a consciousness that might give the mother a life outside the house, is a weakness of the poem counterbalanced by its identification of the broader reaches of economic, social and cultural life in England in the 1980s. Because of her apparent immobility we might never understand the aspirations of the mother beyond her motherliness, but we do understand the ways that her life is variously implicated in the politics of 1980s England.

Notes

[1] Corcoran, Kelvin. *The Red and Yellow Book*. Textures: London, 1986.

[2] 'Catachresis' as the misapplication of a word, especially in a mixed metaphor, is a useful term in trying to read the different elements of the poem whose connections, to use a term developed by Allen Fisher, are an 'imperfect fit'.

[3] Edweard Muybridge is famous for a series of photographs of a horse in motion, work that prefigured the 'movie'.

[4] Waldman, Anne. 'Foreword' in Knight, Brenda, *Women of the Beat Generation*, Berkley: Conari, 1996.

'The Umbrage of Green Shade': Kelvin Corcoran and the Landscape Beyond the Landscape

Jos Smith

In Kelvin Corcoran's *New and Selected Poems* (2004), in the opening poem of a new sequence, *My Life With Byron*, we read that: 'Events left me in the umbrage of green shade' (69): the phrase is a perfect one to encapsulate the unusual collision of different spaces that we encounter in Corcoran's poetry. It is not immediately apparent what we are supposed to do with such an image. It does not do what we expect of it. 'Umbrage' offers us an image of discontent, rancour, offence; 'green shade' offers us a rural, even pastoral space – sleepy, becalmed – in which we are supposed to situate this umbrage. Something in us does not want to compute this and we re-read the image. Was it in fact 'the umbels of green shade'? That might sit a little more easily. But what we have is closer to collage – the pastoral scene is being disfigured in some way. The reclining shepherd/peasant is not reclining asleep; he is fuming, plotting. The umbrage undermines the peaceful effect of the green shade, but the green shade also undermines the umbrage: something about it neuters its anger. The shepherd wants out but every which way is a pastoral symphony echoing around the space of a Claude Lorrain scene. The tensions produce a very striking landscape that is spatially rich and complex. Drawing on the poems published in Corcoran's 2004 *New and Selected Poems,* this chapter will begin to offer a way into the difficult landscapes of Kelvin Corcoran's poetry, exploring these tensions between landscape traditions and a more distinctly late twentieth century discontent. Why does Corcoran's English landscape look the way it does? How does it develop throughout his work? What happens when we lean in and listen to the shepherd 'in the umbrage of green shade'?

The documentary film-maker Patrick Keiller recently curated an installation-cum-exhibition at Tate Britain called *The Robinson Institute,* which playfully claimed to be considering nothing less serious than 'the possibility of life's survival on the planet'. When I visited, a group of American tourists could be heard moving from painting to painting discussing, with a surprising evenness, how beautiful each one was. The installation was composed of work – often juxtaposed quite jarringly – that had been selected by Keiller from the Tate collection and further afield as a complement to his 2010 film *Robinson in Ruins*. Both the film and the exhibition were attempts to better understand contemporary social and economic crises through the medium of landscape. They were overtly and radically political. At one point the film discussed the hanging and quartering of four men in 1596, men who had rebelled against the enclosure of the land on which they lived and worked, while offering a scenic view of the fields today. The effect was difficult for the viewer in a similar way to that mentioned in Corcoran's line above. At one point the installation presented John Slack's 1819 textile print of the Peterloo Massacre on which Shelley based his poem 'The Masque of Anarchy' ('All things have a home but one – Thou, Oh, Englishman, hast none!'). Both of these events, Keiller was suggesting, ought to be remembered in the context of late capitalism and the 2008 financial crisis. And yet, these visitors seemed only to be able to recognise a monotonous thread of aesthetic pleasure. Rather than grapple with the tensions that these two artists present with their uneasy landscapes, there is a tendency to gloss over them and rest in a rather empty aesthetic response.

Yuriko Saito has a term for this. He suggests that the inability to see beyond the pictorial surface and aesthetic composition of a landscape to the real land and its social and ecological significance beyond is to be 'scenically challenged' (238). This isn't intended as a snipe against American tourists – they might have been from anywhere – but rather, we all might recognise and identify with that particular gaze from time to time, one that hopefully we wrestle against: a dopey, unenquiring cultural tourism that wants to *recognise – enjoy – share – move on – repeat*, ignoring anything that does not fit into this pattern, even when the writing on the wall (quite literally in this case) suggests a more difficult and a more uncomfortable story. Corcoran's poetry, like Keiller's films, challenges this tendency in us.

The tendency seems particularly acute when it comes to landscape. Perhaps this is because of the very close relationship between landscape painting and landscape tourism. Perhaps, and more seriously, it is because the very particular rules of sensibility and taste in the tradition of landscape emerge from a crucial optical distance from a framed scene, preventing too much of an inquiry into its living reality. John Barrell, for example, describes the English landscape painting around the turn of the nineteenth century as an 'image of harmony with nature whereby the labourers were merged as far as possible with their surroundings, too far away from us for the question about how contented or ragged they were to arise' (Barrell 16). Recently, however, there has been a re-evaluation of landscape as a tradition, with a host of critics, artists, essayists, film makers and poets revisiting some of its sub-genres like the pastoral, the sublime and the picturesque with an eye to subverting their powerful hold on our experience of the world around us. Patrick Keiller, for example, describes his method in the Robinson films as attempting 'to better understand a perceived 'problem' by looking at, and making images of, landscape' (Keiller 9). Robinson, his fictional narrator, goes further: 'From a nearby car park, he surveyed the centre of the island on which he was shipwrecked: "the location", he wrote, "of a *Great Malady*, that I shall dispel, in the manner of Turner, by making *picturesque views*, on journeys to sites of special scientific and historic interest".'

It is within this contemporary context of subverted landscape genre, diagnosis of '*Great Malady*' and the desire to 'dispel [...] by making *picturesque views*' that I would like to explore the work of Kelvin Corcoran. This might have seemed ill advised, impossible, even absurd, twenty years ago, when we were too close to the aesthetics of landscape to really see the land, but one of the things that lies behind Keiller's, Corcoran's and many others' resurgent interest in a politicised English landscape is the spatial turn emanating out of Marxist cultural geographers like Michel de Certeau, Henri Lefebvre and Doreen Massey. It is a renewed understanding of *space* as organised, produced, managed, mismanaged and reproduced by powerful social relations that has demanded this re-evaluation of landscape. The way that space has become encoded, the way it is now read as a means of structuring our perception and behaviour, have made it, and with it landscape, part of a process of cultural struggle that is politically potent.

Corcoran's poetry offers a scattered and uneasy, kaleidoscopic sense of space that is often in scabrous dialogue with the idea of the nation as a unified landscape, the recurrent 'Eng-a-land' that so many of his voices throw out. It is a space that disrupts landscape by exploring it, not quite as a parody so much as a living dismemberment. 'Eng-a-land' has to it, simultaneously, the wistful, nostalgic diction of a Georgian lyric, a note of paternal, imperial pride ('the triumph of Eng-a-lish classicism' 77) and the nationalist aggression of a boozy football crowd.

The tight, angular, uneasy imagery that we read throughout the thirty years of work that Corcoran's poetry offers us seems set to undermine each of these forms of 'scenically challenged' nationalism. The total view is always broken, something more vivid showing through the cracks. We cannot comment on how beautiful this poem and that poem are, consuming them evenly and moving on. There is a more carefully contorted space that we have to find our way through here, and to get a sense of it is to have certain disharmonies revealed to you. This is a poetry of disjuncture expressing anxiety, anger and uncertainty.

What is perhaps most interesting about this work, though, is that it is unable to entirely let go of the national myth. As the later poems move out to a Greek landscape they become more concerned with speaking back to the homeland (if such a word is appropriate to describe Corcoran's relation to England). A cosmopolitan and Romantic idealism seeps in, a utopianism that wants to believe that the English can be better than they are, a desire, as with Keiller's Robinson, to 'dispel' the '*Great Malady*':

> This is Radio Free Byron on the short wave
> broadcasting to the English shires: wake up.
> We urge war against the west, against Fletcher;
> the Maniots are the men for me, they will do the deed.
>
> Wake up you boys and girls, you sneak careerists.
> ('Myriorama' 14)

The Maniots had been revolting against the Ottoman Empire for many years before the rest of Greece joined in the War of Independence in 1821 (Greenhalgh and Eliopoulis 58). A regional pride and a warrior spirit, one affiliating them with the Spartans, characterised the Maniots, and it is this rebellious pride defying top-down imperial control that Corcoran seems to admire, though war, here, is being waged against an empire to the '*west*' rather than to the east in the wake of the Iraq war. Corcoran's politics seem to find their familial place in the dissenting warrior spirit of nineteenth century Greece, as Byron's did before him, and he sees in this a lesson for England.

This 'broadcasting' back to England describes the space that arises in the later poems very well, a pan-European air space travelled by plane, radio waves, correspondence, foreign relations, trade and dialogue. It is very different from, say, Joyce's relating back to Ireland from France and Italy. It is not an exile. As Peter Riley has suggested, the discovery of Greece for Corcoran is not a 'separate issue, like a travelogue, but a great expansion of resource' (Riley 87). But before we come to the particular version of Greece that is so important to Corcoran, there are the 'English shires', asleep here, that ought to be better understood in the early poetry. The question is that of *two* Englands in fact and the tensions sparked between them: the 'scenically challenged', ideal 'Eng-a-land' and the much-decayed local reality of the late 1980s and 90s that wriggles uncomfortably beneath that scenic veneer.

The difference between these two can be understood in Michael Gardiner's terms as a difference between the institution of 'English literature' and the slow and difficult return of a 'literature of England' in the hundred years after the First World War. The former, 'English literature', Gardiner describes as 'an ideal cultural form which estranged the experience of England by a displacement which continues to structure literary study and marketing today' (1); and as a 'civilising discipline' based on 'an ideal of tradition – but not on tradition itself' (3). An ideal, then, that eclipses the place itself. And with the decline of this ideal throughout the twentieth century, a certain 'literature of England' begins to emerge for Gardiner, 'local, experiential and national again' (1). Gardiner places the most intense arrival of this literature between 1990-2010, though what makes Corcoran such an interesting poet from this point of view is the way the local England emerges with something of the failure of the old ideal about it.

Corcoran's 1989 collection, *TCL*, wrestles with the idea of hegemony in England at the end of a decade of insidious and violent Thatcherite change. 'A man came to feel that he did not fit well in his body; his hands from the outside were not his from the inside' (in *New and Selected* 156). So a 'strange visitor' tells us. Later 'police drive in the eyes' and 'a sort of machinery is at work, / dumb song compulsory / enthralled by vacant ghosts' (162). Everywhere we look in this collection human agency is dulled. There is a form of diagnosis at work here, of another *Great Malady* perhaps. The *TCL* of the title refers to the computer scripting language invented by John Ousterhout in 1988 – 'Tool Command Language'. The ambiguity is clear: this is a language which, to speak, must command, must police and compel at some very deep level. In this picture, language is a rigged game; it perpetuates the broader system. This is not a repressive apparatus of control but something quieter and more intimate, 'dumb', approaching 'from the inside' and all the more dangerous for it. *TCL* comes a little too close to *TLC*.

In the extraordinary poem 'Watching the honeysuckle pour', these anxieties are played out at the scale of landscape. The poem moves between several 'styles' of landscape: a garden; a more expansive regional-industrial vista; a shopping centre; and it ends on an imagined burial scene. Anachronism haunts each of these landscapes too. In the garden that the poem opens with, hung with clematis and honeysuckle over trellises, 'talk of the devil scares the populace / encircles the world set aside' (161). The sense is of a medieval feudal economy and its peasantry, or at least a pre-enclosure, rural poor, bounded by place, to whom 'the edge of the orison' (the phrase is John Clare's) is the edge of the possible world. That is, so long as they believe what they have been told about the devil. It jars with the more modern notion of the garden trellises and flamboyant flowers. In fact the garden as environment becomes interchangeable with the fear of the devil that contains them. Both become a means of social control. We are picturing a diminutive Brueghel crowd huddled with their tools in the grass lawn of a suburban sun trap.

Beyond the garden walls, though, the anachronism continues: 'the future falls from the sky / white blobs drill a Midland or Northern town' – and here we have it – 'attendant lords range rove / cower, smile, laugh full-throat' (161). The brand-become-verb-phrase 'range rove' compounds the wealth and spatial freedom of these 'attendant lords'. They are unconfined to the garden and hence unperturbed by the devil. Are these attendant lords the ones who have 'set aside' the garden space for 'the populace', whatever they can't use? The 'white blobs' are strange though: the choice of words suggests a lack of vocabulary to describe the kind of reworking of the landscape that is taking place. There is a sense that change is taking place in the landscape quickly and covertly and that we are not keeping pace with the changes. We do not know what all these new structures are; we do not know what they do. It was only a few years after the publication of *TCL* that Graham Harvey published his highly controversial *The Killing of the Countryside*, an urgent and informed essay against the way the English government had abused and manipulated European agricultural subsidies to balloon its own industrial scale agribusiness, changing the face of the English landscape forever ('less than 10 percent of farms account for 50 percent of farm output' (15)). The farm-owners, he suggests, 'are neither shrewd stockmen nor horny-handed businessmen […] They are more likely to be wearing Armani suits than overalls, and the closest they get to the fields is driving over them in the Range Rover.' (15) This kind of farming (though it is less like farming than what was called 'improvement' in the eighteenth century) is concerned with short-term, high-profit investment. And yet most of us are quite blind to this when we gaze over the rolling hills.

'Watching the honeysuckle pour' opposes these two classes of people by positioning them spatially in two different orders, the unbridled capitalist free to rove over the landscape with the speculator's eye, unhampered by the garden walls of the 'scenically challenged' and socially controlled peasant class. But the peasant class, in another sweep of anachronism, becomes the consumer class, 'shoppers, dancing youths' on CCTV: 'the dream an endless promise / narrates first names with all accretions […] a hoot and a holler away from paradise'. This is the language of marketing and advertising, replacing the fear of the devil as a means of social control. This is the 'sort of machinery [that] is at work' in *TCL*.

The poem ends with an image of a dead body in the ground 'candid, coiled and waiting / – they fear it's a woman / with shoes to buy, / biscuits and mince in the bag.' (162) In another twist of anachronism, this can't help but evoke Anglo Saxon or Viking burials with their grave goods, though here, pathetically, of 'biscuits and mince'. A 'they' is introduced too, who seem to fear for this woman, but as the line enjambs we find that what they fear is the loss of a consumer. There is the implication of a command, also, in 'with shoes to buy', an almost Ballardian necromancy, as if she is being called back from beyond the grave, as if she is defying the natural order by being dead when she should be buying shoes. How dare she? These are the ghosts we might be 'enthralled' to, 'vacant' but threaded through a form of everyday diction.

Paul Kingsnorth, in *Real England*, describes an epiphany walking around Bluewater shopping centre in Kent when he realises that what he is sensing is 'totalitarian':

And it is, in the original sense of that often-abused word. Bluewater is a total experience. Every aspect of it is planned, controlled and monitored by authorities who you never see but

who only ever have your welfare at heart. Their authority here
is absolute, but unless you abuse their trust, break their rules,
you will never see them. You are here to consume, and as long
as you do so you will be left alone. (5)

The 'ghosts' to whom we are enthralled in this poem are vacant in the
same totalitarian way, and only flare up into sight as the behaviour of
the consumer becomes transgressive (insofar as she is dead: consumers
must not die).

Corcoran's English landscape is one that is fused with this same
kind of totalitarianism. But this is by no means defeatist or cynical. He
attempts to position himself, and us, outside it, if only for a difficult,
glimpsed moment. He manufactures a viewpoint that can incorporate
these heterogeneous spaces, revealing the roving laughter of the
'attendant lords', revealing the trellis walls of the encircling garden, the
'vacant ghosts' and the 'one-eyed camera' watching all; in short revealing
the total spatial regime, however difficult it might be; however much
we have to contort our thinking to see it. In doing so he carves out a
position beyond that regime, however tentatively, and however fragile
and difficult that position might be.

There is a strange rhythm of movement in the poems that follow
throughout the 1990s. They oscillate between, firstly, tightly observed,
unflattering detail – the landfill sites (164) and the retail pavilions (150)
and the 'imperishable plastic, gulls and jaded wrecks' (134) – and,
secondly, the expansive plane-window aerial views. Air space becomes
an ambiguous no man's land ('Who owns it?' (136)) into which we
might read a form of retreat that is also a stepping back for perspective.
(This double function also informs the perspective that looks back from
Greece.)

> What am I doing here flying over England?
> at a nasty tilt, green fields and conservative clubs
> flatten out like a grid to the Irish Sea,
> off the road are houses where children live
> and the heads of the republics return to the centre,
> the country looks like a picture of itself,
> state the name for it, petty towns and news shows,
> drawn in the wake of a commercial van. (140)

The line 'off the road are houses where children live' hangs in the air like an accusation ('can't you see, there are children present!'), as if the flattened 'grid' of the landscape itself is an explicit crime to which no one is shielding the children's eyes. 'Petty towns' seems to have dropped an 'r' under a gaze that sees beneath their facade. You could almost compare this to a *flâneur's* distanced view of the city, but it is not so disinterested and self-assured. It is scathing, certainly, but it is worried. 'What am I doing...?' The self-doubt prompted by Corcoran's reaction to what he sees is as much a question about what he *should* be doing as it is an expression that he could be anywhere else. His engagement in the national question is still strong even if it is melancholic.

In this anxious and scathing altitude 'the country looks like a picture of itself'. There is an interesting paradox here, where to see a country as a whole it helps to have a generalised distance, but for Corcoran to see a country at all we must be intimate and precise. How, then, do we maintain the England that Gardiner calls 'local, experiential and national' (note that it can be 'local' *and* 'national') in the face of the desire to reach after something general and abstract? The answer is to acknowledge, as Corcoran does here, the resemblance to the ideal whilst in some sense re-imagining it, putting it under a certain pressure. The country might 'look like a picture of itself' but rather than the usual metaphor of 'patchwork quilt' here we have 'grid' with all its baggage of identification and control, though also with a nod to the electrical power infrastructure.

This poem comes from the 1993 collection *Lyric Lyric*, a collection threaded through with movement and mobility. If it wasn't for the rest of the poem, this aerial passage might seem more liberated from the landscape below than it is. But all too often in this collection the movement and transport is passive: 'I woke up on the two lane section, roving / westward' (140); 'John Dowland in the passing traffic / goes over my head' (141); 'driven from the capital / under a sky of stupid messages, / sound tunnels with hoardings' (142). Like the 'populace' in *TCL* there is still a sense of being out of control, or rather of being controlled beyond one's own agency. Even that 'What am I doing here flying over England?' has a sense of having just woken up in the midst of a pre-programmed journey.

As if to counter all this though, *Lyric Lyric* has moments of standstill clarity that are intensely local, personal and present. They pierce the otherwise quite frenetic sense of movement cutting back and forth across space. In 'The garden surrounds me blowing' we find ourselves in another garden, hemmed in again, but this time looking up into the air space above wondering 'Who owns it? / Glitzy helicopters come and go / in the Spring drift above the town [...] all day, all day, this grating noise / shreds the sky in filmy strips' (136). Then out of, or under, or right through, this paranoid and highly stressed domestic space:

> I see the small child crouch
> eye to eye with a red tulip,
> in a moment of stillness
> stick her fingers in the cup;
> the flies and bees start up again
> weaving the square of green and trees.
> The world is all that is the case.
> The world is the shrine. (136)

This is not a sentimental epiphany that isolates the natural scene to sanctify it. In fact, it might be the central image's vulnerability to the stressed sky overhead and the subsequent consumerism of the poem's ending, the way it shines out despite these, through them, that makes this scene work so well. The world is not, and cannot be, a shrine for Corcoran unless we recognise that the world 'is all that is the case' first. Again, there is a striking heterogeneity to the space of the poem. It ends by returning to the babble of pop consumerism, paraphrasing and parodying The Beatles: 'I work all day to earn the money / to buy you things [...] I bought my love a fridge, / now there's nothing we won't do' (137).

There is a similar movement in the poem that opens with lines from an old ballad: 'I run to some farr countrye / where noe man shall me know'. A poem that begins in a state of fugitive mobility ends with two stanzas of static luminosity:

> The moon frozen in blue suede,
> framed in a loom of cables,
> left me standing alone
> tilting traffic off centre.
>
> Air filters my window,
> my face, my table and literal sky,

a door into the river night
the site of deep assent. (131)

The first stanza's intense, moonlit landscape has something of a modern Samuel Palmer to it, self-consciously Romantic, the 'tilting traffic off centre' (a phrase that crops up elsewhere as well) almost solipsistic. There is a hint of pastoral about it, but in the form of a poem within a poem, as above, this time 'framed in a loom of cables'. That a landscape like this can be entered, 'assented to', at some deep level, for Corcoran, is not to be taken as a retreat from politics into an immediate tactile intimacy. Such assent is not selective, but assent to 'all that is the case'. The pastoral becomes part of the collaged landscape, the strength of which is in the heterogeneity. Hence we can arrive later at the phrase discussed earlier: 'Events left me in the umbrage of green shade' with its placid, visual-pastoral 'green shade' with the disgruntled, conceptual 'umbrage'. Corcoran's assent is to this form of heterogeneity, through which comes the rupture of the traditional landscape and homogenous ideal England. In the process a space becomes possible again for the local and experiential to speak through the dominating silence of traditional scenery. Challenging the ideal national landscape by juxtaposing it and collaging it with other ways of seeing, represents an attack of sorts, but it is also a form of access for Corcoran, to a richness of experience, one that repays assent by being more plural and chaotic, by being more 'literal'. Rather than being evacuated of politics, the pastoral moments – the moments of luminous beauty and stillness – flare up like a caged animal, a beatific saint on the rack.

The later poems that explore Greek landscapes abound with images of doors, entrances and immersions. These too are ways through the scenery to the literal world beyond. They are often connected to a kind of visionary epiphany: 'In delight a door opens in the air, / we see the whole of Thessaly rising' (81). Or with a sense of portent, power and drama in the land of the chthonic gods: 'A door opened in the ground / releases the great blackness, / first light unfurled the sky' (12). Whether they are cause for delight or alarm, they reveal a world that contains more than has been taken to be the case. The sea is 'chambered' (12); the earth is 'chambered' (22). Writing becomes a way of encountering what lies out of reach, historically, mythologically, experientially, linguistically, even politically; it becomes a way through. Again, this is part of what Riley calls an 'expansion of resource' in Corcoran: Greece, not as an escape from England but a place interconnected with it, a place through which to reflect on England.

Take this stanza from *My Life with Byron*, published for the first time in the *New and Selected Poems*:

> Then a door opens deep in the cell,
> you hear the music of all your life:
> to go in is dangerous,
> to turn away is dangerous. (78)

It is a poem that opens with a familiar image of the garden ('The ivy on the wall lifts in one wave'), but here in the Greek landscape we can't help but think of a fresh significance to the ivy: symbol of Dionysus and the Maenads; ivy decorating the *thyrsus* or religious staff. Immersion, in this tradition, means a momentary letting go of the senses, intoxication, music, dancing; for Nietzsche, it is the Dionysiac stirrings which 'cause subjectivity to vanish to the point of self-forgetting' (*The Birth of Tragedy* 17). For Euripides, those who do not acknowledge the god are punished violently for their arrogance (*The Bacchae*). And yet the necessary excesses of Dionysus can be a daunting prospect to the reserved and rational Englishman. The call is to step away from the pre-programmed self and the pre-programmed language of *TCL* (the language of the 'sneak careerists') and find renewal in a fresh landscape, exposed, perhaps even for a moment, free. 'What scene unfolds in that domed snow shaker?' Corcoran asks in 'The Empire Stores' (26). '[A] limited view of human nature / in a medium of implacable pessimism' (26). 'Oh England on slick rails to the dumb chamber; / put your ear to the ground, your hands in the air' (25).

Greece becomes the landscape beyond the domed snow shaker (an echo there of the English 'air space' again), the Greek gods tempting us off the 'slick rails' of careerism, coddled consumerism and 'Blairprint' duplicity. By no means is this a retreat from the English landscape; it is a rummaging around for inspiration. In fact, it begins to follow genuine connections that implicate the English in Greek history and the Greeks in English history: the theft of the Elgin marbles, the journey of Byron to Missolonghi to fight in the Greek War of Independence and the rise of cheap textile manufacture in Manchester sealing the fate of the Common Company of Ambelakia.

When we imagine a nation we imagine a distinct entity (not unlike the snow shaker), especially an island nation like Great Britain with its brooding uncertainty about its relationship to Europe. But to look more closely – especially in a nation with such a long history of empire and foreign interests – is to reveal networks of influence, dependency, trade, all of which are felt locally wherever that locale might be. Often it serves the national interest to play down such things. This is a kind of imagined community that constructs itself like a snow shaker. Critics such as Edward Said and Stuart Hall have shone a little light on 'the absences and the silences' on which everything that is spoken about a nation is grounded. *English* breakfast tea, for example, or sugar, by far the dominant ingredient of any traditional *English* hedgerow jam: quintessentially English but part of 'the outside history that is inside the history of the English' (Hall 202).

When Corcoran visits Ambelakia in his poem then, he unearths a whole nest of spatial and temporal connections. 'The Common Company of Ambelakia' (the title of the poem) was a co-operative founded in 1778 to help ease the burden of imperial taxation being wielded from Turkey. They were an essentially socialist enterprise providing people with 'Schools Libraries Hospitals Mansions Welfare' (*New and Selected* 75). They represented an empowering localism stepping in to resist the brutality of empire. But it all fell apart when the industrial revolution in England led to much cheaper production of textiles and when the bank of Vienna – who held the co-operative's money – went bankrupt. After such weakening, the Turkish came to raid the village in 1810. An empowered local community is being pitted against an empire here. It is a story that appeals to those asking questions about England after the failure and retreat of the British Empire, even as the partial devolutions of Scotland and Wales bring the union of Britain itself into question. The memory of the Common Company of Ambelakia has a further resonance with the post-war English Welfare State that has, since the 1980s been eroded by party after party. 'Remember schools; libraries; hospitals; mansions; welfare', says Corcoran. He is speaking to his English readers in the year 2004; it is a question and an order.

The final poem in this sequence is titled 'Disclaimer: Byron Never Went to Ambelakia' (with the latter under erasure). It begins with the following from Byron, but it could as easily have been Corcoran himself:

> I saw before me in the vivid occupation of the people of that
> place a living notion of the world made good, a species of
> heresy, a society unfallen – just suppose this were known in
> England – the very thing I had traversed the theatre of war to
> find, here (82)

But the stage is set in the poem for Byron to watch them arrested and
murdered by Ali Pasha's troops. Whether in the form of the warrior
spirit of the Maniots, or the social welfare system of the Common
Company of Ambelakia, Corcoran, like Byron before him, admires
their 'species of heresy' that will fight against domination, and it is this
that he chooses to broadcast back to the English shires in the hope
of stirring them from sleep. This is what Peter Riley has described as
Corcoran 'seeking [...] a visionary extent through the resources of the
powerless of the earth' (87).

Corcoran's attack on English nationalism is at its heart utopian. It
sees the people of England as somehow beset by an empire (at times
British, at times American) in the way that the Greeks were by the
Ottomans. He is calling them to action, attempting to inculcate an
entirely English 'species of heresy' founded on principles that are felt
locally but combined to effect nationally. So we have an extremely
heterogeneous use of landscape, space and place that is – all at the
same time – technological, imperial, national, pastoral, local and angry,
political and radical. The art is in the grafting of them all together into
the same picture, making such genres and styles fit his own overarching
view rather than making his view fit any of the genres or styles. The
result is a landscape that is dystopian insofar as it is infused with anger
and anxiety, and utopian insofar as its sights are on the horizon, and
on how things can be re-imagined and re-made. It is no wonder that
such poetry might be found to be difficult. Ease of reading is being
quite deliberately assaulted in order to represent textures to the given
space that are more literal, that are closer to the textures of instability
and asymmetry that Corcoran sees shaping our experience. A landscape
not for the pleasure of consumption, but one for diagnosis, struggle
and repair. So the poetry refuses its reader an easy ride as it refuses
its English subject an easy nationalism. The reward is a vision of the
English landscape that is alert to its dilapidated and manhandled
vulnerability, inspired by and hoping to inspire a brand new 'species of
heresy' for difficult times.

Works Cited

Barrell, John. *The Dark Side of Landscape: the Rural Poor in English Painting, 1730-1840*. London: Cambridge University Press, 1983.

Euripides. *The Bacchae*. Trans. Paul Woodruff. Cambridge: Hackett Publishing Company, 1998.

Gardiner, Michael. *The Return of England in English Literature*. Basingstoke: Palgrave Macmillan, 2012.

Greenhalgh, P.A.L. and Edward Eliopoulis. *Deep into Mani: Journey to the Southern Tip of Greece*. London: Faber and Faber, 1985.

Hall, Stuart. 'Old and New Identities, Old and New Ethnicities'. *Theories of Race and Racism: A Reader*. Ed. Les Back and John Solomos. 2nd ed. London: Routledge, 2009: 199-208.

Harvey, Graham. *The Killing of the Countryside*. London: Vintage, 1997.

Keiller, Patrick. *The Possibility of Life's Survival on the Planet*. London: Tate Publishing, 2012.

Kingsnorth, Paul. *Real England*. London: Portobello Books, 2008.

Nietzsche, Friedrich. *The Birth of Tragedy*. Ed. and Trans. Raymond Geuss and Ronald Spiers. Cambridge: Cambridge University Press, 1999.

Riley, Peter, 'A Sphere of Abundance'. *PN Review*. 31:3 (Jan/Feb 2005): 87-90.

Robinson in Ruins. Dir. Patrick Keiller. BFI. 2010. DVD.

Saito, Yuriko. 'The Aesthetics of Unscenic Nature'. *Nature, Aesthetics, and Environmentalism: from Beauty to Duty*. Eds. Allen Carlson and Sheila Lintott. New York, NY: Columbia University Press, 2008: 238-254.

Kelvin Corcoran and Greece

Peter Riley

Kelvin Corcoran's poetry of Greece[1] has two sides to it, constantly engaged with each other. One is the relaxation of the northerner in the Mediterranean climate zone: heat, light, sea, stone, wine, music, dozing in the courtyard with a glass of ouzo... and all the rest of that (i.e., Now). The other is the whole of Greek culture: mythology, drama, poetry, ritual, religion, drama, philosophy, legend, history... (i.e. Then). The first of these is rational, the second irrational, but they get on very well together, in fact each normally implies the other. The Now is enhanced and dignified by the Then; the Then becomes visible through the Now and the whole spectrum announces sightings of the extended real. I fear that in a period of drives towards poetical austerity and purity such as we have had in the last 20 years or so in Britain and America, these forms of attention will be dismissed as some kind of indulgence or avoidance, which I don't think they are. Modernist zones might be sympathetic to the poetry in memory of founding fathers, but even here the implied fullness is likely to be disallowed unless contracted into politicised aesthetic inversion, or reduced to a question of language.

I've no intention of asking why Kelvin turned his poetical attention towards Greece. He had a perfect right to and it's not as if Greece is some remote pastoral zone, in fact it's just at the bottom of the garden – we speak its vocabulary every day and we have all lived through its invention of guilt. But it is interesting to trace when this turn happened. There was always a strong autobiographical factor; his poetry followed his life seeking especially the significant and emotionally strong occasions. That was his quest. A few Greek poems appear in *Melanie's Book* (1996), giving the impression of no more than a visit or two, but entirely woven into the fresh qualities of this book, representing as it did a large venture forwards in both poetry and experience, a bid in both for a new life. The word 'literal' is used prominently to indicate his approach to these realities, as equivalent to 'lyrical' – 'Traffic bears us back into lyric / into this explicit, personal experience' (34), 'Then I know love is not a metaphor' (26) – because in the disruption, displacement and new-found-world of the book, the literal emerges as equal to any constructed world of symbol or inference and is best, most authentically, sent into the world on the wings of song. The Greek aspect, the ecstasis of it, evidently chimed forcibly into the whole. There is more than the immediate occasion attached in a small notation such as: 'Eating the fig in the shade of the well / we were drunk with seeing' (*New and Selected* 123).

But this arrival and release (this Now) was not the whole story. The first 'Greek' book is *When Suzy Was* (1999) which is also the book in which old scores are settled, principally in 'The Literal Poem about my Father', the last of a series of poems on his childhood governed by anger and pity. It feels as if this had to be done first and the laying to rest of the harmful father is set like a crucifix in the middle of all the bejewelled poems in which Greece becomes the here and now. Indeed if Kelvin here slays the father he gains entry into the drama of guilt-culture which Archaic Greece re-enacted on a grand scale in the quest for final objective justice and which modern poetry has sought to transcend by comprehending the shame-culture of earlier, Homeric Greece. The poem ends

> My children talk themselves into dreams,
> our hands deep in the sea of glass,
> we rush to the end of the known world
> where the road ends in air.
> (*New and Selected* 93)

a liberation into dislocation and an overwhelming bid for *out*, a washing of hands, as if Britain is finished with, though of course it is not, for 'In my bones the white north sleeps, / each winter I return there' (99). 'The sea of glass' is a phrase from Lee Harwood, indicating a loss of contact with immediate reality in connection with a heart condition. The second poem, 'The Name Apollo' is a kind of preliminary pact with Apollonian craftsmanship, possibly merged into Dionysian imagery. (Jack Spicer's sentence 'I am going north looking for the source of the chill in my bones'[2] is recalled and will be again). So – and this is typical of this poetry's polyphony – nothing is forgotten in this excursion, nothing is erased, the conditions remain.

If we are to ask what difference the turn to Greece made, we must first emphasise important aspects of the writing to which it made no difference. His first book, *Robin Hood in the Dark Ages* (1985) had a preface by Tom Raworth, which is understandable with all those poems of political and cultural protest, unpunctuated and compounded of sparsely connected phrases which suggest themselves as symptoms and sometimes in harsh combinations, so that the reader is jolted through them challenged to locate a path. Yet there is already a habit of reaching a rhythmically strong and emphatic ending, the music of determination, which Raworth would never permit himself – everything had to remain fragmented, suggestive and ambiguous. By the important *The Red and Yellow Book* (1986) he has established the poem as a succession of fuller sentences or lines which may not connect with each other directly but do in each poem seem to belong in the same place, adding up to something, and are free to conjoin into more extended structures and statements. I feel these moves to be acts of kindness towards the reader and that by them he established the particular connected/unconnected way of writing which stayed with him henceforth through Greece or wherever, increasingly cohering the poem or sequence to a particular purpose or acting through a particular subject or occasion. The nervous drive remains, as does the refusal to explicate (the inner speech technique), perhaps obstinately on occasion, but there is relaxation (the Now) and he increasingly realised that the key to this opening lay in the concept of the lyrical, that the unfearingly voiced tropes of songs were not only musically telling but also gained access to sharable realities, language rendered communal. Whatever the Greek poems make possible this is what made the Greek poems possible. Or we could say that there are moments in the poems, or impulses in the poet, which do not allow for verbal cynicism:

> You should know voices when you hear them;
> sparrows, dogs, post vans and neighbours
> lilting and damn the pastoral
> but the dark all round me
> held her head up
> and shrank to nothing in a white bed
> (*New and Selected* 178)

Kelvin was led to Jane Harrison by Charles Olson. Harrison and her associates, the 'Cambridge ritualists', were a late contribution to the vast nineteenth-century search to locate pre-intellectual forces in ancient time which were determinative of modernity, and to locate wider and deeper, collective or subconscious, non-rational versions of mental process (Frazer, Nietzsche, Jung, Herder, Freud, Durkheim, Bergman…). The claiming of a pre-rational, holistic language was a necessary part of this quest, whether in new coinage or recovered *mythos*. But the Cambridge ritualists were distinct because they operated within 'classics', a discipline which had been important to European art and thinking for many centuries and they tore the whole subject open. From questions of literary exegesis and philology, they plunged into the darkest mysteries, proposing archaic tribal ritual (about which little was known at the time beyond descriptive catalogues) as the origins and essential substance, even, of Greek religion, legend and literature. The urge was to 'get behind' (as Olson put it) Homer, Socrates and the dramatists. Harrison proposed 'thought at a level below individual consciousness'[3]: 'Everything can be explained from the analogy of primitive rites of tribal initiation […] A great Art arising from a very primitive and almost world-wide Ritual.' Such voices were to be heard in many other places (late spasms of Enlightenment quest for natural virtue) but the specific invocation of 'art' here and Harrison's belief in poetry as engaging a pre-intellectual and collective comprehension ('a work of the people') operating in a specially favoured zone ('The Greeks – a people of poets') obviously offered a direct connection not only to the classical scenarios of Georgian poetry but to the anti-rationalism of all the modernist work deriving from 1890s aestheticism, which was surely a source for Harrison herself. Not that I'm aware of any non-academic interest for a long time, indeed some modernists were very sceptical and demanded a return to some sense of reality.[4] But Olson took the whole thing on board in a big way and extended it, encouraged by Harrison, into a globalism, inheriting with it the breathless excitement with which this research was conducted. Kelvin was at one time a student at the University of Essex, one of the hot-beds of the Americanisation of English poetry, hosting people such as Edward Dorn for extended periods, and he was taught there among others by Douglas Oliver, who had his own, more poem-centred and morally concerned version of the holistic thesis.

How much of all this Kelvin 'took on' is not important and, anyway, it is all overwhelmingly 'Then'. The results in his poetry seem to me to embrace these projects as access to a Grecian theatre of the poem, but then to back away from them in the face of experience itself, especially as he worked with larger and larger structures. The trouble with Olson's participation, though there are signs of this among the ritualists themselves, was that the projection of quality further and further into the hypothesised past and then spread all over the world, came to involve a thesis of permanent decline, that the Dionysian mysteries and rituals, satyr plays, carnivals, etcetera, came to be of greater regard than their progeny, the more highly valued as they were unknown or fragmentary, and the development from there through the pre-Socratic philosophers towards rational discourse, connected narrative and theatre and, thus, to Socrates, Homer and Aeschylus, was felt as one of degeneration and diminution. This was linked to political theories of ever increasing misgovernment and ultimately to our own condition as a 'pejorocracy'. The Mayan glyphs as a form of writing, which entails the total at every point, make our own writing a thin linear shadow of the possible. His answer to this impatience was, again, poetry, but poetry as a destabilising of language, 'projective verse', a transmission of interrupted and distorted forms as catalysts to the wholeness of the individual spirit which abhors completion and finality. In this the self of the poet was centralised as the achieved contact with primeval power, the bearer of world vision, and fragments of notes chipped off this monolith were valued more than any offering of discourse. The poem full of hiatus might offer the reader imaginative opportunity, spaces to be filled from his/her own resources, but the magician-self of the author presided over the whole thing and dictated the terms. Likewise the place where the poet stood, the local singularity, was newly isolated and enhanced to become the only point at which the self has direct leverage on the world. Poetry thus produced 'at a level below individual consciousness' (or above, which makes no difference) is not for saying, is not for others to hear, or is for them only as they allow themselves to merge into the poet-self. It is understandable that this 'push' as it was called, offered for many a very valuable entry into a poetical language of far more than individual purport, involving global understanding but operated instinctually as an immediacy. The intellectual scope of poetry was quite suddenly expanded almost beyond belief and most of standard issue started to look like the wilful reduction of human potential to domestic economy. But the late Olson ruthlessly pursued inchoation and contempt for merely informative writing to the point where any spare jotting or reference for his own purposes became a poem *without any further intervention* (spacing on the page meticulously preserved by the acolytes, of course). The poet pushed the poetry towards silence because the person, the 'I', was the self-substantial seat of revelation by its mere existence or size. Kelvin's take on Jane Harrison has a very different tone: 'When she gets down to the detail of particular ritual she does reveal a sort of imaginable common sense, that the content of the ritual is its social value, that's exactly what it is.'[5] In Buffalo common sense and social value were not on the menu.

> In the roots of our bright field,
> Jane Harrison is singing
> face to face with the fact,
> the substance of the god is a social custom;
> a worrying thought given the state of things.
> > (*Suzy* 20)

He does enter at times into the ritualists' polemics and even Olson's, but returns them to the lived world as basic tasks: 'I see the ritual, in all its versions, as a blueprint for introspection at the centre of the world – the thought of it' (*Suzy* 32), or transformed into a quite different kind of theatre:

> Beyond my hand and the round eye of light,
> Byron, Jane Harrison and my mother
> stand in the mist of Niagara falls.
> > (*New and Selected* 72),

– revenants, ephemera, who courteously acknowledge the living and then vanish. You're on your own. The poetry is redeemed in such company by the avoidance of austerity ('Now' is always to hand if needed) and above all of stentorian seriousness: 'According to our notions Orpheus has returned from / Egypt melancholic and is teaching weasels to dance.' (*Shadow* 13)

This fond frivolity concerning Orpheus could usefully remind us of Kelvin's general lack of interest in the concept of shamanism, which has so beset avant-garde British poetry and poetico-journalism recently, but which in Greece is, in Orpheus, a late arriving schismatic force, a ritualism resistant to rational discourse, and puritanical as it separates the soul from the body.[6] Kelvin's references to Orpheus capture him more in the Renaissance, as musician and lover, epitome of the power of song and its unkillable succession.

Perhaps at this point it would be useful to insert a sketch of the hamlet of Agios Dimitrios, where Kelvin and his partner Melanie have a house and where they spend part of each year, for it forms the theatre of a number of poems, and details are constantly appearing in other poems, sometimes signalling a return to the conceptual Greece. It is on the west coast of the Mani peninsula in the Peloponnese south of Kalamata, on a small coast road after the main road to Aeropoli has turned inland and up at Agios Nikolaos. It occupies a small round peninsula with half a dozen houses set around a central open space, of which theirs is the first on the right, a very small one-story house, little more than one room but with a small courtyard. Dominating the place on the seaward side is a seventeenth-century tower, the tower of Christeas, the local important person at the time. Kelvin sets some inventive scenarios in it such as Shelley dropping in. It guards a small harbour to the left, blue and white. Traces of a mercantile warrior society in the form mainly of towers are all round you here, especially if you go south into the 'Deep Mani' which is little but stone and fortification. The southern tip of the peninsula, Cape Tenaron, is the site of one of the traditional entrances to Hades. Other and unorthodox faint echoes of myth and legend haunt the area, including a route for Paris and Helen across the peninsula from their island at Githion on the east coast where they first lay together, to embark for Troy from Agios Dimitrios. Little owls inhabit crevices in the walls of the tower and there are also bats. A short walk north by the sea takes you past the taverna of their friend Yannis, purveyor of help and information, to Agios Nikolaos where you go for groceries, post office and Albanian musicians playing in cafés for the workers before they all went back to Albania because things are better there. Behind the thin coastal strip the land rises steeply to Mount Taygetos, 2400m, the central ridge of the peninsula. In the lower slopes there is a string of ancient villages, with sculpted and painted churches, set away from the coast to be safe from pirates and some of the old masonry donkey tracks which connected them to their harbours are still there and walkable.

(There are reasons why Greece has the best popular music in Europe. There are reasons why most Greek engineers, bank clerks, engine drivers or whatever can without hesitation when the occasion arises, dance the *zeibekiko* in a complicated 9/16 rhythm. Or something not too far from it. There are reasons why Greece is the country chosen for the most merciless crushing by international finance, with predictable domestic results of the worst kind.)

From *When Suzy Was* onwards the Greek scenario is established without the prelapsarian implications of Olson's version. The idea is not to devalue our condition in favour of lost paradises of enlarged being, but to specify and clarify it as a complete arena in which the richest memories of long past acts survive as names and stories which elucidate and articulate the present tense. And the grammatical disjunctions when they occur are more like passionate interjections than strategic concealments:

> Deepest octosyllabic land
> oh my heart is, the sea rages
> make me see what's in front of my face.
> (*New and Selected* 86)

The feeling is that an elsewhere, a separate and partly constructed site, was needed from which to think as widely and poetically as possible, breaking apart the sense of a poetical 'home' and the writing becomes a distanced or tangential trajectory which makes possible the most straightforward delivery as something won – not preformatted but worked through the meditative and excitable webs of modern poetry to emerge as messages which comprise the whole. That is, the message is the resulting truth but only as the fruit of a poetical process which encapsulates it in the poem's suspended action and this is a form of personal authentification. The message is held in the suspended moment at the centre of the poem, created by the tensions of the writing, which is a living, pulsating thing. Douglas Oliver spoke of wings, rising and falling, breathing in and out. Kelvin speaks of it as a transformative stage:

> My conceit to make the physical condition of language,
> the arrangement of the struts, curves and sounds, the form
> of discovered truth. Completely simple questions. To think
> about what is always there: reification as a type of behaviour
> in the moment of the poem
> (*New and Selected* 88)

– simple questions receiving simple answers such as 'all thought is thought about something' (*Suzy* 10), which fly in the face of just about everything considered requisite for a respectable contemporary poetry, but which happen to be true. But perhaps the force of the structure itself is less important in reaching this condition than the way Kelvin has totally invested himself in it.

As this process gathers momentum, the structures become more substantial and the terms of reference wider, not only in the Greek poems, though I feel that they furnished the first occasions for this expansiveness. We begin to move into possibilities of monologue and narrative. From *Backward Turning Sea* onwards most of the poetry comes in sections of 20 pages or more which are studies of particular themes, events or figures. *Hotel Shadow* consists entirely of four of them. The technique is something like epiphany, to be possessed by the figure or the occasion (or the music of it) and to trust very little except passionate speech, with an eye on the present tense in terms of war-faring and global finance as much as relaxation in the sunlight.

These poems are stuffed with names of places and persons mostly unfamiliar, but they shouldn't be a problem as they are sufficiently defined in the substance of the poems and they recur from one poem to another, building up their own identities whether sourced or (sometimes) not. I don't see the point in trying to contextualise these, nor do I want to start expounding Kelvin's versions or interpretations of thematic material. I'm more interested in the trajectory towards a more public poetry which manages to carry with it so much of the intriguing stagecraft of modernism.

So the texture may vary from a Poundian kind of cryptic note-making (*New and Selected* 18) through unabashed declared symbolism: 'we'll walk the streets of our burning city / and gather the asphodel of our sweet defeat' (24), to outright declaration, all these participating in a new boldness and confidence: 'Mighty and literal, love burns the world to leave only your face above me in the dark room' (35). Or everything at once:

> If what follows is a metaphor then this is no poem
> – Caspian oil sucked across the Stans to Karachi;
> it's not a silvery zero tube but ignition:
> make the ordinary language good or die. (25)

Against Purity (New Poems 2004) (printed only in *New and Selected Poems*), from which these quotations are taken, ends with 'Four Monologues' which, to me, signal the initiation of these possibilities, particularly the recovery of some of the dramatic and narrative functions which have always been with poetry until the twentieth century sidelined or banned them, or concealed them in the impenetrable ramblings of the unconnected, which they emerge from dripping. The vocal functions in them are quite various but in all of them the story is told: 'Leukothia' spoken by the goddess who welcomes illegal immigrants; the monologue of Pytheas of Messalia, the geographer who discovered Britain ('The great ocean put the chill in my bones') now stranded in a drink shop; 'Helen Mania' a love poem as if spoken mostly by Paris recalling the flight from strife; and most interestingly 'The Ingliss Touriste Patient' which is a first-hand account of a severe health crisis and hospitalisation Kelvin underwent in Greece, which might seem to destroy the function of the indolent Now if it were not for the touching account of the eventual journey back to Agios Dimitrios and life.

The ever-extending theatre that Kelvin makes of his Grecian material never quite loses its first meaning as recovery. I'm particularly struck by some of the non-Greek poems or sets in which at least hints of Greece appear towards the end as the resolution or choral exodus of the whole sequence. One is the extended meditation on Roger Hilton and his art (*Backward Turning Sea*) which, as Hilton fades out of life into his work and the self of the poem begins to sound more like Kelvin, offers glimpses of mountain and sea which are distinctly un-Cornish and 'the ancient world calling'. 'From Where Song Comes or Keeping the Empire in Order', which is about song, ballad and lyrical poetry, reallocates itself to Agios Dimitrios in the section on Pound (which is a masterly deployment of plain common sense). A graphic account of another health crisis, in fact a near-death one, this time not in Greece, *Words Through a Hole Where Once There Was a Chimpanzee's Face*[7] enacts another return to Agios Dimitrios in the last seven poems, referred to by Kelvin as 'four voices from the Odyssey', the wanderer's return. All these shifts act as forms of resolution and an extension of the poetry's field – beyond the subject towards the full present tense, against a back-drop of the 'ancient world' showing various ghosts mimicking our fondest acts and trying to merge into us, an effort in which they about half succeed. ('I was thinking there [Aristomenes] of how we are like and unlike these ancient figures.') The ancient becomes hybrid and the 'ancient rituals' are still with us in at least half of what we do, such as a formal arrangement of lines of poetry. In *Words Through a Hole…* the first section of the poem details the crisis, with all its disorder, and the second, the regaining of life and realisation of its properties, disposes each poem in four quatrains: an appearance of regularity on the page which corresponds to the tone of the imaginative move back to Greece and repossession of its gifts.

Four other major projects are involved entirely with that ancient world. *Alexiares* – an invented person whose itinerary, partly a pilgrimage to Euripides which involves Dionysus (a comment on the surprisingly beatnik features of Euripides' last play, *The Bacchae*) enacts a quest for poetry and its purpose, becoming deeply involved in questions of origins and earth rituals. *News of Aristomenes* is the story of a kind of resistance leader of the Messanians against their enslavement by Sparta. *The Family Carnival* takes in the great festival of wine and license, the *Anthesteria*, to which Jane Harrison devoted an extended study, as a result of running into a carnival while staying at Hotel Shadow in Corinth. ('I thought I saw a goat faced man outside the door in pitch darkness wearing a white veil, I thought his friend was wearing a Dolly Parton-style wig.' Another reason for quitting England, it occurs to me, might be that it has become a land where no real festival is any longer possible[8].) And *On the Xenophone Label* concerns the pre-Socratic philosopher, poet and natural historian Xenophanes. All of these are sequences of substantial poems which derive from purposeful study, experience and both, always in search of a story, but there are no walls round them: the field remains open and the most studied may (but not necessarily) break into a love poem, the relevance of which will be something more than temporal or circumstantial.

To check this I read *On the Xenophone Label* alongside the section on Xenophon's surviving works in Kirk and Raven[9] (which is not a lot – 18 pages of annotated fragments) and really you do get the whole story, the substance of the fragments as well as some matter from the annotations and a lot of poetical extension such as imaginary letters to Parmenides and propositions which take advantage of the fragmentation of the source texts to form a poetical texture. There are no poems from direct personal experience so this must be one of the most strict of the sets. Xenophanes is valued because

> And with my own eyes
> silver jackal black snake
> green lizard spring I saw
> all things with my own eyes
> (*Shadow* 87)

He stands in the middle of the move from mythos to logos, the initiation of rational thought about the universe, the noticing of natural phenomena such as fossils and what they mean – a move probably regarded by Olson and some of the ritualists as a loss. Kelvin does at times endorse something of their polemics by taking pot-shots at Aristotle, Euclid and 'Plato's thought police' but evidently values Xenophanes' skill in disagreement and empirical search, felt to be a pact with the world which has survived on the edge of extinction:

> How gentle is the exploration of the limits of human knowledge;
> from inside such inquiry, a faint ghost in an empty land, we hear
> a transparent whisper of almost nothing through another's history…
> (99)

There is a constant quest for a pact, the possibility of which is enshrined in the Greek home. There are also acknowledgements of the horrors of the world with which it is impossible to reach a pact and which must finally be turned aside from, since the only alternative is to eat and be eaten. There is even direct contemporisation of the ancient histories, implying a formal permanence, as in the story of Aristomenes, the 'scourge of Sparta', where it is made clear that Sparta, always Kelvin's enemy[10], can be made to represent very serious forces of the current world:

> When the Spartans came over the mountain
> and made us their slaves,
> self appointed lords of the way it is
> with their global credit, pipelines
> and smart weapons in phalanx,
> our irrelevance came to an end (49)

and extended further:

> At the heart of it Sparta,
> can only make itself in other lands
> can only enslave, stamping Sparta
> on strangers' faces in rows
>
> At the heart of it system-collapse
> weapons technique, hidden deals… (55)

There is a characteristic movement in the poetry from invocations of harm such as these towards a calm which is sometimes expressed as a more circumspect and caring reading of civics and society – to work through the wildness and clutter of the world, including the most dangerous clutter, to reach a quietude which is the answer, not just personally but in 'what is before my eyes'. This movement is sometimes encompassed in quite short space and at least twice the performance is initiated with reference to the most determined and destructive dealers of contemporary strife:

> Those white breakers falling on us, to make the world invisible.
> You have been duped by Wahhabi cowboys and Yankee Rapturists.
> You were not even a pause in the plan drawn up before election.
> You must think of the good of others abandoned by such vanity.
> You must think of the schools, hospitals and homes of a better
> > nation.
>   (*Backward* 24)

That last line is a far cry from the lone cowboy driving over the western plains spitting satirical jibes at the roadside peasants. It occurred some time earlier in connection with the town of Ambelakia, represented during Byron's (fictitious?) visit as a kind of 18th Century workers' settlement, like one of those schemes of philanthropic mill-owners which Marx detested. It was destroyed by Ali Pasha.

> Remember, the Common Company of Ambelakia,
> the first industrial co-operative.
> Remember schools; libraries; hospitals; mansions; welfare.
>   ('My Life with Byron' in *New and Selected* 75)

and again:

> With the Jihadists and the Evangelicals copulating furioso
> locked in their excuse-me death dance,
> I retired to my home in Egypt
> to dream of my gentle God.
>   ('Two Confessions and a Quotation', in *What Hit Them* 2008)

What is the nature of this peace? The following declaration comes from 'Epicurus is my Neighbour' in *The Family Carnival*:

> Herodotus before you run me down in Athens
> let me give you a summary of my system.
> Ataraxia: I've stretched it on a banner across the street
> ATARAXIA
> for all to pass under and gaze upon in wonder.
>
> There's no point in using words that make no sense,
> that are unattached to the world; we know it, every day
> we know it, that's apparent despite the same old business;
> look at the boundless sky – and my banner,
> look at boundlessness at every turn, bodies and void.
> (*Shadow* 76)

Ataraxia is defined as the specifically Epicurean sense of tranquillity: 'a lucid state of robust tranquillity, characterized by ongoing freedom from distress and worry'. So it is more than the deck-chair and the glass of ouzo. It is both active and passive and the 'freedom' it offers must include the freedom to think and act towards good, as a kind of gravitation. Further, 'It signifies the state of robust tranquillity that derives from eschewing faith in an afterlife, not fearing the gods because they are distant and unconcerned with us, avoiding politics and vexatious people, surrounding oneself with trustworthy and affectionate friends and, most importantly, being an affectionate, virtuous person, worthy of trust.'

When it comes to poetry, this is all very well but I like to think we can also locate such virtue in forms of direct speaking and the realisation of earthly existence as a lyrical fact, which can certainly be found in Kelvin's Greek sphere. Sheer notations of presence as lyrical being:

> Rain has released the smell of wild garlic
> and splashed blue cyclamen across the path;
> mosaic of light on the insect-laden air
> bears the unfinished music of the small gods passing.
> (*Backward* 89)

or, 'nearby a woodpigeon calls and / small birds sing in a chamber of sound' (*Shadow* 54). The placement of syllables and the accession towards rhythmic stability from line to line are faultlessly engaging here. And what is the 'chamber' but the creation of a compass of poetry in a foreign land?

Or the way he begins his lament for Douglas Oliver, the utter no-nonsense graphic simplicity of it, the way it stands within the constructed sphere which is the hope of the writing and the strength of the statements that arrive during the course of the poem which are all, really, epithets of the Greek poetical theatre:

> I saw Douglas Oliver last night
> standing in the shadow of the tower,
> Christeas' tower guarding the harbour.
> [...]
> you hear Doug speak in a land made unstrange
> [...]
> Poetry is the way we think and speak here
> (*New and Selected* 36-7)

'Here' is Ataraxia.

Notes

[1] The books mainly referred to are *Melanie's Book* (1996), *When Suzy Was* (1999), *New and Selected Poems* (2004), *Backward Turning Sea* (2008) and *Hotel Shadow* (2010). A collection of all the Greek poetry, *For the Greek Spring*, has since been published by Shearsman (2013).

[2] Number 2 of 'Seven Poems for the Vancouver Festival' in *Book of Magazine Verse*, 1966.

[3] This and following quotations are from Jessie Stewart, *Jane Ellen Harrison, a Portrait from Letters*. 1959

[4] See Wyndham Lewis, 'The Dithyrambic Spectator' in *The Diabolical Principal and The Dithyrambic Spectator*, 1931.

[5] All self-comment by KC is from recent e-mails to me, late 2012.

[6] See Chapter 5 of E.R. Dodds, *The Greeks and the Irrational* (1951) a book which has been helpful to me in elucidating many points concerning Greek culture in this essay.

[7] Published by Longbarrow Press 2011 in an edition of 25 copies with the note, 'this is an intimate work for a few friends'.

[8] There may be a few small-scale local festivities left, but all of those that I know of are invariably invaded by thousands of visitors, entirely changing the nature of the event, and this includes very recent conceptions such as the Hebden Bridge rubber-duck race.

[9] G.S. Kirk and J.E. Raven, *The Presocratic Philosophers*. Cambridge (1957) 1979 edition.

[10] Why Sparta, the most fiercely militaristic and misogynist of all the fiercely militaristic and misogynist Greek states, should be represented as the prime enemy is perhaps obvious. Additional reasons would surely include such things as the theatrical torture of small boys, which is not mentioned, but the 'cryptaea' is on p.49 of *Hotel Shadow*. This was a kind of official annual peasant-killing festival done to maintain the tone of things.

Kelvin Corcoran's 'Straight Music'

Lee Harwood

Back in 1989, at the suggestion of Ric Caddel of Pig Press, I wrote a sleeve note for Kelvin Corcoran's book *TCL*:

> Kelvin Corcoran examines with a powerful microscope the public and private world we inhabit, and the language we use there and which uses us. His poems – dense, intense, filled with sharp fast thought – expose the horror, the 'swinish morality' of this world, its fraud and pretence, and the cruel greed of its rulers. The outrage is only lightened by the small acts and visions of tenderness in our lives. His vivid poetry shocks us into thought by its sheer intelligence.

Kelvin Corcoran has published many books since then, his poetry has grown and expanded in many different directions, but I still feel this note holds true today. The essential concerns and qualities in a poet's work usually start early and grow from there. No matter what, these strands will be found woven into the fabric of the poems.

This weave of one's loves, one's family, and an acute awareness of the surrounding world 'out there', its politics, its history and its pressures, is to be found right from his first book *Robin Hood in the Dark Ages* (1985). Look at a poem such as 'A political poem' (28-31), or continue to 'World politics or the digestive tract' (37-39) which ends:

> I put my hand to drift in your hair,
> casualty reports coming in
>
>   your hair is cool
>   human hand
>   hear that voice.

The book ends with Kelvin's statement attacking the world 'authorised' by Margaret Thatcher and the Tory government. This statement in turn ends with the sentence 'Where there is no vision the people perish.'

What stands out in Kelvin's poetry is its immediacy, as though the events in the poem are happening now. This is combined with direct and, at times, raw emotion that few other poets can equal. In Kelvin's second book, *The Red and Yellow Book* (1986), read 'the last poem' on his mother's death:

> – no death is an average death
>
> I wish I could get my voice back oh
>
> the fields where you grew are burning
>
> – would you like your bed jacket now?
> Yes   I   think   I   will
>
> fear no more the heat of
>
> the last word –drink–
>
> 8.50 p.m. 9 August 1984.
>
> – we're with you mum (kiss)
>
> in my arms, all gone
> a mannerist portrait
> 58 years old, all gone. (10)

Such feeling, though, is also always put in perspective. It exists in the same world that later in this collection tells of:

> the revolting confidence of ownership,
> each turns a page of English history
> it fingers you and gets it wrong (18)

and further, in the poem 'the sound at the end of waiting':

> the brutality of facts in the box of delights
> will open bright in your face (22)

'Nobody thinks hard enough for poetry' is the title of one of the poems in Kelvin's next book *Qiryat Sepher* (1988). The poems in this collection and *TCL* (1989) set out to shake such complacency. They are poems where emotion and thought and communication exist. They contain clear, direct speech that's openly searching and asking questions. The poems also have the rhythms and language of natural speech. In such a world the reader becomes involved, is taken beyond the words. The poems are not hiding behind unquestioning cliché or the word wallpaper so common today. Words do actually mean something, have precise value. There is little excuse for the abuse of language. Contrast such literary games with the lovely clarity and humanity of poets such as Yannis Ritsos, Cavafy, Elizabeth Bishop, Borges, Paavo Haavikko, Miroslav Holub, Frank O'Hara, Wisława Szymborska, and so many others, including Kelvin Corcoran, whose poems stay on and on in our hearts.

In 1990 *The Next Wave* was published. As you progress through Kelvin's books you realise he has a very distinctive voice. Here, as elsewhere, there is an anger and violence. An intense pace. In the hard and cruel world of business, economics and politics he portrays:

> The idea was simple;
> banish feeling to the borders (22)

but within this same world are vivid scenes of people's lives:

> I was talking to you but couldn't see your face,
> engulfed by unformed stars and signal mess (16)

See, for example, the poem 'In the lazar house' (17) and the beautiful poem on the birth of his daughter Madeleine (25). I think of Ed Dorn, one of the few other poets who has this same balance in his early poems of the political and the personal.

Such ambitions for poetry are even more clearly stated in Kelvin's 1993 collection *Lyric Lyric*. In the first poem:

> I go the straight song
> straight music drives me,
> …
> the human meaning
> out of the dark dream
> breathing immediate words (3)

Later in the poem that begins 'The garden surrounds me...', while the prime minister's helicopter arrives and security barriers are erected, a small child crouches to examine a tulip close up in the nearby park.

> The world is all that is the case.
> The world is the shrine... (27)

And this too set beside memories of his father in the piece starting 'My father waits at the gates of the Midlands Electricity Board for the forgotten sandwiches'. This yet another layer in these many-layered poems that cut across the strata and show a full world that includes so many strands, so many forces.

Melanie's Book (1996) and then *When Suzy Was: a book of answers* (1999), for me, move up several notches. As though Kelvin really gets into his stride. You can hear his voice in these clear, vivid poems. The power of the love poems is intense. But love that's not isolated in the lover's dreams, but is earthed, lives in this world. In *Melanie's Book*:

> Estate by estate, family by family
> the poor turned invisible,
> in the hard blue sky above the stadium
> currencies vanish, nations appear. (4)

> The bosses have all gone for the season,
> one block of light falls across the corridor,
> quiet after business   don't walk away from love. (11)

> There I'm thinking with my hands
> and the room's flying over the city,
> over the bridge, the parks and zippy motorway
> your open face floating before me.

> Every time I see you
> something happens and I can't speak,
> like birds in the air
> calling and calling your name out. (14)

> there your face is changing above me;
> love pours into us and we cross the threshold

...
You're the Queen of Heaven and Earth, I thought you'd
    want to know.
– You know how to stop a girl eating her breakfast don't you.
    (16)

The Greek landscape, that has become such a central ground for
Kelvin's poetry, is first seen in *Melanie's Book*, but it is in *When Suzy Was*
that its presence is felt to the full. It's the Greece that is now, its people
and landscape, but side by side with this are all the Greek myths and
ancient history. The two worlds, as he discovers, are so closely bound
together. The past still feels real and close in this landscape. It allows
him a lovely freedom to range through time and still be here. As he says
early in the poem 'In the red book'

We kept to coastal routes, in sight of meaning
around the shores of the various world.
    (15)

But while, as in the poem 'The roadside shrine' (35-37), there's a Greek
setting, the world of 'back home' never disappears. It is a continual
background, sometimes more obvious than others. And within this
book is a poem so clearly set in England, in that strip of land facing
the Welsh border. This poem is 'The literal poem about my father' (27-
29). A poem that whenever I hear it read I'm close to tears. That poetry
should move one this deeply, a poem that is intensely personal yet not
exclusive or private, is for me the proof that poetry really does matter.

Kelvin's *New and Selected Poems* (2004) includes several later poems
that move back and forth between Greece and England. 'The ludicrous
placation of ghosts' (72) is one example of how this can work so well.
But others stay in one place – the directness and passion of 'Melanie
I've been thinking about when we first met' in England (35). And in
Greece, 'Four Monologues' (38-44). A sequence that includes 'The
Ingliss Touriste Patient', a vivid account of Kelvin's collapse and time
in the Kalamata hospital. After he leaves the hospital the poem ends:

From Cambos, the air heavy with eucalyptus rolled over the car,
sweet pine and burnt dust off Taygetos drenched the road
and through Kardhamyli jasmine in waves fell upon us;

so you kept driving and I lay down and the full moon
made its path across the water and I was there. (44)

It seems that after 2004 Kelvin more and more starts to create a
series of monologues, or portraits of other people, ancient and modern.
They may be loose and wide-ranging, but they're centred around one
individual. A precedent I think of is Robert Browning's poem 'A Toccata
of Galuppi's' in his *Dramatic Lyrics*. But the form Kelvin chooses – a
book length sequence of poems – allows him even more freedom to
wander and include all sorts of associated concerns. It's perfect for the
way Kelvin writes and what he cares about.

Roger Hilton's Sugar (2005) is the first obvious example of this work.
The energy and passion and bloody-mindedness of the painter Roger
Hilton set against a hard cold world. But within this portrait the
mask or persona is set aside at times to allow a beautiful love poem,
'Melanie I want to say in plain words' (23). The poem a parallel in the
writer's own life of the force of human warmth and love that counters
the 'torture gardens and out of town shopping' (13) and all that Hilton
rages against.

After the Hilton volume Kelvin continues to explore the lives of
other figures that create resonances in him. Xenophanes of Colophon
in *On the Xenophone Label* (2009), which includes the stanza:

> The limits of human knowledge
> do not excuse inquiry
> you are not off the hook
> the rim of the world burning
> ('Propositions 1')

Other portraits are included in the later collection *Hotel Shadow* (2010),
such as Aristomenes and then Byron. And in the book *Backward
Turning Sea* (2008) he even invents a figure, Alexiares, created from all
of Kelvin's readings of ancient history, mythology and contemporary
history. These poems are immediate and convincing and the very
opposite of dry scholarship.

It would be an error to think that Kelvin's progress as a poet follows
a straight path. He ducks and dives and you can never be quite sure
what he'll turn to next. And while, I know, I'm repeating myself yet
again, the mix he creates never narrows. Love, family, politics, and

now Greece weave through and around each other. Memories of his mother and father are continual strands in amongst it all. Read the poem 'Hearing Mishearing Doug Oliver' in *Hotel Shadow* (66-68), to see this weave yet again. A weave that is always fresh and surprising no matter how much we think we know the story. A weave that talks to us.

In *Backward Turning Sea* just read such perfect poems as 'Helen Mania' (11-16), telling the story of Helen's flight and journey to Troy. Then read 'Aphrodite's Bay' (20-22) for Kelvin's own journey. A journey that includes ancient Mediterranean history, modern Greek history and a Birmingham bargain stall. And then after this read the recent booklet *Words Through a Hole Where Once There Was a Chimpanzee's Face* (2011), a sequence of poems mapping Kelvin's experience of (and recovery from) an ischemic stroke, and asking all those questions that follow such an event. It's immediate and personal, as are all three poems I've talked of here. And always in these poems is the music,

> I step over the silver thread between two worlds,
> I walk to you across water and open the door.
> ('Aphrodite's Bay' in *BTS* 21)

There are poets whose new work one *always* looks forward to. They can usually be numbered on the fingers of one hand. Kelvin Corcoran, for me, is one of those poets.

PART TWO

ON SONG AND LYRIC

'I think the writing occurs as song,
in a musical part of your mind and
you're not fully in control of it, but
you struggle to be.'
—Kelvin Corcoran

Second Conversation

AB: *Kelvin, on the one hand commentators like Andrew Duncan clearly support your work and, on the other, Don Paterson has also reviewed your work very favourably. How might we begin to position your work on the map of contemporary poetry, or does it not matter?*

KC: I don't know the answer to your question about positioning and whether it matters or not. If there is anything consistent in what the commentators you've referred to say, it would be about the poetry being lyrical wouldn't it? That's not a million miles from something I'd admit to. That might make sense. I wonder if there are a couple of assumptions behind the question, which are to do with something about a league division of poetry and its commentators; or the division, the categorising, of the mainstream and the others? My publisher, Tony Frazer, is amusing on this: he thinks he typically publishes people who are too straight for the avant-garde, and too avant-garde for the straight. Doomed in other words!

AB: *The poet's pegs are too square for the round holes and too round for the square ones?*

KC: Yes, but if you think about what shape the poetry is for the defined 'market' while you make it, deliberately positioning yourself, then you *are* probably doomed; there are lots of shiny and taste-free supermarket apples. I don't think of the reception of it in that way.

AB: *Do you have a reader in mind at all?*

KC: I've wondered about that. And some people are very straight about it, aren't they: they *know* who they write for, and they can probably guess how many readers there are, and in some cases *who* they are. You know, you turn up and there are three people at a reading and you know two of them! But I don't think there's a reader in your head when you write. I think that a stronger tendency, a curious inclination, is the way in which a mind wants to entertain itself. I don't have a clear idea of the reader, which is not a wilful or belligerent ignorance, neither do I think the reader carried in the mind is a useful or necessary device – but some supposedly advanced writing appears to dismiss the reader before the game begins, I think. What's the purpose of that I wonder?

AB: *But those divisions we mentioned, the round and the square, do exist?*

KC: They certainly exist in the minds of some of the combatants who put themselves in those camps, those holes, and it might be, in part, to do with your question about regard for the reader. On that score there is certainly plenty of poetry around which merely flatters a lazy reader for immediate emotional confirmation. There's more of that around than the 'reader exterminator' variety.

AB: *Yet over recent years there* has *been a significant move away from this binary of 'accessible' and 'difficult' poetry – to decamp – so that you now get people talking about 'cusp poetics', poets who write on the boundaries between different kinds of traditions.*

KC: I'm not interested at all in the 'poetry politics' business. I'm aware of some of it because it's gossip, but, in all truth, if we played that game on this table and said "Where do you place so and so?" I could say, "Well, they're about there, and so and so is over there, nearer the salt." I suppose one aspect of this that receives attention is the level of difficulty or challenge perceived.

Ian Davidson had this very amusing idea, if I remember it correctly, describing seven categories of the difficulty of a walk, taken from a real example of categorising the difficulty of expeditions. Something like: *1) Easy stroll through the park on Sunday afternoon wearing your comfy shoes* and, at the extreme seventh grade (or the first grade) it's: *7) Unpredictable and hazardous territory, be well equipped, be accompanied by professionals/experts in the field, or armed guards, sudden pitfalls can be expected, and life-threatening changes of climate, you will be disorientated and feel almost constantly under threat.* I might exaggerate a little here. But we know who that is, don't we? Geoffrey Hill and Roger Langley, perhaps? And we're over here at number one with whomever? Roger McGough, Carol Ann Duffy? But that's to rely upon a taxonomy of difficulty, and that's not the only issue. I know who I prefer, in these rather stark terms, if we have to resort to them. There are rather obvious differences on offer aren't there? Ed Dorn also had a useful categorisation conceit based upon the different grades of beef – from prime through to utility – which sounds about right.

AB: *You've talked about the significance of Basil Bunting to you before, and W.S. Graham. Picking up on your 'taxonomy' above, are those the poets of your tradition? Does that word 'tradition' mean anything to you?*

KC: Yes tradition of course. I'm always trying to write various accounts of the lyric tradition as a poem. And, yes, there are people you read repeatedly, aren't there, but it doesn't mean you want to write as they did. You read them repeatedly because you want to, for many reasons. This is about pleasure, straightforward admiration and enjoyment, an unlimited engagement, perhaps because a single reading seems not to exhaust what's there. Reading poetry by the likes of Bunting and Graham, again and again, is the contrary experience I've found elsewhere. Sometimes with other poets I've ended up thinking, well this isn't quite what I thought it was ten years ago, you strip off the enhancement of memory of a particular reading at a particular time, and it's disconcerting. And there's the great thing of coming to something for the first time. I've just read some early Anne Carson. Why didn't someone tell me about this before? Oddly enough, rereading all of William Carlos Williams lately has given me both responses: the knockdown brilliance *and* some moments of clunkiness, but overwhelmingly the former. I used to read some of whatever-the-poet-I-was-reading read. That can be curious. As for tradition, a tradition a poet may be foolish enough to claim, I don't think so. I recently read *Paradise Lost* and *Paradise Regained*, but I seem not to have written a blank verse theological epic yet.

I suppose there are those who write with a very clear idea of the reader and his or her capacity, the enforced reader of the exam text anthology, for instance. But that is a form of industrial production, of utility; another poem about a troubled childhood, my lovely teacher, how lovely but sad nature is. But that's not poetry is it; it's not worth our attention is it. That's just doggerel. So I don't have an idea of the reader in the moment of writing. Who does?

AB: *There's a fair amount of reference in your work, particularly your most recent work, to other works of poetry and art, to philosophy, and to historical or mythical figures?*

KC: I'm sometimes bothered about the specific idea of difficulty related to reference and allusion, of how much you can expect a reader to know... Well, go and find out. It's so much easier these Google days, at least as a starting point, and then go and read something more useful. Don't be lazy, just go and find out. You don't want to just read something in the poem that tells you what you already know, do you?

Having said that, when you read Pound's *Cantos* it's endlessly frustrating, because Pound is such a terrible user of historical sources. It's frustrating because he can turn a line and break your heart with sheer beauty. For instance, in the *Cantos* there are eight or nine references to Plethon or Gemistos, a late Byzantine philosopher in whom I've become interested, and I've used him in a poem 'Sea Table'. And you might think it's not Pound's job to instruct me about Plethon for the purposes of referring to him in my poem, but there's a problem. If you're really keen and curious about something and you don't even realise that he's referring to that person or idea (because the references are so scrambled and the possible significance so buried and confused), then you just won't find it.

What I found out about Gemistos I didn't find in *The Cantos*. If poetry is to include history then it has to work differently to dumping barrow loads of archival material in the poem, which is only to the detriment of the argument of the whole work. Pound of course partly acknowledged this fault himself later on in interviews when he's gone back to the work. But the possible difficulty of reference and allusion is only peripheral perhaps. The real difficulty is more to do with the uses of the poetic imagination and what initially makes some sort of sense to a reader; it's with *this* that everything or nothing is available to the reader.

AB: *Does the political interest in your work come from research and reading like that, or perhaps from other 'political poets' like Douglas Oliver who tutored you when you were at Essex University?*

KC: No, I don't think it's through that. It's to do with the contrast in my experience as a kid, at school, and with family, and then changing with an education. But I did have one good teacher in school who woke me up. I'm the cliché; you can put me on the poster: one good teacher can change everything. He was a very interesting character, a Canadian who had been a Spitfire pilot. He used to wear spats and dress very formally to teach at a very ordinary secondary modern school in the Midlands; he was unique in that certainly. He got me into the Labour Party and interested in ideas. He made me work. "Work Corcoran, or I'll throw you out the bloody window!" And you thought he meant it, so you worked. I still think about him. And he said he had no imagination; he wrote textbooks on proper usage and grammar. I can remember one afternoon, he did a lesson on Keats' 'Ode to Autumn', and I got it! I got it! I got it like sunlight bouncing off the desk in the classroom. And there was this moment when I thought *OK, I've got it now, move on. I've really got the shape and meaning of that poem.* It was like the most beautiful girl in the world had just smiled at me. It was just like that.

AB: *So, thinking about how readers can 'get the shape and meaning' of a poem, what about the reader – or listener – when you are giving a poetry reading?*

KC: The experience of reading in public is a different issue. You know that you have certain poems that, if you read them in a certain way, will possibly have an impact on an audience, well at least you hope so based on previous responses. For me this is very different to the writing experience in relation to the reader. There are other poems perhaps, which you worry won't work in the context of most readings. Perhaps I've got this completely wrong, but it's a matter of the poet's confidence and the audience's confidence, and you end up thinking *actually this is really quite comical and quite witty*, now and again, but often an audience won't laugh, either because your sense of humour is no good, and you've just discovered that sobering truth; or you get an audience, like I did in Canterbury the other week, which gets every joke. They got every joke, every hint or innuendo, in these otherwise quite bleak poems. And they laughed. That's a beautifully confident audience. I'd take the lot of them home with me.

And you know that there are other poems which you might hesitate from reading in public, because you think that sometimes this is just not going to work. And yet at the same time I think everything should be able to be read aloud, shouldn't it? No ideas but in song! But then again it partly relates to an audience. I'm happy to go away with about five percent of what's been read as understood in some way or other. When I heard Bunting read *Briggflatts* it was the first thing I knew about him and that poem, I think I understood about five percent, and yet it was completely electrifying. The song takes us along. But the question is, at what level of difficulty are you happy to operate, and are you aware of the difficulty, and do you care about the difficulty, or are you mistaken anyway? I can't work it out. The title 'Sea Table' – the poem I'm working on – part of it is that everything should be able to come to the table, and off it.

AB: *OK. So, perhaps along with some perceived difficulties, there's also something that critics have noted about your work all along – this word 'emotional' – and the meeting of the personal with the impersonal.*

KC: Yes, that does interest me. Those two factors seem to intensify one another as well; the completely intimate as utterly common, shared. But having done several readings of late, I read that very personal yet completely impersonal set of poems about my stroke and the recovery from the stroke, so you go down in the first half and come back out in the second – *katabasis* and *anabasis*, the going down and the coming up – and I've been struck by the way people have reacted very emotionally. *Words Through A Hole Where Once There Was A Chimpanzee's Face* is an example of that. Some of the poetry I like the most does this; it will go beyond those terms, personal and impersonal, and approach a sense of risk. You're not quite sure what's going to be said next; I like that. Maybe there are things you say which are so disclosive, or so remote, that they stop being so, they just come back into view. I wonder if this is related to the point where a poet becomes *more aware* that they might have to acknowledge there might just be a reader who's going to try and read this one day? So you can't just obliterate the reader. You can't just play some clever senior common room game with them. Well I'm leaning back the other way now, aren't I? I don't know. But writing poetry is for delight. It's for the unbound physical pleasure of making something which delights the mind.

AB: *Let's start to talk then about how you do that then; about the making of a poem.*

KC: OK. First you choose a form of writing that will give you no money at all...

AB: *And the medium which is most slippery and resistant to saying what it means?*

KC: Yes, which is going to give you the biggest heartache and trouble with your mind... So why do you do it? Well, it's for delight.

AB: *Delight in the lyric. One can identify lots of song-like structures in your work. But also lots of sonnet-like poems. And prose poems. Are the processes of writing those different types of poem the same? Is it the same process with each to tap into that delight? What processes do you use?*

KC: At first, when I started writing a few poems that I sent off to magazines, they were tight, short lined, ten or twelve lines at the most, and you're going on in the dark, feeling one step at a time, wanting not to make a complete hash of things, but still getting that same pleasure from it. And whether it's shorter poems or the longer, connected poems, or even the pseudo-narrative pieces that I've written more recently, I don't think the procedure is very different. You go into it half dumb, half blind, even as you purposefully pursue specific sources or deliberately construct a certain prosody, line length and stanza, it seems to make no difference. At best you still only half know what you're doing. But without working the fabric of the verse in this way you don't know what can be said at all I think, submerged in it where metre and the other phonic qualities of the words themselves, and how they are combined, actually make the meanings. I think the writing occurs as song, in a musical part of your mind and you're not fully in control of it, but you struggle to be. And if you use processes or methods, they are probably attempts to reach into this activity, to make it look as if it's something you can handle and talk about. I don't know. And it sounds like I'm being a Romantic and talking about inspiration, but there's also a marked degree of making, of artifice in this experience. If you just sit here and wait for inspiration to arrive, gift wrapped and grinning, it won't show up: 'I'm a radio, just turn me on, I want to play!' But I think there's a partly unknown enigmatic blindness, in which you can see; a hidden meeting somewhere else, or a sort of coming together of the given and of artifice. Or sometimes more or less a whole poem will come along, word for word, one time, bang! It's as if it's just made itself. But it might be like that because it's already there, in some odd sense.

AB: *That artifice and process is clearly present in a technique like collage, which you've often talked about using; a deliberate process of making. What has that allowed you to do in your work?*

KC: I think at some point you acquire a notion of the possible direction of the poem you are writing, no matter how digressive, or finally mistaken it might turn out to be. So collage is one example. Not getting in the way of the words as they come out is another. There's also the taking and twisting of sources; the games of the palimpsest are a popular and shared preoccupation. They're examples of keeping going in the writing of the poem and its extension. That's the queue outside Jack Spicer's shop – not only for the poetry itself, but also for his account of how poetry is written. He seems to be a pervasive influence, and for the poets whose work I'm always interested in, he's a considerable figure I think.

AB: *So there's an emergent structure, and that then gives you the permission to carry on?*

KC: Yes, and you find the echo and the anticipation in what might emerge and the elements which might talk to each other through the book. Another device, a form of apparent digression, is *parabasis*. John Hall has mentioned this term to me. It comes from the chorus in Greek theatre, interrupting what is being said in the name of something more personal, or intimate, or urgent, appearing to cut across the artifice. But actually it's just redefining and intensifying the artifice. It might just turn out to be what you really wanted to go on about. It's perhaps a way of keeping open the diverse and plural ways of the poem and resisting over-determination, for the pleasure of the contrapuntal perhaps. But the single, isolated poem might also be a perfectly respectable thing without all this, or it might not exist at all. After all, if it exists within a tradition, it's already in touch with and alert to other poems, and it's doing its own work; it simply isn't singular, it can't be.

AB: *But the bigger structure, using other techniques of collage and* parabasis, *for example, allows a poetics with a bigger world vision, is that what you're saying?*

KC: Well, perhaps it's about the common and traditional ambition to extend the range or possibilities of the poem and wanting to play up and down through the different layers of tradition that are always there when you try to write a poem. For instance, I'm fairly sure that I'm not the first person to hear a nightingale singing in the single lyrical moment. So I've written a short poem about a nightingale singing and I'm trying to let the poem have its way with other meanings within the sequence and outside of it. The poem is in a run called *A Short History of Song Set to Music and Abandoned*. Well, that's my ambition anyway. The poem is clearly about Keats, and about the nightingale singing to me in my ear; the intricacy and simplicity of the song, in the middle of the night in May in Greece, and it's overwhelmingly beautiful. I can't put it in quotation marks and enter the postmodern moment. It's that nightingale and it sounds astonishing. But at the same time I've interleaved the songs with instructions for musicians to play an impossible music made up of unlikely sound collages and other elements, as a commentary or self-conscious accompaniment to each poem, singing a ridiculous history of song. But also I think perhaps the nightingale poem might require a conventional musical score, real, possible, congruous music.

'MY HEAD WAS AWAY AND SINGING': KELVIN CORCORAN ON AND IN SONG

JOHN HALL

What does it mean to describe a poet as 'musical' and for this to sound uncontentiously approving, as for example, 'theatrical' might not? On the back cover of Kelvin Corcoran's *Hotel Shadow* (2010), for example, a snippet from Andy Brown praises the work for being 'alive' in a number of ways, the last and most significant of which is 'poetically (musically)', where the brackets suggest that 'poetically' can be a synonym for 'musically'[1]. I want to attempt, in relation to Corcoran's work, to respond to my own question: what can this mean? Mostly I want to narrow the question down to be about the relation of his poems to song and I am not expecting a single or simple answer. It will become clear that I don't find it helpful to treat poetry and song as interchangeable terms.[2]

You don't have to read many pages from any of his books to recognise that this is a poet who takes song and songs seriously, as giving pleasure, as shaping and joining lives, and as being at the heart of the category of the evolving human. The words 'sing', 'song' and 'music', together with a wider lexicon that becomes attached to them, sound as refrains almost throughout; songs are quoted or alluded to; autobiographical scenes are connected to song; specific songs are the source and topic of some poems, while other poems make song itself – an idea or figure of song rather than any particular song – their topic. There is also something about the shape of these poems that is itself *in some ways* song-like, perhaps revealing an ear that brings to its rational judgement of sense, as Campion, one of Corcoran's chosen song-writers (*Hotel Shadow* 15-22), nearly said, years of attentive listening to songs.[3] You don't have to read many syllables or lines to hear that this is a poet for whom thought operates through hearing and for whom speech designed for listening must be *measured* (though not necessarily *counted*). At its simplest, there are two ways into the question: song as written into the poems, as vocabulary, quotation, topic; and 'song' as a term used in analogy for a mode of writing whose care for sound brings to mind qualities that have parallels in the two practices. I have already suggested that the first of these two is itself multiple.

In a brief essay I shall need to be selective and shall concentrate on the last and first sequences in the first set of poems from *Hotel Shadow* (2010), 'From Where Song Comes or Keeping the Empire in Order'. As its title indicates, song here is also topic. At times this is approached through autobiography and biography (particularly the last sequence, 'Learning to Play the Harp'); at times through other poets (MacDiarmid, Campion, Pound); at times through specific songs ('A Thesis on the Ballad'); and at times through speculative theory, history, anthropology ('From Where Song Comes'). Like so many other poems of Corcoran's, these also incorporate fragments of song and sustain an already established associative lexicon. The second half of the set's title, offered as an alternative, suggests the connection of song with order, very much including political power. I shall try to touch on all of these aspects, some of them glancingly, others in more detail.

First, I want to comment on what is by now a familiar structuring arrangement for Corcoran, which may have a bearing on the song-likeness of the lyrics that make up his work, and also on the way that they are read as lyric poems rather than as, say, epic, even though the longer structures increasingly 'include history' and have evident civic and rhetorical purpose.[4] A group of named poem-sequences is constellated by theme or motif under a single title in what I am calling 'a set'; each sequence within the set is itself divided into more closely related, usually untitled, sections, often separated only by asterisks. These 'sections' are often readable as relatively autonomous lyrics, so that far from there being a whole that is cut into sections, what we have is a constellation of related lyric movements. These lyric-sections are divided into regular blocks of text: stanzas of two, three, four or five lines, usually three or four. Within any one lyric there tends to be relative visual uniformity of line length of the kind associated with metrical verse. The number of lyrics within sequences varies, as does the number of stanzas within them, so signs of measure, order, regularity apply more at this median level than at the higher levels, which seem to be openly responsive to poetic contingency. The relative visual uniformity of the lines on the page might suggest, and thereby encourage a reader's ear to hear, an order within the lines too, with some form of patterning at syllabic – even phonemic – and phrasal levels. There is close syllabic attentiveness, with a possible and perhaps inevitable undertow of iambs always ready for transformation and variation through inversion into trochees or springing into spondees or extension into longer rhythmic units, but

the stress patterns of his lines are so open to variation that the notion
of foot does not win out over the Poundian 'musical phrase'. (Pound 3)
The rhythmic units that I hear are in interplay between syllable, phrase
and line, and the shortness of the stanzas allows the lines to work against
each other, as John James' *A Theory of Poetry* (James 135) suggests they
should. Despite this emphasis on prosodic features, I would say that
most of Corcoran's poems appear to respect the grammatical ordering
device of conventional syntax and its related punctuation protocols. It
may become clearer later why I say 'appear to'.

An autobiographical approach to the first alternative in the set's
title could be phrased as 'where song seems to come from in my own
life'. Even though it is the last sequence of the set, I shall start with
'Learning to Play the Harp', a poem in three sections, with explicitly
autobiographical passages. The title refers to 'The harp that once
through Tara's halls', a song by Irish poet Thomas Moore that laments
the loss of national integrity and pride, symbolised by the harp that no
longer plays through the mythic halls but hangs instead on the wall:
empire kept in order by the silencing of song, or the wilful silence of the
oppressed. This is a familiar trope: the loss of music is the consequence
of, and metonym for, even greater losses and, in melancholy paradox,
music that is supposed to be lost provides the means for mourning. The
poem opens with a related loss, that of specific poems.

> The lost poems of W.S. Graham written
> as a boy in Govan and in all of his life,
> the shipyard night-shift listens still
> to John McCormack on Radio Éire sing
> The Harp That Once at closedown.
> (*Shadow* 37)

This is Scotland in the 1950s and the radio is tuned to Ireland, to
Irishness, to an Irish catholic tenor. At the time, the two BBC channels
would have closed down with the imperial national anthem.

This first section has only two five-line stanzas and no first person
pronouns. The assumed topic at the outset is these lost poems; third
person pronouns are likely to refer to Graham. The second section has
twelve longer lines, grouped in pairs. A first-person presence is at first
implied in what could seem to be a direct aside to the reader but that
also has the ring of formulaic citation about it, sounding perhaps with

an 'Irish' accent: 'Have you ever heard anything as sweet as that?' The citing of sayings may not be that different from the citation of songs; this citation has sweetness in it. Honey is one of the words in Corcoran's lexicon of song. The OED's first entry for *melody* starts with 'sweet music'. *Melody* and *mellifluous* (honey-flowing) share a first syllable, though probably not an etymological connection. That first syllable is plenty to be getting on with.

In the second couplet the first person is introduced explicitly, though by way of the slightly refracting formulation (another re-citation of a 'form of words') of 'that would be':

> And that would be my dad around the house somewhere
> singing the same song,

By the time *Hotel Shadow* was published in 2010, Corcoran's readers could already be aware of the frightening and unpredictable behaviour of the poet's alcoholic father, for example from *The Red and Yellow Book* (1986; *New and Selected* 180) or 'The Literal Poem About My Father' in *When Suzy Was* (*Suzy* 27). The section continues:

> he drones in and out of the tune.
>
> It was all taken from us you know, by the English, the war
> of loss and burnt letters, the despised and disappearing past.
>
> His voice steps in and out of the tune, up the stairs
> making still the house, the garden in deeper silence. (37)

Loss, stillness, silence are ideas and sounds already present in the first section.

In going straight for the thematic node of the poem and its explicit motivation I have left so much out on the way. And this is a difficulty with writing succinctly about Corcoran: it is in the detail, in the deepening grain, and also in the asides – lines and phrases freed from linear discursive consecution – where the main work of the poems takes place:

> Fixing the boy in place counting down he sees
> the grain in the black wooden chair deepen. (37)

So let me go back now to at least some of the detail. These two juxtaposed scenes, one from biography, one from autobiography, that are connected by a song that is indeed the 'same' song but that is also different because of the difference in its performance and the context of that performance, could so easily be presented as anecdotes with an accompanying commentary that spells out their connections. This is not what happens. There is too much else going on in vocabulary and in an interplay between syntactical phrasing, prosodic line and phonological contour. In that first stanza of the sequence ('The lost poems …' *Hotel Shadow* 37), already quoted in full above, for example, the syntax of the first two lines seems innocent, giving us a likely subject phrase (around the lost poems) with a qualifying clause (where and when they were written) that will in due course head for a main verb. But there is already an alert issued in the unreliability of 'and' and 'in'. Biographical knowledge of Graham might resolve some of this, but there is something especially troubling about the idea of a published poet writing 'lost poems' 'in all his life'. As an alternative reading, though, the phrase might be, despite the punctuation, an adverbial qualifier for the next line: 'in all his life / the shipyard night-shift listens still'. In this reading, memory of the scene in the shipyard stays with the poet (Graham) all his life. The main clause never arrives; something is not being said. This kind of undecidability makes for close listening: 'the shipyard night-shift listens still' (37). There is a gathering of like sounds in this line and a recall of already heard sounds from the previous lines. Is it a coincidence that all the component sounds in the title of Graham's *The Nightfishing*, are here? '[S]till' almost reverses 'list' and its position, suspended at the end of the line, encourages another ambiguity between its temporal sense ('Now … as formerly', OED), its kinetic sense (motionless), and its sonic sense (quiet). While 'still' hangs there at the end of line 3, the next line ends with the contrastingly propulsive 'sing'. The stanza closes down on 'closedown'. That final 'n' is a nasal continuant: it hums off. This is just one example of the attentiveness to the sound-shapes of words and phrases that prompts the term 'musical'.

The second stanza re-opens quietly:

> Silent now, night tenor of silence
> shed on the dark waters of the Clyde,
> as if words might launch the boy across

> the black river, another world, no more
> at closedown and dawn, they're gone, as the smoke. (37)

As an event in the world – as signified and referent – smoke is a 'continuant'; it lingers, and the idea of it lingers, even though the final 'k' in the English verbal signifier for this kind of event does not, in contrast to the sibilants that end 'silence' and 'across', and the open vocalic ending of 'more'. The song itself has not been stilled, resonating paradoxically as the 'night tenor of stillness' ('heard melodies are sweet but those unheard are sweeter'), in which the precise choice of the various meanings of 'tenor' is left open. The after-effect of the song is 'shed on the dark waters of the Clyde / as if words might launch the boy across / the dark river.' 'Silence' ('mute') and 'shed' both come from Moore's words:

> The harp that once through Tara's halls
> The soul of music shed,
> Now hangs as mute on Tara's walls
> As if that soul were fled.
> (Moore 16)

For Moore, 'the soul of music' is not autonomous; it is bound up with 'the pride of former days'. Nearly audible in Corcoran's stanza is another song, cited several times elsewhere and given its own place in 'A Thesis on the Ballad' earlier in this set (*Hotel Shadow* 34):

> The water is wide, I cannot get o'er
> Neither have I wings to fly
> Give me a boat that can carry two
> And both shall row, my love and I
> (Trad.)

Water (especially wide and dark), song, loss, the impossibility of distance, smoke, words as means of transport towards desire and away from fear, these are refrains in the work. What is the power of song to annul loss and distance? And who, before the grammatical first person has entered, is 'the boy'? The second, autobiographical section, may have more to say about this. The threat of the father in his 'alcoholic box' is projecting through his 'droning' and '*step*ping' in and out of tune, where 'step' is associated with two senses of *scale*, musical scale and stairway. The word is derived from the Latin word for ladder (*scala*), and is closely related to *ascend* or *climb*.[5] Is the father threateningly climbing the stairs or is it his unscaled voice that does so, the physicality of his sound standing in for the rest of his threatening body? The combination of step and 'untune' recalls the famous speech on 'degree' by Ulysses in *Troilus and Cressida*:

> Take but degree away, untune that string
> And, hark, what discord follows!
> (Shakespeare 1.3, ll.109-110)

The root of the second syllable of 'degree' is the Latin *gradus*, a step; in other words, a scale. Rising (soaring) and falling (dropping, sinking) do not have to occur in steps. Musical notes can slide into each other, as can phonemes. Smoke, which has a strong association with the vertical prayer intended by burnt offerings, including incense, does not visibly rise in steps. Variants of 'rise' are very often to be found in association with 'sing' in Corcoran's poems; some imprecise but strong quality can rise *into song*; and song itself can rise, as though from the ground. There are these two movements, one vertical, one horizontal: the pitch of syllable or note; the crossing of the line from syllable to syllable, from note to note, as in the crossing of water, wide or not.

The third and last section of the poem, in short-lined quatrains, gestures towards the escape from a past that turns back on itself by introducing a new – presumably autobiographical – scene, one with an unnamed 'her', whose 'mouth made me dumb'. In this case, the mouth is not the projective place of voice, as with John McCormack or a drunken father, but the sensuous, receptive place for a kiss, neither quite introjective nor projective:

> her mouth made me dumb
> —will you come across the water to me.
> (*Shadow* 38)

The water is still there, but green now. 'Dumb' is another kind of silence, closer to Moore's 'mute', though with connotations of stupidity. Mouths and voices both belong to registers of sensual – and of course sensory – exchange between people who are present to each other or who remember or imagine each other's bodily presence. The scriptural domain of the page needs surrogates for this sensuality, which it may find in an erotographic lexicon and/or through the erotics of rhythm, intonation, and voicing. A voice, like that of John McCormack, carries a signature, can itself be sensuous, erotic, an idealised display of gender. Those who know a voice do not mistake it for that of another. Many of us fall in (rise into?) love with singers – at least for the duration of a song – by virtue of the qualities of their voice. *Voicing* is something else: the sounding in speech and song that is produced by vibration of the larynx and whose significance is partly derived from a phonic interplay with voicelessness, rhythmic switching between voice and non-voice. On the face of it, to be voiceless is: either to withhold speech, to whisper, or to eschew all vowels and voiced consonants, being left with the restricted sound palette of the voiceless stops – p, t, k – and the voiceless continuants: s, sh [ʃ], f, ch [tʃ], th [θ]. Sure enough, phonological analysis shows that sibilance and voiceless alveolar stops ('t') account for a high proportion of the consonantal sounds of these stanzas ensuring a rhythmical switching between voice and voicelessness.

I now want to move to the first sequence in the same set, 'From Where Song Comes' (*Hotel Shadow* 11), whose register is more thetic than autobiographical, in that song – not any particular song, songwriter or poet – is the declared topic. I shall not have time to consider the other case-study sequences: on Thomas Campion, Ezra Pound, ballads (mostly border ballads), and an excursus on war ('From the Hen-Roost'). The first alternative in the title of the whole set – 'From Where Song Comes or Keeping the Empire in Order' – names the sequence I shall visit in a moment. The second has no named sequence but runs as a thread throughout. There is, for example, a negative presence of *empire* behind 'Learning to Play the Harp'. The two sequences dealing with, or taking off from, Pound, encounter the latter's belief in a relation between the musicality of a poetic line ('melopoeia') and sound political order. Charles Olson's aphorism (in a poem dealing with his relationship as poet with Pound), 'as the line goes so goes / the Nation!', succinctly catches this sense of correspondence between poetic and civil order (Olson 319). In his cross-cultural speculations, Blacking, one of the acknowledged source for 'Where Song Comes From', sets up a comparable chiasmus through which he crosses 'humanly organised sound' with 'soundly organised humanity' (Blacking 99, *passim*).

Corcoran had long previously expressed such an order at the level of the 'heart':

> using order
> using calm
> mastering the heart
>   (*Melanie's Book* 24)

This assumption of a homology between clarity of poetic line and civil and personal order has no obvious connection with the origin or geographical provenance that are suggested by 'From Where Song Comes'. The sequence has six sections, each of between three and five stanzas, with stanzas of a fixed number of lines, varying between 3 and 5. The final section is grouped as three quatrains with a couplet, suggesting a sonnet. The author's note on this sequence cites Hugh MacDiarmid's 'In Memoriam James Joyce', Maurice Bowra's *Primitive Song*, and John Blacking's *How Musical is Man*: a poet, a classicist and literary scholar, an ethnomusicologist (*Shadow* 104). I want to look at – and listen to – the opening section in some detail in order to try to catch some of the complexity of a thesis in poetic form that does not appear to operate either through the logical progression of an argument towards its conclusion, or through the unfolding of chronology or (hi)story. I find myself looking for pattern and relationship between disjointed phrases, hearing lines which follow as sounded but which, as logic or syntax, are in parallel rather than series. This prompts in me an uncertain, questioning reading that often needs to go back on itself since 'the song's never the same twice' (*Shadow* 11).

The first line of the whole set seems to provide an immediate answer to the implied question, 'From Where Song Comes',

> Descended from the tribes of the Tarim valley

only to be diverted in the next into a local and economically complex scene:

> lost in town, open mouthed at the end of
> someone else's tether (11)

These seem to be itinerant musicians, caught up in history, not originating it, and the scene is local rather than globally anthropological. Point of view is obscured. Who is seeing this? Or who knows? When, in historical time, is it taking place? Who, in the third quatrain (below), are 'we' in relation to 'a chorus of phonemes, not even ghosts'?

> A chorus of phonemes, not even ghosts,
> we stand disjoint, signatures broken
> drilling holes in work, family, the whole lot;
> those first words cling like a jacket of smoke. (11)

This is suggestive but condensed and is certainly not easy to paraphrase into discursive prose. The prosodic stress derives as much from repeated conceptual charge associated with significant terms as it does from strong assonance (phonemes in sequence rather than joined in chorus). Under 'significant terms' come all of 'chorus', 'phonemes', 'ghosts', disjoint', 'signatures broken', 'work', 'family', 'first words'; under 'assonance' most noticeably the long 'o' [əʊ] in phone[mes], ghosts, brok[en], holes, whole, those, smoke; the sounds shared by 'word' and 'work' [wɜːk]; the play of 'l's (liquids, tongued continuants) in the second half. This is working suggestively rather than precisely and the imprecision lends itself to undecideability. 'Drilling holes' is presumably a metaphor and for me at least an unsettled one (Is this a joiner's drill? Or a surgeon's? Or a geologist's?). And those 'first words': are these the first words sought by a palaeontologist (of the kind relied on by Bowra in his confident interpretations), or the first words of any one infant? In either case those origins cling 'like a jacket of smoke'. For someone of my generation, that jacket of smoke evokes the olfactory signature of father.

The first words offered in the next quatrain are indeed a shortened list from Bowra, who in his turn drew them from a book by the Austrian linguist, ethnologist and theologian, Wilhelm Schmidt, on language in Tasmania: 'woman', 'arm', 'speak', 'weep', 'hit', 'stone' (Bowra 28). These were words, apparently, that shared roots across otherwise differing languages: 'differing in fundamental forms, thick with roots'.

From linguistic anthropology, the scene jumps to a street, a home, a setting where there is a 'you' for the poet to address. Perfectly intelligible words become unintelligible shouting that needs to be shut out by a refusal to listen, or by a banged door:

sound unintelligible, shut out—you were shouting
I didn't understand, doors banging in the street.
(11)

A lyric continuity is allowing jump-cuts and sudden re-orientations
that lead in the last quatrain to some of the formal components of
refrain, finding resolution through (choric?) repetition: 'we' repeat
because this is how it repeatedly is:

If we sing our belonging and away,
listen to the neighbour's rising call;
the song's never the same twice,
if we sing belonging and away.[6]
(11)

Song is associated with both settlement ('belonging') and migration,
including walkabout ('away'), reproduced perhaps in the dual locations
of England and Greece, of the contemporary belonging and the
'away' of the researched past. The language of belonging is particular,
concrete, favours proper names over abstract nouns, resonates within
the sociability of domestic – or quasi domestic – affect. The language
of 'away' can be just as full of affect: of loss, of pain for the left home
(nostalgia), of regret. The ballads that Corcoran selects for attention
have narratives full of regret, of threat to settled domesticity. But there is
another variant of 'away' and this is the transcendence of the particular
that scholarly knowledge and abstract conceptual schemes can offer.
Corcoran tends to cut between these two registers of the 'restricted' and
the 'elaborated', and this cutting both intensifies and unsettles the lyric
coherence of his work.[7]

In this particular section, the neighbours' slammed doors have
become one neighbour's 'rising call'. A call is the opposite of a shut-
out; a call is a come-on, a come-in; a call demands a response, not
necessarily in kind (and very likely the call is itself a response, and so
on, recursively). And 'away' can be conceived again on the two axes: the
horizontal, across surface; the vertical, in the 'rising' of song, and the
penetration through drilling, or the past conceived as down. Although
for Kelvin Corcoran song usually rises, the songs he cites and enjoys
often have a 'dying fall'[8]. They also tend to be 'thick with roots', to have
migrated through history and also to come from or otherwise engage

with the poet's own past. As metonyms of the left place, songs can offer an often plaintive form of symbolic settlement for migrants such as his own father, such as Graham. 'Away' needs its belonging, which the sociality of song can re-call.

Bowra looks for signs of the origins of song among surviving hunter-gatherer people, and relies for his source data on the work of linguists and anthropologists, codifiers at the edge of the dark forests of capitalism. The short, though longer-lined, second section of Corcoran's poem is a laconically succinct economic 'history' of language, if not song. An originating 'moment' is provided, where agriculture arrives as an imperative, bringing with it 'telekinetic supply chains' and the 'long slow lines' of the plough and, above all, 'code' (phonemes rendered intelligible):

> There was a moment, perhaps as polyphonic flocks rose from the
>   dark
> edge of the forest at dawn, an impelling code fills the sky, a code
>   that
> previously didn't exist when things were themselves.
>   (*Shadow* 11)

In doing so the 'flocks' instituted an arbitrary code which separated things from themselves. Sound became *phone*, with an implication in the use of the word 'flocks' that this is learnt from bird-song. The acquisition of code is represented as a great loss and terror, instigating the concept and percept of strangeness. Strangeness is not-belonging. First there is agriculture and then trade over distance:

> A conspiracy foisted on them from the wet earth itself had them
>   invent
> the seasons. They take their place in the telekinetic supply chains and
> the plough sings it, the long slow lines in classical tropes of ridge and
>   furrow.[9] (12)

The phrase 'telekinetic supply chain', bringing together parapsychology and the pragmatics of business and military procedures, suggests the causing of movement (of objects) from a distance.[10] When things are no longer themselves they can be moved, let us say, by the power of speech and song: word magic. Poetry.

According to the OED's draft supplementary entry (2003), the first recorded instance of 'supply chain' is from a 1910 publication called *Railroad Administration*. When applied to human organisational or taxonomic systems, 'chain' implies systematic connectivity along a line rather than, say, through that more recently salient metaphor, a 'net'. A chain's linear linkage provides a suggestive trope and is used in all sorts of ways – 'the great chain of being', 'chain-reaction', 'chain-smoking', for example; not to mention 'take these chains from my heart' (*New and Selected* 169). As a metonymic rather than metaphoric operation, a 'chain' was adopted as a lineal measure of 66 feet (or the length of a cricket pitch), very useful for measuring out and dividing up land, with multiples producing furlongs and acres. In connection with the plough, that appears soon after in the poem, there is the related technology of the chain-harrow (first you plough; then you harrow). The key associations, as I see them, are movement at a distance, connectivity, order, measurement, and all identified with the plough, a device that inscribes cleared land with the ordered lineation of ridge and furrow (line and stanza, plan and circuit), in a movement that *turns* (*strophe* as in *boustrophedon*) systematically, back on itself.[11]

The fourth section, which shares the format of the second, returns to this explicatory register, drawing directly on Bowra, on choral song, on the link with prayer, on a moment of change, this time to do with rituals of offering that depend upon the placing of honey and 'other animal products' in trenches set out in 'scandalous patterns'. The word 'scandal' is derived from a Greek word for a trap (or at least the spring of a trap). Ploughing is aimed at purposeful growth, not chance spontaneity like a certain kind of song:

> He said—the words
> come of themselves, shoot up of themselves, a song. (13)

The third section, which I have passed over, is in an expressly lyric register, established, for example, though the phrasing of its third line: 'into the dreamed sea of lyric voices' (12). This seems to celebrate a line of nameable poets, but keeps in play two ideas, that of trap, and that of edge, the two placed together ambivalently. Edges are, you could say, where there is neither fully 'belonging' nor fully 'away':

> is that you girl leaping from the world's edge
> hair spread like a dark net to catch the little poets? (12)

'Is that you girl' will bring to mind and ear for many readers a familiar song (Chimo 1969), and citation of the shared familiar is always an invocation of 'belonging'. Into the bodies of those who know the song will enter quite specific rhythms, intonations and voice qualities of the remembered singer and of the musical accompaniment, with its strong rhythms. As a consequence, these enter the event of the poem, the performance that is any act of reading. Some readers may lose themselves in the cited song and abandon the poem. The rest of us return from the (virtual) sung, after its due snatch, to the virtual spoken of the continuing poem.

Another song in this sequence that comes in as a brief snatch or sample, is 'What the world needs now', in the final section (13), where Corcoran's, 'What the world needs now is a theory of song', ends the line rather differently from the original song's 'is love sweet love', perhaps casting doubt on the need for a 'theory'.[12] In the same section, there is also this:

> Let it unruin many a poor boy, standing next to the gap
> an oasis or total knowledge maxed in the echo chamber (14)

with its twist on the line from 'The House of the Rising Sun': 'And it's been the ruin of many a poor boy' (Trad.). For many of us at this point Eric Burdon's voice joins the chorus of phonemes.[13] A gap is a name, you could say, for internal edging[14], and is ambivalently both break and/or join.

This final sonnet-like section lists what would need to be covered by a 'theory of song'. First in the list is 'a thesis on the ballad', which Corcoran himself provides later in the set, with poems on 'Barbara Allen', 'The Water is Wide', 'Edward Edward', 'Lord Randall', 'Little Musgrave and Lady Barnard', 'Lamkin' and 'It Takes a Worried Man'. The traditional anonymity of ballads makes them less likely to be exclusively attached in memory to a specific singing voice, though many readers will have full bodily memory of singing the songs themselves, perhaps many times, both alone and in chorus. Here we have a poem, a text on a page read perhaps silently by a reader in solitude, which triggers recall of a whole (other) song, and perhaps along with the song, at least one context in which it was previously experienced. Songs, in other words, are situated, and not just the 'primitive' ones; they do things; they travel. In the list are examples from Blacking when discussing the purpose of song among the Venda of southern Africa (Blacking 40-43). Poems, which are not songs, can try to engage with the full situatedness of the songs that haunt them.[15]

> From the licensed street corner, a version of a version
> from another country rings out many voices in one
> (*Shadow* 13)

Being haunted by song and being very carefully shaped as a sounded thing does not make a poem a song. A poem is a poem.[16] But poems can welcome song and allow it a resonating if spectral place in their own poetic proceedings.[17]

Notes

[1] The comments by Andy Brown were extracted from: "'I Was There and Not There": England, Greece And Myth in Kelvin Corcoran's *Selected Poems*'. (http://www.stridemagazine.co.uk/2004/September/brown-corcoran.htm) (accessed 25.8.12)

[2] Zoë Skoulding sets out the terms for considering differences and possible relationships in a forthcoming essay (Skoulding 2013 est.) that compares citations (including mis-citations) of songs in poems by Denise Riley, John James, Sean Bonney and Caroline Bergvall. The chapter on Sound (Chapter Two) in Stewart 2002 is also very helpful, drawing on a wide range of reading.

[3] 'The eare is a rationall sence and a chiefe iudge of proportion' (Campion 36).

[4] I have in mind here Ezra Pound's well known definition of epic as 'a poem including history' (Pound 86).

[5] The unattributed brushed-ink drawing on the cover of *Melanie's Book* is made up of a set of splodged dots in a rectangular grid overlaid with what looks very much like a short ladder with all its rungs except the topmost one missing a middle section: a partially unscaled scala. It *rises* all the same, an effect partly achieved by a slight angle.

[6] This echoes, and twists, an earlier citation of Burns:

> My head was away and singing:
> an' war'ly cares an' war'ly men / May a' gae tapsalteerie, O.
> (*Selected Poems* 44):

7 Basil Bernstein set out a sociolinguistic distinction between two 'codes', the 'restricted' and the 'elaborated' in *Class, Codes and Control vol 1*. London; Paladin. 1971.

8 'That strain again! it had a dying fall: / O, it came o'er my ear like the sweet sound' (Shakespeare, *Twelfth Night*, 1.1, 4-5)

9 This is how the stanza appears in *Hotel Shadow* 2010. My sense is that 'furrow' should end the third line and not sit on a line of its own but that page-width forced the wrap at page-setting stage.

10 As long before as 1986's *The Red and Yellow Book* there had been this:

> telekinesis and country music
> spark across the imperial world.
> (*Selected Poems* 184)

'[...] one can see subjects coming to an agreement in an imaginary struggle, in which there is, between adversaries, a regulation at a distance, transforming the struggle into a dance.' Jacques Lacan. *The Seminar of Jacques Lacan, Book 1, Freud's Papers on Technique. 1953-1954.* trans. John Forrester. New York and London: W.W. Norton and Company. p. 281. 1991.

11 Susan Stewart (Stewart 85), for example, refers to the 'long-standing western relation between poetry and plowing. [...] This deep analogy between the turning that opens the earth to the sky and the turning that inscribes the page with a record of human movement is carried forward in the notion of verse as a series of turns and in the circling recursivity of all lyric forms.'

12 Written by Hal David and Burt Bacharach and first recorded by Jackie DeShannon in 1965 (http://www.youtube.com/watch?v=vp1F16_7lO0). (accessed 21.8.12)

13 http://www.youtube.com/watch?v=TcY-uo51QTE (accessed 21.8.12)

14 'Any opening or breach in an otherwise continuous object'. (OED)

15 I am borrowing the use of the term from Skoulding (2013 est.).

16 Skoulding cites Jacques Roubaud (ibid): 'A song is not a poem and a poem is not a song... It's an insult to poetry to call it song. It's an insult to song to call it poetry.' cited in 'Prelude: Poetry and Orality', in Marjorie Perloff and Craig Dworkin, *The sound of poetry, the poetry of sound*. Chicago: University of Chicago Press. 2009. p.18.

17 '[L]yric is not music – it bears a history of a relation to music – and, as a

practice of writing, it has no sound; that is, unless we are listening to a spontaneous composition of lyric, we are always *recalling* sound with only some *regard to* an originating auditory experience.' (Stewart 68)

Works Cited

Blacking, John. *How Musical is Man?*. London: Faber & Faber. 1976.

Campion, Thomas. 'Observations in the Art of English Poesie' in *The Works of Thomas Campion*. Ed. Percival Vivian. Oxford: Oxford University Press. 1966.

Chimo. 'Is That You Girl?' 1969. (http://www.youtube.com/watch?v=ZlMJOeJUFCw). (accessed 21.8.12)

James, John. *Collected Poems*. Great Wilbraham, Cambridge: Salt. 2002.

Moore, Thomas. *The Works of Thomas Moore, Vol. IV.* Paris: A. and W. Gallignani. 1823.

OED. *Oxford English Dictionary*. Second Edition. CD-ROM Version 3.1.1. Oxford: Oxford University Press. 2007.

Oliver, Douglas. *Poetry and Narrative in Performance*. Houndsmill, Basingstoke: The Macmillan Press. 1989.

Olson, Charles. *The Collected Poems of Charles Olson*. Berkeley and Los Angeles: University of California Press. 1997.

Pound, Ezra. 'A Retrospect' in *Literary Essays of Ezra Pound*. New York: New Directions. 1968.

Shakespeare, William. *Troilus and Cressida*. Cambridge: Cambridge University Press. 1963.

_____. *Twelfth Night*. New York, Toronto and London: Signet Classics. 1965.

Skoulding, Zoë. 'Misremembered lyric and orphaned music' in *The Oxford Handbook of Contemporary British and Irish Poetry*. ed. Peter Robinson. Oxford: Oxford University Press. 2013 (est.)

Stewart, Susan. *Poetry and the Fate of the Senses*. Chicago and London: Chicago University Press. 2002.

THE PLEASURES OF REIFICATION: KELVIN CORCORAN'S *LYRIC LYRIC*

SCOTT THURSTON

In 1990, at the tender age of sixteen, I sent a questionnaire to Kelvin Corcoran in order to find out more about his poetry for a piece of A-level coursework I was writing under the tutelage of Robert Sheppard, which also involved writing to the poets Ken Edwards and Elaine Randell. In response to my somewhat naive but qualified question: 'what can you say about the "content" of your work, e.g. if there are specific long-standing preoccupations in it?' Corcoran responded:

> Preoccupations is a clear enough word. Thinking inside the physical form of the language for the pleasure of reification. Whatever is happening – most recently writing about driving on motorways. You tell me. (Questionnaire response 1990)

The phrases 'clear enough' and 'you tell me' reveal a terseness that characterised Corcoran's overall response – reluctant to be drawn by my schoolboy questions, impatient with my grasping at notions I barely understood. As he put it in his accompanying letter:

> [I] trust you can excuse the apparently abrupt tone in some of the responses. I wonder if you might be better off with the poetry and ignoring the poets, certainly this one anyway. I could more usefully respond to specific comments on one of my poems I think. (Letter to the author 1990)

That said, 'you tell me' is not an entirely inappropriate division of labour directed at the would-be critic. As it was, the rather richer second sentence of Corcoran's questionnaire response gave me a highroad into writing about his poetry, illuminating the series of depictions of the book as an object in his 1985 collection *The Red and Yellow Book*. It enabled me to think about the relationship between literature and the world, and to attend briefly to the politics of 1988's *Qiryat Sepher*.

A few years later, having by this time gone up to read English with Linguistics at university, I received a copy of *Lyric Lyric* in the post with a friendly note from Corcoran which read: 'here's a *Lyric Lyric* for you as you are responsible for a good line thinking back to your letter of sometime ago.'[1] The good line in question appears in the opening stanza of the third to last (untitled) poem in the book, and turned out to be the sentence from the questionnaire, only very slightly altered:

> In blue September between blue blinds
> I write and drink, thinking of money,
> thinking inside the physical forms of words
> for the pleasures of reification.
>   (*Lyric Lyric* 38)

Aside from the thrill of feeling oneself to have been somehow instrumental in the creation of significant poetry, this episode reveals something about how the discourse of poetics works in relation to creative practice. Here I am following one of Robert Sheppard's many definitions of poetics as: 'the products of the process of reflection upon writings, and upon the act of writing, gathering from the past and from others, speculatively casting into the future' (Sheppard 99). As Sheppard has argued, poetics lets writers 'question what they think they know' and allows creative work the possibility of 'dialogue with itself' (Sheppard 100). By responding to my youthful questioning, Corcoran articulated an idea which fed directly back into his creative practice, and his overall approach to poetics is also revealing of the dynamic and sometimes tense relationship between the discourses. In the same year that he responded to my questionnaire, Corcoran was interviewed by Peterjon Skelt for the book *Prospect into Breath: Interviews with North and South Writers*. Skelt's introduction to the interview reveals a fraught process of negotiation:

> The following text has been extensively edited and nearly did not appear at all. At one stage the author requested that only a short series of poems be printed, which he selected from each of his books except the first, with the introduction: 'In response to questions about his background, writing processes, politics and audience, KC offered these poems' (Skelt 156).

There is a pervasive shortness on Corcoran's part throughout the whole conversation which includes remarks such as 'I don't really have a view of my work. I can't see it' (158) and

> If I had to try and say what I thought I was doing in a book in
> terms of the sections or the forms, it would be unidentifiable
> in the end. I don't think there is any other version of that
> experience apart from the poem (158-59).

There is an almost defensive anxiety here that to probe the creative
process too much would risk destroying it – a familiar refrain in
university Creative Writing workshops throughout the land. However,
Corcoran's attitude reveals something suggestive about his view of the
respective roles of writer and reader. In response to Skelt's question
about whether his work has changed over the years, Corcoran uses the
same labour-dividing phrase as in his response to my questions: 'You tell
me. You read me quite closely' (162). Replying to Skelt's question about
the social responsibility of the poet, he adds: 'the responsibilities to the
reader are [...] not to confuse what can be said in a poem with what can
be said in an interview' (165). To this end, Corcoran seems to finally
get his way when, in response to Skelt's final question – concerning
his subject's aim to work out 'how poetry can be a political weapon to
attack my enemies' – he offers a poem as the last word of the interview:
'The only way I can answer you is this' (166).[2]

    This strategy is replicated more fully in Corcoran's response to
Denise Riley's broad invitation to contribute to her 1992 edited
volume *Poets on Writing: Britain 1970-1991* with, as she puts it in her
introduction, 'anything to do with the working processes of poetry and
the surroundings of those processes' (Riley 2). Corcoran submitted a
further four pages of what was still yet to become *Lyric Lyric* under the
title 'Sometimes a Word will Start it' – also presented as an epigraph
from John Ashbery. In fact Corcoran had reflected on this phrase in
the Skelt interview and added his own qualification 'sometimes a letter
will start it' (Skelt 157) which is presented here after the epigraph as
simply 'Sometimes a letter,' suggesting another line of feedback from
the articulation, however reluctantly, of poetics to develop creative
thought.

    Riley's own reflections on editing the volume reveal a sense of
uncertainty about the status and genre of the writings collected:
'they subside, a bit uneasily, between being critical pieces which can
be tampered with, and expressions of belief which can't' (Riley 3).
Moreover she finds there is a 'real uncertainty as to what the standing
of these writers' prose pieces to the poetry is' (3). Whilst assuming that

what a writer says about writing will have a 'different kind of interest' from what a non-writing critic might say, for Riley the real value of the discourse lies in its relationship, however myriad, with the poetry:

> The penumbra of writing around the poetry here *is* the extended material of and for the poems, for their life and working conditions; so that to put it forward could strengthen the understanding of these for both readers and writers. (3-4)

This sense of poetics as the 'extended material' of and for poems accounts very well for the fact of Corcoran's questionnaire response turning up in one of his poems. Certainly my encounter with Corcoran's poetics as articulated in his letter to me was enabling for my critical writing on his poetry, but it is also interesting to note how his practice blurs still further the already fraught boundary between poetics and creative work that Riley reflects on, and which continues to be a focus of debate within the context of teaching and research in Creative Writing in the academy. In the case of *Lyric Lyric* in particular, the conditions under which it comes into being are a clear theme, and will be considered below.

In a move characteristic of my own critical practice, and reaching back to my use of Corcoran's remarks twenty-three years ago, I want to examine his use of the word 'reification' as a key into the poetics of *Lyric Lyric*, and his poetics more generally. Reification in its basic definition means to convert a person or abstract concept mentally into a thing, to materialize it. The origins of the word and its common usage however point more specifically to its occurrence in Marx's writings, and the concept was later developed extensively by Lukács and also finds expression in Adorno's writings. In addition there are significant later treatments by Frederic Jameson and Gillian Rose. What is at stake in the concept in a Marxist usage is the way in which, due to the commodity exchanges that take place in a capitalist society, a relation between people takes on 'the character of a thing' (Honneth 96). In Honneth's reading of Lukács he identifies three directions of reification:

> Subjects in commodity exchange are mutually urged (a) to perceive given objects solely as 'things' that one can potentially make a profit on, (b) to regard each other solely as 'objects' of profitable transactions, and finally (c) to regard their

own abilities as nothing but supplemental 'resources' in the calculation of profit opportunities. (96-97)

For Lukács, under capitalism, reification has come to constitute our 'second nature' (in Honneth 98). The implications of this analysis are profound, and constitute an important aspect of Marx's theory of commodity fetishism and theory of value. Other accounts of reification, including Rose's, bring into focus the huge questions of the relationship between substance and subject (object and concept) and between actuality and change as what is really at stake for this term.

Andrew Duncan has indicated that Corcoran has a background in Marxist theory[3] but it seems unlikely that the sense in which he sees the process of writing as one that engenders the *pleasures* of reification would be in accordance with a strictly Marxist use of the term. The key instead seems to lie in Corcoran's material sense of language – the physical forms of words that are the agent of this pleasurable translation of thinking into a poem – and in this his poetics seems engaged with an enquiry into the relationship between substance and subject, and what follows from this as a politics.

This concern with reification also occurs in a short poem contained in 1999's *When Suzy Was*, and represents another instance of a discussion of poetics presented as a prose poem.[4] The original volume has the subtitle 'A Book of Answers' on the flyleaf, and it is the (almost) eponymous poem that I want to attend to, whose opening paragraph reads:

The Book of Answers

We sat at the truth table in the quiet house and I told Lee about The Book of Answers, as a way to try to think about what is always there: the alphabet, an etched model of silence that speaks. (Nonnus) My conceit to make the physical condition of language, the arrangement of the struts, curves and sounds, the form of discovered truth. Completely simple questions. To think about what is always there: reification as a type of behaviour in the moment of the poem.

(*When Suzy Was* 10)

The 'truth table' – a device used to determine the logical validity of propositions – appears several times in *Lyric Lyric*, but here also functions as the scene of an exchange between two writers, that is, between Corcoran and the poet Lee Harwood. Harwood was later the subject of a series of six interviews that Corcoran conducted between 2007 and 2008 and published as *Not the Full Story* in 2008.[5]

The focus of the conversation here discovers the Book of Answers as an enquiry into the alphabet, the image of which seems to derive from the following lines of Nonnus' *Dionysiaca* (Book IV, verse 261-265):

> But Cadmos brought gifts of thought and voice for all Hellas;
> he fashioned tools to echo the sounds of the tongue, he mingled
> sonant and consonant in one order of connected harmony. So
> he rounded off a graven model of speaking silence; for he had
> learnt the secrets of his country's sublime art.
> (Nonnus 1940)

This evocation of the power of the 'graven model of speaking silence' is pervasive in Corcoran's oeuvre, where a concern with the materiality of text is often explored through the history of writing systems. In *Lyric Lyric* there is a reference to the thirty incised graffiti in a Proto-Sinaitic (19C BCE) script found in the turquoise mines of Serabit el-Khadem which are considered to be the earliest known alphabetic script. Corcoran's line 'ten years to read one word' (*Lyric* 8) reflects a situation in which, a hundred years after the script's discovery, still only one phrase of the script has been translated. In the Skelt interview, he describes the organisation of 1990's *The Next Wave* as 'an absurd way of saying this is a clay tablet, with the illegible inscriptions on it.' (Skelt 160) 'Tocharian the I-E Enclave' refers to the ancient Indo-European language of Tocharian discovered in eighth-century scripts found in Chinese Turkestan which confounded assumptions about the Western provenance of centum languages, leading to Corcoran's reflection on 'another language like ours, / used by people unlike us' (*Lyric* 17).

Continuing this thread, 1998's *Qiryat Sepher* ('city of the book') is named after a city on contested land in the Middle East, mentioned in Joshua and Judges, a large number of whose contemporary occupants are devoted to scriptural study. In the Skelt interview Corcoran refers to Qiryat Sepher as the 'city of the letter,' and 'the site where a very early alphabet was unearthed' (Skelt 160-61). The translation of the city's name is implausible as letter, given the clear sense given to 'sepher' as 'book' in transliterated Hebrew. In correspondence, Corcoran speculated:

> Qiryat/Kiryat means city, town in Hebrew and I imagine in other Semitic languages. Sepher as in glyph or suggestively an etched letter. (The meanings of cypher spin everywhere, secret writing, magic and beyond) [...] I read a book on the history of the alphabet, an encyclopaedia of the alphabet, a library copy. There was some speculation about a site in Northern Syria where fragments of a very early alphabet were discovered. City of the Letter: Qiryat Sepher may well be my invention of a name for that place [...] Serabit el-Khadem in the Sinai is a better literal candidate. It is an actual place. [...] In the book *Qiryat Sepher*, the poem of the same name, alludes to this speculative etymology. The scene has shifted to the contemporary but the archaeological dust still drifts and there's something to be unearthed to set things right. The poem on p8 in *Lyric Lyric* is more of a literal claim about the possible origins of the alphabet, I think, than the *Qiryat Sepher* poem.
>
> (email to the author 2013)

Qiryat Sepher nevertheless abounds with images of the material nature of text: 'ideograms pinned on the dock wall [...] the fiery circuit of the word' (*New and Selected* 169); 'the articulate speech you taught / my kind king, I send you a line' (170); and, in the poem 'Qiryat Sepher' itself: 'signs and values abound / unearth the native script / to free the falling crowd' (171).

This concern with the ancient origins of writing systems underwrites the depth to which Corcoran feels the pleasures of reification. His poetics, fascinated by the micro-architecture of writing – its 'struts, curves and sounds' – is also committed to the 'form of discovered truth,' as if truth resides in writing like an ancient script lies in the earth, waiting to be revealed in an act of Heideggerian unconcealment. That said, Corcoran wants to wear this truth lightly as if it is part of the everyday: 'completely simple questions.' The repetition of the phrase 'to think about what is always there' draws a parallel between the objects of both sentences in this passage: first, the alphabet, and secondly, reification itself. This identification suggests a poetics concerned with reflecting on the act of writing in its most fundamental material form.

This poetics is radically dramatised in the prose poem which appears on page seven of *Lyric Lyric*, which also forms the first section of 'Sometimes a Word will Start it.' Here the act of writing is figured as a physical excavation:

> I could write through the table, cursively gouge down to the hieroglyphics living in our capitals. B, E and M are some of my favourites; house, man and water. Dusted with logic and sand I set them right against gentlemen thieves burning in the east. The dirt piles up at my back, tradition blocking the stairs and the light at the bottom of the stairwell.
>
> (*Lyric* 7)

This extraordinary image is historically correct in that the letters B, E and M can be linked to hieroglyphic symbols. The Egyptian hieroglyph *per* – ⊏⊐ – meaning 'house' was used to write the sound [b] in Semitic, because [b] was the first sound in the Semitic word for 'house,' *bayt*. The letter E can be traced back to a hieroglyph of a man with arms upraised – 🛉 – which meant 'joy' or 'rejoice' and was transformed through Semitic *hê* (related to *hillul* – 'jubilation') and then into Greek *epsilon*. M has its origins as the hieroglyph – 〰〰 – (actually equivalent to n) transformed via the Semitic *mem* for water. As this process of cursive extraction takes place, the dusting of logic suggests the table that has been written through could be another truth table like the one in 'The Book of Answers.' The dusting of sand however is used to make an allusion to more troubling relationships to the ancient world through the nineteenth century theft of Egyptian antiquities by the British aristocracy in the form of Henry Salt – appointed British consul-general in Cairo in 1815 – and his accomplice Giovanni Belzoni. As if on an archaeological dig, dirt piles up behind the narrator in his upper room study, blocking the light down the stairs. The pile of dirt is also seen as 'tradition' – as if the intervening accretion of material that has obscured the hieroglyphs is the outcome of a ritual repetition which has obscured the originary brilliance and truth of these symbols, and risks hindering the narrator's freedom and security. Indeed in the next line the narrator calls out to someone downstairs: 'Are you alright down there Linda? Is the baby alright?' (*Lyric* 7). There is a possible link here with a moment in Corcoran's interview with Peter Riley when Riley asks: 'Do you think Linda's all right sitting downstairs by herself all this time waiting for us?' (Corcoran/Riley 16). The enquiry about the baby perhaps also reflects an anxiety about the narrator's own contribution to history, if the baby is also his.

Here the poem risks a fantasy of return to an original shared truth, a vision of a language in which meaning is unambiguous, and yet the tone seems largely unironic as the narrator descends into a kind of tunnel, hoping that 'all things will settle into all things' and that he will arrive 'at absolute normal breathing the air of a new speech.' (*Lyric* 7) The equation of 'normal' and 'new' here – elegantly across the shifting noun-verb 'breathing' – suggests something of the interest in 'The Book of Answers' in discovered truth as something simple and always there, an amalgam of a 'make it new' Modernist poetics alongside a more Wordsworthian interest in the 'language really used by men' – and indeed 'lyrical ballads endure' is a line in the first poem of *Lyric Lyric* (3). Later the poem appears to comment on itself as 'entirely sincere and doesn't feel like a fetish' (7) – as if countering the more negative implications of the concept of reification, i.e. that it turns poetry into a fetish. Reification however seems to be applied to the narrator's neighbours who are described as having a substance that 'you can't see through' (7). Whilst this suggests a metaphor for inscrutability giving rise to slightly more ironizing questions: 'Are they agents? Are you?' the narrator also questions an implied Marxist analysis: 'It doesn't look like economics' (7). Via a remark in the Skelt interview which explains the phrase 'verbal substance' in *The Red and Yellow Book* as part of a quotation from Merleau-Ponty (Skelt 160), it might be possible to read this attribution of substance to people as a recognition of their embodied nature as opposed to a Marxist analysis of their economic determinism.

As it is, the powerful image of gouging through a writing table to reach hieroglyphic symbols is returned to in another prose poem which appears in both *Lyric Lyric* and 'Sometimes a Word will Start it' although the sequence of the lineated poems between and after the prose is different in each presentation. Here the hieroglyphic letters are folded back into what reads as autobiographical disclosure as the narrator offers an account of his father waiting at the gates of the 'Midlands Electricity Board' for his son to bring him 'forgotten sandwiches':

> A small, strong man anxious to get back inside out of the rain. I
> remember this on the edge of town where the river ran through
> water meadows and layered silence in live trees. The woods
> rose to a story sky behind factories and industrial plots and the
> grey road shone like a dark mirror. Here's your sandwiches dad.
> How much the drinking as percentage of the packet?
>
> (*Lyric* 9)

The use of setting here poises this exchange between the pastoral
landscape of the river at the edge of town and the industrial cityscape,
with the metaphors of a 'story sky' and the 'dark mirror' of the road
figuring the creative activity of the writer. The 'layered silence' is also
suggestive of Nonnus' vision of the alphabet as 'etched silence.' The
question about drinking is addressed elsewhere in 'The Literal Poem
About My Father' which identifies Johnny Corcoran as an 'alcoholic
given to violence' (*Suzy* 27). In the present poem he is seen as 'A bitter
man, a rum man, an anything man in fact' (*Lyric* 9), with devastating
puns on the tipples seen as personality traits. It is at this point that the
hieroglyphics return as a kind of exegesis of the initial letters of the
phrase 'Midlands Electricity Board':

> M   the wave sparkles
>   burning the time
>   drawn back to land
>
> E   man with downcast arms
>   Ireland, India, Burma, England
>   at the gates to nowhere
>
> B   house given up, empty
>   doss house, boarding
>   no home kept without her
>
>   (*Lyric* 9)

There is a haiku-like feel to these stanzas. The 'M' symbol evokes water,
although this time a wave on the sea, rather than the river already
mentioned. The image of sunlight on water that 'sparkles' suggests a kind
of ambivalent agency for the wave, that is 'burning the time' – perhaps
brilliantly and exuberantly, or wastefully – before it is 'drawn back to

land.' The incorporation of part of the mapped-on word ('Midlands' to 'land' here) is also found in the next two stanzas. 'E' treats the figure of the narrator's father in close comparison with the hieroglyph, but giving him 'downcast arms,' instead of upraised ones. The places mentioned suggest initially his Irish origins, and India and Burma may be places visited or post-colonial parallels as England hoves into view. Whatever the role of these places they leave him rather haplessly at the gates to nowhere, the refigured gates of the Electricity board. Finally 'B' very clearly concerns the house glyph – but in this case a house 'given up,' leading to other more transient modes of accommodation – the board of 'Electricity Board' returning as a 'boarding' house, after the loss of the mother (also described in the 'Literal Poem'): 'no home kept without her.'

These largely downbeat stanzas nevertheless show Corcoran very clearly thinking inside the physical forms of language – drilling down into the hieroglyphic substrata of the initial letters of his father's workplace to overlay their past and present meanings together in an enquiry into the truth of his own personal history, as well as the origins of written language. This process is echoed later in *Lyric Lyric* in the poem 'Hysterisis Loop':

> It was the time of end pieces,
> the time of folding away the truth table
> from which they had eaten
> and scored into its surface
> a name that belongs to something else.
>   (33)

That the two prose pieces should be offered as a contribution to a book of poetics – as well as retaining their life within the environment of *Lyric Lyric* – is revealing of the extent to which Corcoran's interest in reification as a 'type of behaviour' in the moment of composition as both the means by which his poems come into existence, and the subject of those poems.

Throughout the book environment of *Lyric Lyric*, however, this concern with the physical materiality of writing remains entangled with the other materiality of poetry as a sung (i.e. lyric) and spoken art. The repetition in the title perhaps hints at this duality – its excess inviting us to make a comparison, to find the dissimilar in the same. Following the evocation of *Lyrical Ballads* at the opening of the book, the narrator of the first poem declares 'I go the straight song / straight music drives me' (*Lyric* 3). Taken together with the notion of sincerity, this seems to be another kind of statement of poetics – a commitment to straight talking, elsewhere caught as 'an exact measure, a direct road' (6). Yet, this is not as straightforward a position as it might seem, as another prose poem in the collection argues:

> Do you think I'm trying to make this difficult? You are not watching the disintegration of anything, where the first push went opening sound reduced to the scabby politics of acquaintance. Stuff it. The ripped voice makes us free (20).

The narrator here appears to be answering a common criticism of innovative poetry as being wilfully difficult, despite his own commitment to the 'straight song.' He challenges this view by stating that his poetics does not reflect a breakdown ('disintegration') in communication. The syntax of the second clause of the second sentence is slippery, but seems to hint at the fate of a certain kind of Modernist poetics, if one identifies the 'first push' with Pound's famous line 'To break the pentameter, that was the first heave' (Pound 532). One might expect Corcoran to align himself with this 'push' and the 'opening' of the sound-world of poetry that resulted, and yet this poetics appears reduced to the 'scabby politics of acquaintance' – perhaps a critique of the exclusive aspects of Modernist literary culture. Nevertheless, the piece concludes with a self-reflexive 'stuff it' as if to reject this reservation, making a bold assertion of the liberatory aspects of a disruptive poetics – 'the ripped voice makes us free.'

Despite the seemingly de-politicised use of the term reification in Corcoran's poetics, *Lyric Lyric* nevertheless operates a profound critique of contemporary society, which sees the narrator 'bash my head on England' (6) and cite Tom Raworth's damning lines from 'West Wind': 'colourless nation / sucking on grief' (35) whilst stating baldly: 'what I want doesn't exist' (37). Such a poetics confirms a belief in poetry as a force for political engagement, despite risking its own reification in the Marxist sense. As such it could be compared to Adorno's view of the double character of the art work: that it is a fetish but also resistant to fetishism. As Adorno states in *Aesthetic Theory*: 'artworks are plenipotentiaries of things that are no longer distorted by exchange, profit, and the false needs of a degraded humanity' (Adorno 298). It seems to be in the light of this view that Corcoran is able to share with us his pleasure in the manifold delights of a reification that is both aesthetically and politically liberating.

NOTES

[1] Corcoran reflects on this kind of gesture in the Skelt interview: 'I send poems to people [...] because conversations turn into poetry. Or things that have happened and I may have mentioned to somebody, later appear as a poem anyway, and they may have a hand in it themselves. It seems like a friendly gesture' (164-5).

[2] The poem, beginning 'The garden surrounds me' appears on pages 27-28 of *Lyric Lyric*. In the Skelt volume it is printed with two attributions to embedded quotations from Wittgenstein and Ben Okri. The poem describes an urban lockdown prior to the visit of the prime minister in an unspecified location, but is punctuated by visionary and lyrical moments. The poem ends with the litany: 'Shame on you. Shame on you. Shame on you' (167). It could be read as a response to Margaret Thatcher's 1982 visit to Cheltenham in the aftermath of the Falklands conflict.

[3] In a review of *Lyric Lyric*, Duncan writes: 'Other members of the class, taught by Ralph Hawkins at Essex University around 1978, recall Kelvin as being theoretically worked-out to an amazing extent: he had a position, based on Adorno, which he could apply to everything.' Viewable at: http://www.pinko.org/12.html. See also the poem 'Adorno' in *Qiryat Sepher* (*New and Selected* 172).

[4] In the Skelt interview, Corcoran makes a claim for his use of prose sections alongside lineated pieces: 'I want the thought to jump out of its skin, and sometimes you can do that with prose, to stand aside from the poetry, but sharpen the tension as well. To say something that is not normally said' (159).

[5] Despite his previous reluctance to engage with Skelt, it is worth noting Corcoran's interest in the interview form as an occasion for poetics as also demonstrated by his important conversation with Peter Riley published as 'Spitewinter Provocations: An Interview on the Condition of Poetry.' In the current volume of course, Corcoran seems much more at ease with the interview as a mode for articulating his own poetics.

WORKS CITED

Adorno, Theodor, W. *Aesthetic Theory*, trans. R. Hullot-Kentor. London: Continuum. 2004.

Corcoran, Kelvin, 'Spitewinter Provocations: An Interview on the Condition of Poetry' with Peter Riley, *Reality Studios* Vol. 8 Nos. 1-4 (1986), 1-17.

——————. Letter to the author, 3 November 1990.

——————. Questionnaire response, 1990.

——————. Email to the author, 15 February 2013.

Honneth, Axel, 'Reification: A Recognition-Theoretical View,' The Tanner Lectures on Human Values, delivered at University of California, Berkeley March 14-16, 2005. Viewable at: http://tannerlectures.utah.edu/lectures/documents/Honneth_2006.pdf

Nonnus. *Dionysiaca Books I-XV*, trans. W.H.D. Rouse. Cambridge, MA: Harvard University Press. 1940. Viewable at: http://www.theoi.com/Text/NonnusDionysiaca4.html

Pound, Ezra. *The Cantos*. London: Faber and Faber. 1990.

Riley, Denise, ed. *Poets on Writing: Britain 1970-1991*. London: Macmillan. 1992.

Sheppard, Robert, 'The Poetics of Writing: The Writing of Poetics,' in *Creative Writing Conference 1999 Proceedings*, ed. John Turner, Danny Broderick and Peter Hartley. Sheffield: Sheffield Hallam University. 1999, pp. 99-109.

Skelt, Peterjon, ed., *Prospect into Breath: Interviews with North and South Writers* (Twickenham and Wakefield: North and South, 1991)

ACKNOWLEDGEMENTS

The author would like to acknowledge the valuable assistance of Andrew Duncan and Kelvin Corcoran in preparing this essay.

KELVIN CORCORAN AND THE LATE MODERNIST LYRIC

SIMON SMITH

Between 2008 and 2011 Kelvin Corcoran published two major collections of poetry from Shearsman Books, and a pamphlet of poems from Longbarrow Press: *Backward Turning Sea, Hotel Shadow* and *Words Through a Hole Where Once There Was a Chimpanzee's Face*. The first two collections map Corcoran's further engagement with Greek culture, ancient and modern, the pamphlet charts a major interruption to that engagement, and a life threatening illness, an ischemic stroke the poet suffered in September 2010. Beyond Greece, in all its manifestations, there are various poets, with whom Corcoran is in constant dialogue through these volumes; major figures from Modernism, like Pound and Eliot; further back in time the masters of song like Campion, Byron (and Byron's Greece); contemporaries such as Douglas Oliver, Peter Riley and Alan Halsey, and near contemporaries such as Basil Bunting, W.S. Graham and Dylan Thomas. Other artists also occupy the shadows from other art forms: Bach (especially the keyboard music, and specifically the interpretations of Glenn Gould), and the St Ives painters, specifically Roger Hilton. Whoever Corcoran engages with at various moments in these books, it is in a spirit of keeping the channels open and the dialogue going, unjamming the frequencies, in a Spicerean manner, to repeatedly examine and unlock the shifting present and its pressing circumstances and contexts in the light of key texts and artefacts. The poems themselves work through sequences that seek to 'speak' to one another in each volume of poetry, and across volumes, and across time. All of these preoccupations reside in Corcoran's habitual concern with, and return to, the lyric, what it is, what it means, how it works, and how it can be brought to have relevant purchase on the world we live in now. Here is a literary form, which has changed over time to fit particular and present circumstances; indeed, this seems to be a form most suited for Corcoran to registering mutability and change. In this regard, the most original and striking feature Corcoran's work has to offer is its examination of how the lyric can be used as a tool, a weapon, perhaps, to take on the other topic that runs the length and breadth of his work: politics. For Corcoran to write the lyric is itself a political act.

The focus on Greece in the work and its culture dates back to roughly the time of *Melanie's Book* from 1996. Greece and lyric become closely associated from this moment in the work. The interest here is in a minor key, as a radio station, radio Athens (37) (echoes of Jack Spicer here), and the poem on page 30 of the book, reflecting on the story of Theseus and Ariadne; but the technique of meaning-making will become familiar, as Corcoran uses the lyric, the act of saying tipping almost into song, to bring about a simultaneity or collapsing of time into a space of timelessness:

> By the harbour an off-shore island,
> out of the air above the waves
> Theseus abandoned Ariadne
> [...]
> Beyond the causeway, out of the sun,
> the swimmer can see the submerged town;
> [...]
> step through marbled light, on the blue threshold
> into deeper pressure I heard: Hello boy.
> 			(*Melanie's Book* 30)

Here the poem allows the poet to be released into the place of seer, to be witness to the 'deeper pressure I heard,' and the ambiguity of the address, 'hello boy' – does this refer to the shadow of Theseus, or is it a recognition of the seer and the seer as poet? The place of the lyric is the 'harbour', the 'off-shore island', 'the causeway' and, most importantly, the 'blue threshold', either places discreet, small and contained, or places which present a location or moment of transformation.

The interest in Greek culture also has an antecedent in the work of a poet Corcoran has a great enthusiasm for: W.S. Graham. In 1993 Faber and Faber published *Aimed at Nobody*, revealing Graham's unpublished poems to be about, in part at least, the associated Mediterranean, and Greek-influenced island of Crete. Graham describes in his poem 'In Crete' the process by which the lyric comes to have presence, a shaping presence in the world, and describes very well how lyric, and latterly, Corcoran's use of lyric, operates. It seems likely that Graham's poetic here comes to shape Corcoran's. This poem uncannily names and enacts this aesthetic process of the Late Modernist lyric:

> It is always strange when some other
> Voice comes in on the silence we think

> Is natural to us, is our home.
> I heard. I hear. I long to hear
> The Greek owl say his say.

And later:

> You see here I am lonely in another
> Land. I am lonely in another
> Full stop period. We are all
> Moving or circling what we go around.
>   (W.S. Graham, *New Collected Poems* 308)

Again the emphasis is on the contained, the isolate, the discreet as location, the idea of 'home,' the precision in 'full stop period'. In Corcoran's lyric he teases out, and traces the contours of a language coming into being where, 'It is always strange when some other / Voice comes in on the silence we think / Is natural to us.' This movement of the voice is manifest in features such as refrain and repetition, the return to particular themes (free market economics, wars, Trojan read through present conflicts, the work and life of Roger Hilton, etc.), the intertwining of formal language and poetic structures in the quatrain and tercet (favourite stanzaic forms for Corcoran), and through problems of 'music' in the language, where 'we are all / moving or circling what we go around'. The Late Modernist lyric, in the way Corcoran uses it, and the way it has developed over time in his work, enacts these modalities of voice and technical expression; and in this way his work takes up Graham's challenges.

By the time of *Backward Turning Sea* (2008) Greece and its lyricism (now in a major key, as Greece has become more of a presence in the books) offers an alternative earthly paradise to the grey austerities of the British Isles. Here the Helen myth of 'Helen Mania' (11-16) graphically portrays 'the alternative escape route' (11) in Corcoran's re-write of the story, with a radical multi-layering of voices, and a simultaneous clarity of narrative in a Troy-meets-Anglo-American-foreign-policy, a blurring of the ancient with the contemporary: 'it's Priam's turn for regime change' (14), 'Helen a black outline in the blast' (14), 'I think I hear armour clashing by night, / see smart bomb snapshots of Trojan bunkers / [...] / reconstructed it's just as real' (15). The space cleared by lyric and Greek light means the country the imagination can now occupy is one where 'the belief in mythology as fact' (22) prevails, and more crucially, where 'Sappho entered the western lyric', the effect of which is a sharpness of vision, a peeling back and clear astringency in the connections of the world: 'I can see the coast of Asia minor, / low blue hills, an apron of light // [...] Where my language was made' (25). Or as Corcoran states later in a poem about Alan Halsey's visual work (and other contemporaries), Greece and this revitalized lyric impulse offers fresh ways of seeing he can bring back to England, a *foreignising* film superimposed on the familiar. Corcoran's forms of perception have fundamentally shifted, so he sees Halsey's work in the terms of the Greek:

> these ikons open a second front
> an unknown country we might
> with a racing chance inhabit (28)

What is taking place is a 'republic of the poem' (30) with Greece at its fault line, where 'in Agios Dimitros the faultline sounds' (36). What breaks out beyond that fault line in the poem titled '*Over the calm, clear shining water*' (the title itself an Ancient Greek lyric fragment) is a way to see the world afresh: 'we go out into the world in the name of the first wave' (39), to resolve itself in one of those discreet places, the harbour, calling back to *Melanie's Book*:

> Leukothia, steady my sight,
> let me align the arms of the harbour
> and fix the point in mid blue
> where all nonsense is washed away.
>
> In that telescopic ellipse
> swim all the living things,
> our quick lives coming and going
> in the unpeopled cities of stone.
>
> It is light, morning light
> comes walking through the village,
> out of the folds of the mountain
> into the folds of the sea. (40)

This way of seeing through the Late Modernist lyric finds its parallels in other art forms, particularly in the work of Roger Hilton, the St Ives painter. 'Roger Hilton's Sugar' is more than simply *homage*, it is an enquiry into the earthly paradise presented in the late gouache pictures, blazing with colour and movement, and yet lyrical in their discreet scale, delicacy, and vulnerability. The place is Cornwall, but the light and vision Mediterranean:

> On the secret island, in the middle sea,
> two figures dance on the Cape of No Hope,
> Hilton sets out, feet first, on the bed of last days,
> – the fun is over, what else have I got?
> Miraculous pictures leap from his hands.　(43)

Or in 'From Botallack Out': 'as I cartwheel on the canvas of despair; / at different depths the light changes / aqua, marine, and the green gods' (59). At the centre of this poem is the crucial section 2, where Corcoran creates an 'interview' with Hilton, reminiscent of the dramatic positioning of voices and method of address to be found in Jack Spicer's book *After Lorca* (in *My Vocabulary Did This to Me* 105-154):

> Q1
> Is the text of your painting perception itself, so that we see the
> work of the mind only in the act of painting?
>
> A1
> I thought when I was dead
> I would not have to explain anything;
> green branches shoot from my wrists
> instruments of truth or nothing
> [...]
> text? text of what? paint?
> 　　　　(*Backward* 60)

Here is Corcoran's poetic, a kind of gentle manifesto, catching us unaware, so to speak, thrown via another voice, a 'poem,' an 'interview,' which is made present through 'layering', the accumulations of filmic surfaces referred to earlier. Question 2 is 'Is it the layer of living things, through which other people and things are first given to us?' To which the answer comes from the ghost of Roger Hilton: 'Layer of living things, that's good, / up to my elbows in that, paint' (60). Here the intervention of the body in the process of meaning comes into presence, as the lyric impulse becomes the form by which articulation takes place for these elements of figuration:

> I'm shipped up, skin flaking off
> float me away in bloody bedroom,
> the hidden life made apparent
> free as painting the air blue, red,
> vitamin B injections useless
> first person lost down the lane boy I.

> Q3
> Are you conscious of the body as the unperceived term in
> the centre towards which objects turn?

> A3
> No getting away from it there
> [...]
> I saw the ghost body under the boat
> at one with the waves, the fatal current
> all my life, that face emerging
> [...]
> I sailed around the cirkle islands (60-61)

In this section of *Backward Turning Sea*, the reader is returned to the world of *Melanie's Book* (1996), that *primal scene* for the lyric, the clear, underwater vision, collapsing together the Mediterranean, the Atlantic, Troy, Crete, Greece, Antibes, Cornwall into both history and the present moment of utterance, inscribed in their simultaneity: 'the shape of morning rises / [...] momentary chart of all the sea lanes of the world' (66). The result is a cleansing of language, a clearing of the decks, and the ability to see the world anew, straightforwardly and whole again:

> Melanie I want to say in plain words
> [...]
> How on earth did I find you?

[…]
My mouth hanging open in a new world. (68)

And:

smell the sea in the air, we could live like this
[…]
the light in waves making the hidden form apparent
[…]
saw the days sail by like painted boats
at a jaunty angle in a square of painted blue.
[…]
And with my right hand and my left hand
I made the picture of it all. (72)

Further investigations of the lyric take place in *Hotel Shadow* (2010), particularly in the first section, 'From Where Song Comes or Keeping the Empire in Order' (11-38). There are meditations here on the origin of lyric, Campion, Pound, economics, politics, war (historical, recent and contemporary), the poet's father and his alcoholism, W.S. Graham, and Jack Spicer. This section marks the culmination of years of practice of the lyric to articulate what amounts to a theory of the form, and is, perhaps, the clearest statement Corcoran has made about lyric poetry to date. As he plangently, earnestly states (with a cheeky nod in the direction of Burt Bacharach, as well as Campion, Dowland, and the song tradition): 'what the world needs now is a theory of song' (*Hotel Shadow* 13) and, to extrapolate from the sequence, a politics of song. Indeed, one of the things this opening series to the book unveils is the politics *in* song/lyric. Lyric, well Late Modernist lyric at least, reveals the lyric act as a political act: 'but imagine a common purpose in breathing the next breath' (15). Lyric becomes the locus of the 'commons', a *polis* or city in the act of utterance. Earlier in the sequence Corcoran has meditated on the origin of the lyric, as its articulation changes its relationship to the land, its physical place. Here the lyric is transformative in relation to a civic purpose, with the past coming into the present: 'the other time we enter now is everything' (14). In this regard Late Modernist lyric is quite different from post-Modernist lyric, by which I mean that popularized in the *Penguin Book of Contemporary British Poetry* edited by Andrew Motion and Blake Morrison, and latterly characterized by the work of poets like Simon Armitage, where the lyric is singular without reaching out and across, making the connections of series, or through history to the tradition of lyric poetry. There is something innately cut off, separate about this kind of post-Modernism, conservative even, and more akin to the Georgians championed by the anthology's editors.

Corcoran actually is in direct argument or dispute with High Modernism, particularly and explicitly the High Modernism of Ezra Pound. He directly addresses Pound's work in 'Reading *The Cantos*' and 'From the Hen-Roost' (*Hotel Shadow* 23-33). What Corcoran takes from Pound for his making of Late Modernist lyricism is the hard, jewel-like technique in verse and image-making of the Pisan and later Cantos, to shape a clarity in the form of the poetry, a clarity that clears the way for his present political context, and integrated political analysis and vision, a politics of the lyric. Pound mistakes anti-Semitism for economics, ideology for politics:

> What does Pound find to admire in Sigismundo and the Medici?
> Hands grasping the rods of power, banking and patronage,
> polishing the azure air for the faces of Tuscan gods?
>
> I woke up in the cherry season, ate the cherries ripe and wet,
> the sea breathing in the olive groves, clouds rising from the hills,
> to see ants hoist crumbs to a depthless sky.
> (*Shadow* 23)

Pound's Modernism is identified as a force 'grand to propound the big idea', and a 'species of modernist ambition / to synthesise the culture's cache, / a gesture, anti-Semitic and parochial' (23), a force misguided and specious. Corcoran remarks on the nightmare of high Modernism gone bad, 'and then in Canto XLIX his genius / breaks your heart', which results in the fragmented, broken lyric, its remains bleaching in the sun, 'everywhere/ scattered song' (24-25). The whole project ends with the ignominious death of Mussolini and his mistress, and the desecration of their bodies: 'In Pisa at night the modernist preference for antiquity over the present was stuffed and hung upside down from a lamp-post' (25). Corcoran identifies Pound's high Modernism in the end as vanguard (backward looking), not avant-garde (of the present), facing forward into an ever-changing future, and this fundamental difference marks the distinction between Pound's Modernism and Corcoran's.

'Pound's [aesthetic is] out there, gone ape in the Broken Ant-Hill Book of Reference' (26), an Über-Culture as a heap of rubbish. And later:

> Vatic recital of bank rates does not
> make for the revealed truth of history;
> this ideogram means overbearing insistence
> about a pile of broken sticks
> does not make a tree. (28)

Corcoran's aesthetic is, on the contrary, one of simultaneity, of all politics, myth, history, all converging on now, formed in a discreet, and yet connecting (and connected) act of seeing:

> You could sit still in a village abandoned under waves of summer,
> Just look at things – people and animals and trees tell you everything
> > (26)

and:

> Ezra Pound is rolling rocks down the mountain
> at the edge of the European mind, rubble, empires of rubble
>
> the empty house where the sky spreads
> stands in the dry river bed abandoned
>
> saved by foxes and cicadas
> > their parliament (29)

If much of *Hotel Shadow* (2010) addresses the broken mind of Ezra Pound, *Words Through a Hole Where Once There Was a Chimpanzee's Face* (2011) is an account of Corcoran's ischemic stroke suffered in September 2010, a literal breaking of the mind and its serious consequences. If Corcoran's lyric poetry has been a negotiation of rupture and fracture in aesthetic terms relating to Modernism up to this moment, then this pamphlet is an enactment of rupture and fragmentation at the level of the real, and how that can affect the lyric. After engaging with Pound, the figure from high Modernism who Corcoran comes back to consciousness with is William Carlos Williams, who himself suffered a series of strokes towards the end of his life. Lyric and its articulations of culture are no longer the pressing issue. Instead, memory, the memories that constitute the individual become all-important:

> *Memory is a kind*
> *of accomplishment,*
>
> Oh Dr Williams you clever man
> your words came to me in hell
> to feed the insubstantial dead.
> (*Words Through a Hole* 7)

The subject of this short book is about a literal coming back from the dead, and how the lyric form anchors the Self in the world, and how the experience of this terrible episode transformed Corcoran's sense of the late Modernist lyric. Whereas Pound suffers the mental and physical depravations of first the cage at Pisa and then incarceration at St. Elizabeth's, Corcoran's is a very real descent to the underworld and then a return: 'And when I was down there / this was in my head / even though I was not' (8). And the underworld in this case is a fundamental loss of the mind, a physical loss of memory, which comes to be represented in the sequence by a gift from poet Lee Harwood, a book called *The Wonder Book of Wonders*, which starts to take on a whole new status, as the biggest wonder is Corcoran's literal return from the dead. In this book, 'on page 88 someone has cut out the face of the chimpanzee' (9). The chimp's absent face comes to represent the burning out of neurons, literally obliterating the poet's memory of the whole episode as well as other physical effects such as (temporary) blindness and then oddly experienced visual effects relating to colour spectrums. What is important, is that like the chimp, this loss of facility and data changes how Corcoran can think about words and therefore lyric: 'he dreams of words through a hole' (9). The question for the lyric now becomes: what can we be sure of? What things are best avoided? Familiar points of reference become crucial, so friends and the faces of friends – this sequence (11-13) is central to recovery; so coterie is important, and cultural acquaintances are anchors:

> John Coltrane bends time
> Bach straightens it out again;
> stay with me boys
> be at my side, my left and my right. (12)

Things to be avoided are the things that shift around, de-stabilise, embodied in a figure who rises from the chimpanzee's absent face, as a kind of horror, the unfamiliar bogey-man:

> Herr Forelegs made his smell.
> – Do you really mean to keep fighting this?
> on the other side of seeing
> in the crowded darkness, you belong to me.
>
> I can wrinkle the world in front of your eyes
> make the familiar unfamiliar,
> spit you out like gristle
> like a knuckle bone, like nothing. (13)

After the stroke the world looks not only terrifying but also constructed, as the poet has to reconstruct for himself, and his brain rewire, the channels for perception and connection to the world. At the end of the first section of the book the descent to the underworld is explicitly one associated with the disruption and chaos of language and dissonance of the lyric: 'katabasis song plays backwards… this last word last katabasis' (18).

With the second half of the book, 'And Coming Back,' the reader is invited to witness recovery and follow a process of return; the process of the poetry is not loss and elegy, but return to an engagement with moving forward (an avant-garde, not a backward-looking vanguard):

> And if it was today the sky failed, the year
> turned a bed of darkness and more darkness,
> under it all the learning of the world waited,
> all the learning of the world, packed and ready. (21)

The tear in the fabric of the brain, the rending of culture, and the fracturing of the perception of culture takes the Modernism, the late lyric Modernism of Corcoran's work, into a new dimension, not just a new direction. The last section of the book is a series of sixteen line poems, which grow in strength as the poet grows in strength mentally and physically. The points of reference here are the Arctic explorer Nansen (an important figure for W.S. Graham's *Malcolm Mooney's Land*), and the pianist Glenn Gould (also struck, fatally, by a stroke), guides to literally a new landscape for the lyric, a starker one, but more defiant, with a new clarity. Here is poem '1.3,' in its entirety, registering how far the late Modernist lyric has paradoxically been strengthened by the experience of this terrible episode, where song has become light:

> To walk away from all of that
> and to say I know you, I know your names;
> the mind making its own patterns
> along a low horizon of muted light.
>
> I think I taught that girl, worked with that man
> but no only in Apophenia, not in the world;
> and then to walk away from the buried life,
> the trees designed and the light contrived.
>
> I know you, I know your names,
> dark ones at the door, sharp ones at the gate,
> shadow swallower, eaters of the thinking meat;
> that my legs hurt tells me I'm coming through.
>
> From here you turn left, then right at the lights,
> the cars pass in a dance, a sports ground there
> and here are the shops and the banks of the day,
> as almost remembered on the other side. (23)

WORKS CITED

Graham, W.S. *Aimed at Nobody*. London: Faber and Faber, 1993.
_____. *New Collected Poems*. London: Faber and Faber, 2004.
Morrison, B. and Motion, A. (eds.). *The Penguin Book of Contemporary British Poetry*. Harmondsworth: Penguin Books, 1982.
Pound, Ezra. *The Cantos*. London: Faber and Faber, 1987.
Spicer, Jack. *My Vocabulary Did This to Me: The Collected Poetry of Jack Spicer*. Middletown, CT: Wesleyan University Press, 2008.

Personal Response –
'The Singer Tears Your Heart Out'

Kat Peddie

Kelvin,

I've been reading your Greek poems, following you through the coastal routes and oceans of the place and the sublime literal you sustain, thinking of your letter-poem to Peter Riley.[1] It's the voice I want to hear in poetry, free from the grandiose and where everything matters. It is exactly the most intimate and the most shared experience, as you've said elsewhere – singing around the shores of the various world.

Here, after days of storm, a perfect Mediterranean Summer is with us. So I read your poems outdoors, & among the fig trees & wild flowers it is a place that might make me think of you even if I weren't reading you. Though I am very much the tourist here – I mean no goddess has yet emerged from our 8 by 4 metre pool. In writing this, I wasn't sure what form a personal response would take &, as most of my writing is academic, how far a personal response differed from an academic response.[2] So I decided to take my cue from you – because your responses are always so personal, so filled with the desire to communicate intimately and directly to a friend, a reader.

I wrote to you a while back, when I didn't know you very well (though I still do not, & given that this knowledge is mainly through reading your poetry, I am more intimate with you than you are with me – which makes this letter necessarily different to yours), that I had listened again to a recording of you reading 'A Thesis on the Ballad' & cried.[3] There were provisos about having listened to Barbara Allen repeatedly and a gin intake to match. I told you this in a way that was designed to be self-deprecatingly comic. I worried about the possible mawkishness of sentiment. (I still worry about this.) You were more moved than I had expected you to be. I think this is why I am writing this. I hadn't thought too much, then, about why I had had that emotional response, and why you might responded to it in the way you did. This response, then, is an attempt to think about this.

§

Kelvin, this is no longer written directly to you. To continue this as a letter now feels rather like whispering praises in your ear in front of the reader.

§

That Kelvin can praise, in his letter-poem to Peter Riley, precisely the things that matter in his own poetry is a testament to how aware and in control he is of his own poetic. This would come across without his having given me the terms of praise. What moved me, firstly, and most simply, was that it was the voice I want to hear in poetry – & voice in a literal sense – that it was Kelvin reading. Which isn't just to say that he is a very good reader of his poems, but that his poems seem to be composed in concordance with the rhythms and syntax of the audible word – whether spoken or sung. I'm sure others in this book have talked about Kelvin in terms of song – only one of the ways in which this seems true for me is that his poems always have a sureness of sound, a knowledge of how quite simple words, often put simply together, can create exactly the right tone, pitch, and pace to make their meanings resonate. I am often pulled into one of Kelvin's poems by an arresting line or phrase, usually short – maybe five words long, and plainly put, that illuminates all around it, and bears its often huge intellectual and emotional weight so much better for doing so lightly. These words stick in the memory.

What sticks in the memory is the subject matter of the poems. I was moved partly because the ballads he used are lodged deep in my memory: I have listened to them since I was a child: they resonate with me, as they do for many others, and Kelvin has a way of using folklore at its fullest, of bringing its figures and rhythms to presence. This is as true of his Greek poems as of his English ones: the gods and heroes of Greek myth and history don't occupy a privileged position in antiquity, but inhabit and are of the present landscape.

Kelvin's Greek poems are often inhabited by the same figures as Pound's more Italianate Cantos – though not, of course, Sigismundo or the Medici – as Kelvin asks, 'What does Pound find to admire in' them: 'Hands grasping the rods of power, banking and patronage, / polishing the azure air for the faces of Tuscan gods?' (*Hotel Shadow* 23). Kelvin's difference to, and dispute with, Pound, as this quotation suggests, lies precisely in their similar interests: economics and myth. That Kelvin's economics differ utterly from Pound's hardly needs saying. But myth is related to this – it is an attitude towards history: for Pound, mythical figures exist as a nostalgic yearning for an age prior to that of the economically, and thus morally, corrupt age he finds himself in – as Kelvin writes,

> In Pisa at night the modernist preference for antiquity over the present was stuffed and hung upside down from a lamp-post.
> (*Hotel Shadow* 25)

It's an attitude that deserves no better treatment than Mussolini, in fact is a part and parcel of extreme (and not so extreme) right wing politics. In Kelvin's poetry, antiquity is important inasmuch as it is a part of the fabric of the present: it is myth that refuses the forces of abstraction usually placed upon it; that refuses to be reified into something that no longer relates to the spheres of economics and politics that came to shape it, and which it shapes. The fictionality of myth, its history, is insisted upon, and in doing so its force in the present becomes clear: not only does examining the dissemination of myth have very deliberately suggestive parallels with contemporary politics – often offering ways of talking about it explicitly, but there is also an understanding of the power of myth and story, not as fact, but as exerting an imaginative power, as emotive presence. What much of Kelvin's poetry tends toward is thesis on the ballad, on song, myth, & stories told, the reasons and powers of their telling.

§

Even Pound, though, has some saving graces:

> And then in Canto XLIX his genius
> breaks your heart
> (*Hotel Shadow* 24).

That what should be prized in a poet (who otherwise is found to be politically and poetically bankrupt) is a Canto that not only goes against this political grain, but also provokes an emotional response in the reader, is telling. Kelvin is, and very deliberately, a personal, intimate and emotive poet. He is lyrical in all senses of the word. I said that I worry about sentiment becoming sentimentality. Kelvin's poems help to overcome this fear. They are, as he says to Riley, 'the most intimate and the most shared experience' – their intimacy being inexorably linked with their being shared. Two aspects I have talked about – his ability to write directly to a reader, wife, friend, and his investment in shared myth – constitute a part, though not the whole, of this feeling. Another part is, as he praises his daughter for in 'Madeleine's Letter to Bunting':

> You already have the trick of writing from the body,
> of not explaining that you are you and not you in the poem
> but trust to the shape and weight of words as you go
> (*Hotel Shadow* 80-81)

His honest responses to other poets and poets is of course a facet of this intimacy – and he both manages to bring out what is important in their poetry in a way that is both generous and genuine (even to Pound) and indicate the values towards which his own poetry strives and achieves.

What this poetry *is* is not the emotion of the solipsistic castings-off of a confessional-lite verse. This is important because as this sort of verse has come to monopolize emotion, self-articulation, and the recounting of event – all of which Kelvin does so well – these aspects become suspect. These are things, Kelvin reminds us, that it is vitally important not to lose – in the spheres of political thought and action that Kelvin rails against

> The idea was simple;
> banish feeling to the borders
> (*The Next Wave* 22)

Here they are central. I think in articulating this I came to realize why what I had said to Kelvin mattered to him – why it was a legitimate and welcome response rather than a slightly embarrassing one. And I also came to feel glad that I had been asked to write a personal, rather than academic, response.

I think that is all.

Notes

[1] 'Alstonefield' is a letter-poem by Kelvin Corcoran addressed to Peter Riley, published in *Backward Turning Sea* by Shearsman in 2008. 'Alstonefield' is a long poem by Peter Riley, published in the eponymous book by Carcanet in 2002.

[2] Should it, for example, have endnotes?

[3] The recording can be found at:
https://soundcloud.com/free-range/kelvin-corcoran-9th-feb-2012?in=free-range%2Fsets%2Fzone

PART 3

APPROACHES

'The key is that they are page-sized… it seems, for me, to be the size of affordable human attention.'
—Kelvin Corcoran

THIRD CONVERSATION

AB: *Hieroglyphics, the origin of languages, alphabets and scripts, cuneiform,* Qiryat Sepher, *boustrophedon texts; these related things tie together all sorts of ideas in your work about which we'll talk today...*

KC: Yes, *Qiryat Sepher,* 'City of the Letter', somewhere to the northern border of Syria, where an early alphabet was discovered...

AB: *These things relate to the clay tiles you are using to write from today in 'Sea Table'?*

KC: Yes, and back to *Your Thinking Tracts...* For that book, Alan Halsey sent me a book for my birthday: a collection of 14 of his properly idiosyncratic graphics. The idea was to write the poems to illustrate the pictures, not the other more conventional way around. Previously I'd had images from Alan and others to illustrate the poems, as book covers and section markers, but this time the plan was the other way about. And if you look at Alan's pictures, they do look like odd, graphic, scripted... collages... of something you might have found on a cave wall, or hidden in a lost library somewhere. One thing I like in writing about pictures in this way is that it's a project and you have to go and *do* something about it! We were talking earlier today about Phillip Terry's novel *Tapestry,* a really striking and sustained ekphrastic work. With *Thinking Tracts* it's as if you're following a set of clues and pretending there's something to be solved. Meanings are constructed in that fashion and, sometimes, you find yourself writing things you didn't know you wanted to write until then. And at the same time you have to get up and go out and find about things in order to write anything, about these very particular 14 pictures for instance which don't yield up everything at first glance perhaps. It's certainly one way to work, to work against my natural idleness and indolence.

AB: *You also have an ekphrastic project in* Roger Hilton's Sugar...

KC: Yes. In a way, *Thinking Tracts...* relates to the Roger Hilton book. The Hilton book was definitely a go out project, visiting galleries, correspondence with Rose Hilton, reading at galleries as part of a touring exhibition of St Ives art whilst writing the poems, talking to people involved in what to us is a very curious world, the art world, it's not just the jackpot money either. I often found out that the one picture that they do have in the Swindon art gallery, or elsewhere, is in the back of the store, but if you come back in March we might be able to retrieve it for you to have a look at. Another link between these two books lies in my interest in Hilton's late works, the gouaches, the informal drawings, mixed media, which are all page-sized, small. So are all of Alan's 14 pictures. It's almost a form of reading to look at the images. I also read Hilton's book *Night Letters*: it's full of different moods and anxieties and fears and pleasures. And he's clearly very, very unwell, on the point of death and he knows it. The recently published facsimile of it is a great thing itself. It will repay endless reading. There are letters, diary entries, notes to his wife left on the table, tender, ill-tempered, everything: *Don't forget my fucking sugar. Where's my paint?* There are moments of deep remorse. I like its apparently unedited or unmodulated verve. Once inside that material, and inside Alan's graphic pages, you become completely absorbed. It's the world you are in, writing yourself in to and out of. The key is that they are page-sized… it seems, for me, to be the size of affordable attention.

With Alan's work there was a sense of a sequence, those pictures followed one another in a certain way, and allowed me to make up other connections. And the circumstances of Hilton's last work also made a sequence, a total environment. I wonder if the fascination with visual art, the actual physical object or made image, is closer to what is happening in the mind; closer than words, which seem pale ghosts in comparison as a version of what is actually happening, chemically and structurally in the brain, in the moment of making and inventing. (Well, future reading suggestions by email please.) I can see how in art and in music the hand is an extension of the mind. I don't see that with poetry, which is not the same made object; it's a verbal construct, a written one. Handwriting will not determine the quality of the poem, though I prefer hand-writing drafts over word processing, typing – which it isn't, because there's at least some direct physical connection between the thinking and the action which is simple and unlike 'typing'.

AB: *So in both of these books of ekphrastic poems you are interested in the difference between the materiality of paint/sound and its relationship to the mind, which is a different kind of struggle from the one that the poet has in terms of the relationship between materiality and text?*

KC: Yes. In this new poem 'Sea Table' I'm reading a sequence of twenty clay tablets, signs, to solve an unnamed problem, in order to understand what's happening. 'Sea Table' began as a visual poem, laser cut on a plank of wood and painted, which taught me I couldn't paint! And it leans on other various visual sources throughout the body of the poem. There is a connection between the actual physical struts and angles and shapes of the word and the impulse towards music. Writing in response to music, or about music, musicians and composers, is straightforward, but it's very hard to write about where your mind is when you listen to Toumani Diabete playing kora improvisations, which are complex and beautiful, the B minor Mass, or Glenn Gould playing Bach. There must be a neurological literature about these processes, and not just on the benefit of the Baroque for the brain's workings. There's a technical language of description of music, which gives you everything and nothing, but I haven't read any of the books. Anyway, the technical language doesn't do. When I'm in the audience and hearing music being played and it's the music I need to hear, I sit there grinning like an idiot, a transported idiot. As with the Toumani improvisations, you are there and not there, taking a deep draft as he pursues the music, making it up, deeper and deeper and then returning, compresent to the music, and almost holding your breath – which is ill-advised. Who said music is all the pleasure of mathematics without having to count? It's a great thing. And when I listen to Glenn Gould playing Bach, I know everything and nothing in all that architecture of sound. It's the nearest state we can reach out to in understanding what absolute human inventiveness means, it seems to me – the wordless language. So pictures, visual art, and music, lurk there in the origins of language, altering the brain's construction and chemistry. It seems to me that poetry always wants to return to this original moment, it's always trying to reach back into music, to change back into pictures, like it wants to go home. Who said that? Well, more immediately, a series of pictures can be a constraint or a provocation; it can deny *and* give you the way forward at the same time.

AB: *Taking another slant, however, if we go back to an early use of hieroglyphs in your work (the Egyptian glyphs for M, E, B in* Lyric Lyric*), those symbols become a way for you to write about Thatcherite economics, waiting outside the Midland Electricity Board gates for your dad. The symbols become a way into your social politics... it isn't about the rather* *philosophical things you've just been talking about... it's actually very gritty, and grounded in a tough, real economy?*

KC: Yes. Well, it's punning away isn't it and who would separate abstract speculation from the gritty, the given? In trying to grasp the very precise economic circumstances of a father who is an alcoholic and works as a store man for the Midlands Electricity Board, and from time to time doesn't work at all, I don't have to abandon anything. And there may well be a connection between the shape of our letter W and the original Egyptian hieroglyph for water. So there are roots. That's part of it. It's a good question. I want everything there, but the mediocrity that passes for poetry that swills around our culture, doesn't want everything, it excludes in the name of consumable immediacy, homogenised run-off topped with a few token gestures.

AB: *That's why I wanted to ask you about your other ekphrastic work, the chapbook* What Hit Them. *I know you say that you don't overly care for those poems any more, but in this ekphrastic sequence based on* The Geometry of Fear *art exhibitions, you overtly challenge that sort of artistic complacency, which you associate with Hirst, Emin and Saatchi. You should read Julian Stallabrass' brilliant debunking of the Young British Artists in his book* High Art Lite...

KC: I'd be interested to see that. But as if Tracey Emin or Damien Hirst would pause, at all, on their way to the bank! Part of that project was for me to read the poems next to the pieces of art that lay behind the poem. I did that several times in galleries around the country. I became interested in Lynn Chadwick and Kenneth Armitage.

AB: *So why is their art not glib and easy in the way you and others criticise the work of the YBAs?*

KC: I don't know. Chadwick and Armitage had been through the Second World War and their experiences read directly into the work... the quality and the torment of the experience and the total pleasure of having survived is there. Some pieces look like some strung together rickety aeroplane, and indeed Chadwick served in the Fleet Air Arm over the North Atlantic in aeroplanes that must have felt quite like that.

AB: *You seem to be saying that Chadwick's and Armitage's sculptures find 'the geometry they shaped to help them cope' with the Second World War, but that contemporary art is not a sufficient shape to help us cope with the traumas of our own time?*

KC: I don't know. What you've described is true of those artists I refer to in the poem, yes, but I don't know enough about contemporary art to say further.

AB: *Do you think that poetry is up to it? Is that partly why you don't much care for these poems, because you fear it might not be? Can poetry shape a geometry to help us cope?*

KC: (Very long pause…)

AB: *Answers on a postcard please!*

KC: (Laughs). That's really a very good question and… (Another long pause). I don't know, I haven't thought about that. Does poetry have to be equal to anything? I wouldn't look to poetry for therapy; the malady will be long if you do. I haven't discarded those poems, some of them reappear in a later sequence about those political events. What's obvious is that poetry can be reduced, stifled by a parochial lack of ambition, as by over-ambition, a certain type of which is nothing more than the starry egotism of the poet, a tendentious and displaced notion of poetry's mission, as hieratic disclosure of what we all need to know for our own good, to set us free and dancing arm in arm into a linguistically reformed future.

Here's an example to the good. I've just edited the next issue of *Shearsman* magazine, and read a lot of poetry by younger poets and others previously unknown to me. I was knocked out and it was a great thing to do. There's nothing lacking in the poetry I read and it might be an answer to your question, it doesn't dodge what I think you're referring to as present circumstances. Certainly you can never know what's coming along from the future, what someone will write that changes everything. I don't know that poetry has to be equal to anything and I think part of my hesitation is that some poetry that doesn't quite work doesn't fail for lack of ambition, something is being worked out, and I admire the ambition… but the description of the role of poetry as a form of truth-telling, as heroic gesture, is inadequate. There is an ideologically-bound poetry which is like that and it's to do with a mistaken and inflated view of poetry's public profile. If you are exaggerating who you think is listening to what you are saying, and that it's of any importance to people at PricewaterhouseCoopers, or in the other boardrooms and new Satanic mills and lobbies with their representatives in Westminster, if you are imagining that you are going to make a difference by singing your heart out, then you've lost the poetry by projecting a grand role for yourself which doesn't exist in the world; the poetry is lost through the poet being over concerned with an audience who turn out to be largely imagined in order to pump up the poetry into some unexamined notion of relevance.

AB: *In the Hilton book you write about the thwarted attempts to see the paintings. You're seeing Hilton ironically there, and resisting the obvious sensational biography that often accompanies him. Is that what you were after in these poems, instead of a traditional ekphrasis in which you just* write *about* paintings?

KC: Well not seeing him, actually. Partly, yes, but knowing poetry about Hilton by W.S. Graham and others also interested me. The other part of that was, perhaps a slightly misplaced ambition, to write as Hilton paints: the exuberance of his works and the appealing mixture of the representational and the abstract. In the *Night Letters* there's a fairly graphic picture of the domestic circumstances in which those drawings and informal paintings were made. The art of Hilton and Nicholson and Barnes-Graham and Barbara Hepworth and others all working in Cornwall… there's nothing like that hugely ambitious, confident modernism, it puts most poetry then and now to shame doesn't it.

AB: *Hilton's works and writing can be quite lewd too?*

KC: I really like that! When we were looking at the Hilton exhibition in Tate St Ives, 2006, one of the attendants said to Melanie that she thought the paintings were aggressive, in some way threatening towards women. Melanie's view was, no, I don't see it that way; they're very exuberant and tender and lusty and just full of zest. That's what I like them for as much as anything.

AB: *OK. Let's talk about your prose poems, because I guess that with those types of poem you are also giving yourself a form, a way forward, a provocation and a challenge, but also a shape?*

KC: There's a particular thing about the passages which become prose. They are often circumstantial pieces that can be about grief, or unexpected circumstances of illness, and indeed about love as well. Lurking behind such poems is biography, which arises from circumstances and events. For some books those events took over entirely and what I thought I was going to write about changed, so I found myself writing into something that I didn't think I was going to do. The events took over and the poetry derails and the words jump out of themselves on the way to where they thought they were going. They teeter on this moment of possession and dispossession, that you are not in control of, because of what has happened. For example, the prose poem 'The Vaccination Queue', in the waiting room, remembering my parents. The ambition is to take you behind the scenes of the poetry, as if I've got to say this to you directly. I can't be putting this 'into poetry'. It's not poetry. It has to go behind the scenes and become a different sort of poetry. It turns around on itself. This notion of dis/possession then swaps around anyway, because you say the unexpected. I don't think these are purely personal experiences at all: they are utterly shared; utterly common; they're not about the person writing them, they're everybody's common lot. It's a misconception to think of them as personal – the most personal is the completely shared. Others have said this, Peter Riley amongst them, and I agree.

AB: *So this is our queue, our history, our 'class system as vernacular drama' in that poem?*

KC: Yes, it's a political piece. It's about the NHS!

AB: *And then you also have the utterly straightforward prose of poems like 'I was with my mother when she died'.*

KC: It's bare isn't it? It's saying this is without artifice; or an almost vernacular, idiomatic artifice, which is almost transparent.

AB: *That strikes me as wonderful within a form that is often thought of as one of the most artificial of poetic forms. I like the way you strip that out.*

KC: It's about complete disclosure. Why pretend it's just about you? There's nothing individualistic about those experiences. If I didn't know that already, I'd know it from the way people respond to them in readings. It's as if I'm opening my house to you, I'm playing no tricks on you here.

AB: *Because prose is a more 'democratic' form than verse?*

KC: Maybe, or maybe because we are not aware of standing off and engaging in that business of 'writing a poem' or listening to a poem. Or maybe I just don't understand the craft of writing prose and I don't worry about it as much. You're not so concerned to play a certain move, or deliberately stage a line in a certain way. It's only quite occasional – I haven't really written any sustained prose.

AB: *I'm interested that some of your prose poems have a medical theme, so perhaps we could move on to talk about that... you said that 'The Vaccination Queue' is a poem about the NHS. Is that what's behind these poems; the social role of medicine?*

KC: Apart from the inevitable individual experience which, as I've already said, is not really personal at all, they are about the identity of this country. The NHS is a quite remarkable feature, which seems to be right in the middle of the sense of national identity. It comes wrapped up in those incidental experiences of any life story. It's also under threat.

AB: *This returns us to the individual-collective which is present throughout your work... you often have medicine placed in its social setting in your poems.*

KC: Yes. It's a mark of a civilised way of life, isn't it? I also think modern medicine is a statement about rationality and the political advance which established the NHS is unmatched. I know, of course, there are real failures, but the whole pejorative account of the NHS is a political campaign of a very tendentious and divisive kind.

AB: *Yes. In* Backward Turning Sea *there's a prose poem in 'About my country' which tells of the neighbours bringing around food, ending with a line about 'the memory of common poverty beaten'. This theme is intrinsic to your work.*

KC: It does keep coming back in the work, you're right. It's partly dealing with the vulnerability of the past – a family in the past – subject to the 'chance' things that happen and aren't chance at all.

AB: *If medicine in your work can then represent this individual-collective line, then it's also where the public and private come together again?*

KC: They're intense moments, aren't they? You wake up in a hospital bed, surrounded by people caring for you just because you are there. Illness does make you see things beyond your will or control; the moment of the collapse or the condition. Although there's nothing to recommend that! If you're in a clinical situation, your privacy is reduced, and there are other people in similar conditions, it's intensely personal, and not.

Waking up one time in hospital, there was a young woman standing there, she worked in the hospital, and she said to me: 'Sir, do you remember me?' And I said 'No, not really.' Anyway, she told me her name. 'You taught me,' she said. And then I *did* remember her. 'I saw your name,' she said, 'and I was sorry to see you were ill. I remember when you made me read a book, and I still read books because of what you said.' And that was brilliant. I thought, I'm being elevated here.

AB: *Your poem 'The Ingliss Touriste Patient' is in some senses anecdotal in a similar way to this story about your ex-student, but it also plays around with discontinuous time frames, floating voices, literary figures... and you create a lyric meaning out of that mix.*

KC: It's a type of derangement that is actually appropriate to the condition, rather than a literary move. But ultimately you are writing about it afterwards as an act of reclaiming, pulling yourself back in. What access do we have to those experiences outside of ourselves? There's no privilege in it, but only a fool would just walk away and treat it as if nothing had happened. Everything that *is* is in there. Everything that happens must be involved. As an aesthetic it clears away any narrowness of attention. You are subject to the competencies of others, you are afraid for your life, and the hallucinatory aspect of it... the delusions you suffer under clinical treatment are pressing...

AB: *So Ezra Pound entering the poem is akin to other similar 'imaginings'?*

KC: Pound is the poet of the Mediterranean. I think about him when I'm in Greece, so he comes into that poem set in Greece. These are *unbidden* experiences. I'm not constructing it, or looking for it. Why would you? I don't plan it. When you walk away, it's like escaping another car crash, breathing.

AB: *This business of the form of the illness finding its appropriate expression in the form of the poem... that's even more true of* Words Through A Hole... *Lee Harwood sends you a book in which someone has cut out the face of a picture of a chimpanzee, and there you are yourself, effaced by the stroke?*

KC: Utterly depersonalised. The poems take some of the words that happened to be visible through the cut out shape of the chimp's face. The first half of the book is deliberately fragmentary, tending towards incoherence and deliberate mistakes, and ends with a love poem. That's the end of the journey underground. Then part 2 is the journey back, above ground, where everything is ordered. 16 poems of 16 lines, foursquare, interspersed with something I thought I could get away with: two prose poems of 8 sentences, so I still have 16. They're mostly about journeys: into London to see an exhibition of the Egyptian Book of the Dead (always a jollifying experience in November in England) and then to Norway on a boat up to the Arctic Circle, and back to Greece.

AB: *There's a lot of the Arctic in these poems, both real and as metaphor: your own Norwegian trip; Nansen, the explorer from W.S. Graham; Glenn Gould dragging a piano to the North Pole...*

KC: Ultima Thule. And it's damn cold, but... to see the Northern Lights! In the right conditions the Arctic itself is a three dimensional hallucinatory experience. You're knocked completely out of your frame by what you are seeing. You can't be finished with it. I knew I was going to be alright then, and it worked its way into the poem, and then we headed off south to Greece for some warmth.

AB: *So were you listening to Glenn Gould at the time; is that why he's there on a literal level?*

KC: Yes. I'd started listening to Glenn Gould. He died of a massive stroke when he was fifty. The experience of the complexity of that music, its shapeliness, which can make other music sound plain, is counterpoint, the realisation of simultaneous ideas. Counterpoint interests me in writing. Which is why it can be quite hard to single out subject matters, like 'the Greek poems', because you lose some of the threads. On the other hand, you can also lose everything by pursuing ten channels at once, so you don't see one damn thing; it's all just dispersed.

AB: *Does this relate to your use of the condition, and technique, of 'apophenia' – a way in which we generate meanings from apparently random information?*

KC: That's what happened to me temporarily and immediately after the stroke. I remember saying to Melanie, 'I know these people here.' They were visiting the patient in the next bed. 'I used to teach their children,' I said. And Melanie would say, 'No, Kelvin, you don't actually know them.' This happened again and again when I was in the hospital. It also gives these unreal connections a heightened sense, a charged sense of meaning. The brain does it.

Essentially apophenia is a neurological term, it means being unwittingly subject to the brain's endless inclination to make patterns and relationships between phenomena where no such connections exist and it can be caused by neurological damage. If I've understood it, what happens is that the brain – in trying to fix the damage, to reboot itself – forces relationships in our perceptions which are irresistible in thought, but don't actually exist in the world. Where some translation of apophenia might be useful is as a term for thinking about Modernism; whether Homeric mythology can usefully be played against the events of one particular day in Dublin in 1904? Can you write a long poem, *The Cantos*, with history included in it? Maybe, by analogy, it's a critique of a certain kind of modernism: a grand poetry driven by these nonexistent connections between ideas, characterised by ill-founded, heightened revelations. So there's the immediate physiological meaning of 'apophenia', the clinical experience; and then I had this flash of an insight into the ropey nature of modernism itself. Pound is such a terrible researcher in the archives but beyond that, there's no core argument either!

AB: *The katabasis /anabasis journeys – the descent and return – are also key to the* Chimpanzee *poems. You make that an Odyssean journey home.*

KC: Yes, although I'm sufficiently recovered and intact to realise I'm not the Homeric hero. Neither has the insight from apophenia stopped me looking for such patterns – irresistible, as the doctor says. The issue is the return; a persistent trope in Western literature. Again it's not personal.

AB: *But you're also a kind of Telemachus, Odysseus and Penelope's son, writing about your own father?*

KC: Yes and no, unavoidably, although it's not agonised at that point. The etymology of the name Telemachus is interesting: 'far from the fighting'. I just thought it was an intriguing pattern, a reliable pattern given what we were saying before. What's interesting for me is how much we do, and do not, recognise in it, how like and unlike these people we are.

AB: *We've talked about music a good deal today and, like visual art, it's everywhere in your work. You're working on two new groups of poems informed by music:* Glenn Gould and Everything [an excerpt appears towards the end of this book] *and* A Short History of Song Set to Music and Abandoned.

KC: Yes, and on a collaboration with songwriters in Canterbury, which began with a reading I gave there. Sam Bailey played behind my poem about Barbara Allen from 'A Thesis on the Ballad', and since then we've turned a set of poems into a set of songs. It's marvellous. I read with some music behind, then I sit down and shut up and they play and sing the songs. We'll record it and take it from there. I was wary of this to begin with and was, of course, completely wrong. In the *A Short History of Song* poems, as we said before, each one comes with a set of impossible instructions for impossible music. The *Glenn Gould And Everything* piece is a ham-fisted attempt at counterpoint, it can't work as in music: in one column there are accounts of Glenn Gould's musicianship, and in the other column my walk around to the Co-Op and thinking about something I've just heard in the news, or music coming out of the dance school around the corner, to try and run the two threads simultaneously.

AB: *This is what I've always admired in your work; its sense of looking out; of counterpointing the lyric with history, politics, myth, literature, Greece, the NHS, painting, music. That outwardness is still strong in your work with editing and interview projects?*

KC: Yes. Poetry is dialogue, I think, imagined or actual, it's to do with what you can only know because of dialogue. The educationalist Professor Louise Stoll talks of 'knowledge animation' and makes the point that you simply can't know, can't experience certain things on your own, it depends on dialogue. I'd say dialogue with living and dead poets. Perhaps it's a conversation, like being bowled over by the exciting work of new poets in editing *Shearsman*. That was entirely pleasurable. We'll see what's made of it. And, similarly, I'm developing a series of interviews with poets, out of my own enthusiasms really. I've always enjoyed interviews – doing them, if not receiving them…

(Laughter…)

Only in *Apophenia*: Medicine and Meaning in Kelvin Corcoran's Autopathography

Andy Brown

Kelvin Corcoran's books provide numerous poems that deal directly with medical themes and personal, or family experiences of hospitals and clinics ('autopathography'), as well as many poems with incidental medical references. Many of the poems are characterised by techniques of collage and discontinuous time frames and locations, or voices that invite the reader to find their own patterns and, hence, make meanings – a technique we might term *apophenia* (from Greek, *apo* = away from, and *phaenein* = to show). This has specific psychological connotations but, in general usage, means 'the human tendency to seek patterns in random information'. Corcoran specifically uses the word as a place name ('only in Apophenia') in *Words Through A Hole...* (2011), towards which this essay progresses with *apophenia* as a guiding principle.

Corcoran's references to medicine range from incidental instances such as 'a cure for pain [...] that morphine song' ('The Empire Stores', *New and Selected* 28), or references to 'bubonic plague' in 'Power Lust and Striving' (*TR&YB* 2), to other passing references to 'antibiotics' (*TR&YB* 25) and other medical vocabulary:.

> she sleeps it down over the bridge
> which crosses a dry river
> aim your gun, answer me
> heaven comes in a myth of light
> of diamorphine
> I hope
> (*TR&YB* 9)

with a later recurrence of the 'waters of oblivion/Lethe' imagery in the lines:

> I dreamt of a rowing boat that rocked me skyward
> I didn't want to float into that anaesthesia
> (*TR&YB* 24)

Corcoran often cites medicine in conjunction with other social institutions, as in 'Schools Libraries Hospitals Mansions Welfare' ('Ambelakia' *New and Selected* 75) or, an early poem 'from the Red and Yellow Book' which presents the reader with 'marriage, divorce and public health' (*TR&YB* 26). In 'Is this the breaking of my first life?' (1999), we witness the people in our lives being whisked away:

> One by one the characters exit
> by ambulance, dispute or indifference,
> though many walk off into nothing
> you must allow the discontinuous past
>   (*Suzy* 13)

– the unsettling vision of our fellows transported off to an uncertain future, just as they came from an uncertain, 'discontinuous', past. With ambulances, our most private moments are played out in public. This poem begins with lines about the poet's mother:

> I stood at my mother's grave
> a door closed for ten years,
> the remembered town arrayed
> I see her black hair still (12)

in which these feelings are tied to statements about 'Bright stations of the Tory economy' and a river so polluted that it's 'liquid shit' (12). The dystopic suburban picture is haunted by the poet's parents – 'my parents' voices buried in the wall' – just as much of *When Suzy Was* is haunted by these ghosts that 'clamour at the window' of the title poem (30).

Corcoran's parents are everywhere in his autopathography. *The Red and Yellow Book* specifically treats of the death of his mother, who is often pictured in this collection, either prostrate in bed:

> but the dark all around me
> held her head up
> and shrank to nothing in a white bed (7)

or sitting in a chair, waiting for the inevitable:

> by the window in an easy chair
> spectral grey and thin as light
> her eyes fixed alive on her grandchildren. (16)

In the more recent 2008 poem 'About My Country' (*Backward Turning Sea*), Corcoran presents another sequence, including a prose poem about his father and family, amidst a wider array of subjects as diverse as Octavian at Actium, Saddam Hussein, Blake despairing in London, and the war-torn cities of Mogadishu and Jerusalem. We reach an ending that describes 'the valley of song of how we could have lived', an exhortation for poetry to lift us beyond the brutal realities of such locations. Nested in the heart of this sequence, we find the prose poem about the father, which begins with a medical subject:

> I remember when my father was ill with an abscess on his lunges. Neighbours brought food to us, shepherd's pie wrapped in the dish, warm in my hands, and another time ice cream. How can this be? The neighbours standing at the door urging my mother to take the food for her children. Her own stories of childhood sounded like Thomas Hardy. Talking with her brothers, the same faces laughing at the intimate memory of common poverty beaten. And of course there is a limit to what can be hammered out on the anvil of autobiography – but not the memory of common poverty beaten.
> (*Backward* 23-4)

The archaic spelling of 'lunges' admits the 'discontinuous past' to the poem again, wherein the father's medical plight and the consequences for the family are played out at a public level: the fate of the individual is part of wider social, and historical, poverty. What happens to the individual body is symptomatic of the health of the social body.[1] And where do we often experience the personal and the social meanings of family health and medicine but in death and childbirth? These two bookends to life's medicalised experiences feature strongly in the poems. Consider these lines from the poem 'Pale hole winter sun' from *The Next Wave* (1990):

> ultrasound interior
> dark heart beats

> as though unfixed
> in monochromatic inversion
>
> blind, buried alive
> already kicking
> we saw a head, spine
> stomach, limbs and organs
> > (*New and Selected* 145)

which capture the common experience in minimal, materialist terms and pitch pregnancy against the image of the foetus 'buried alive'. Later, in the same collection, Corcoran writes 'I hold the baby in my arms', in an intimate private/public moment, just as 'our lives attendant and detailed / sleepwalk the amnesia pretone' (152): our lives are 'attendant' (waiting) as much as they are attendant (care-taking, over-seeing) the 'next wave' of individuals. The poem seems to challenge us: do not sleepwalk through forgetfulness ('the amnesia pretone'); do not blink and miss these moments.

These private/public medical contexts recur, as in the short lyric 'Shakespeare clouds bank abstraction' from *TCL* (1989), which includes the public figure Roger Scruton in the foyer of a theatre:

> What are you thinking Roger?
> Balmy white man rhetoric
> nailing the victim to the crime,
> bound for the terminal hospital
> hands and heart made private
> > (*New and Selected* 160)

which echoes the earlier 'ambulances' and plays pointedly with the political meaning of medical 'privatisation' – a social health service made private *and* a personal, private experience. It also points towards the hospital interiors that colour many of the poems in *The Red and Yellow Book*:

> paintings in hospitals can help;
> local scenes, the haywain, a good frame
> or the two cartoonish kids looking at the moon,

> they are folksy and sit on a bench
> they are rumpled and happy
>
> – I am not joking
> (*TR&YB* 5)

We have now reached 'the terminal hospital' (of the Scruton poem), where the individual and the social rub unhealthy shoulders. One poem in the collection draws attention to the language of doctors:

> they really use this language
> they mean to do these things,
> show me your leg, how it feels inside (13)

the idea of language here representing that very (internal) space where the private pain and suffering meets the public domain of medicine. Yet as 'The last poem' from *The Red and Yellow Book* tells us, 'no death is an average death' (10). We may be united in our common fate and our private moments may occur in the public view of an ambulance, or hospital, yet we remain individuals. It happens to each of us and each of us alone, even as we are 'attendant' on each other:

> the last word – drink –
>
> 8.51 a.m. 9 August 1984.
>
> – we're with you mum (kiss)
>
> in my arms, all gone
> a mannerist portrait
> 58 years old, all gone (10).

As an expression of personal grief made public, Corcoran's poetry is, perhaps, nowhere more moving than in the prose poem 'I was with my mother when she died', which begins with straight talking: 'I was with my mother when she died, by the bed in the corner of the ward. Quiet after visiting time; her brother and sister and my sisters' (20). The poem continues in a quotidian fashion, dealing with the enormity of the moment (another one we must not miss in 'the amnesia pretone') by detailing several small acts of kindness and connection: 'I went up to town to buy the ginger beer she wanted, small bottles with screw tops. My final thing for you, and until this last day you held the glass yourself. In the teeth of death a human act' (20). The clash of the private and the public is then made painfully evident with the short stanza:

> The day before I'd been called back to the hospital to get rid
> of my father, drunk and talking about euthanasia. Only the
> medically qualified understand alcoholics. He left noisily, but
> she was beyond embarrassment then (20).

those last words relegating the drunk father's actions to a containable, if awkwardly objectionable, box. The mother's death itself comes quietly, unremarkably and, *as poetry*, all the more powerfully for that: 'I watched the last pulse in her neck, kissed her forehead and said, 'We're with you mum.' Then the sister said, 'She's gone, she's at peace now.' (20) As we might expect of Corcoran's work, however, this is a non-linear sequence – *The Red and Yellow Book* does not end with the mother's death ('the last poem' comes on page 10 of 29). Surely the poems wish to portray our commonly-held belief that we are in the midst of ongoing cycles of life and death, and the deeply personal can become the impersonal, through death so quickly:

> the newly dead look dead so soon,
> her black black hair
> over the gone face,
> not my mother then (16)

or, as the prose stanza at the foot of the same poems shows us, the heightened emotional moment can so quickly turn to the mundanity of the everyday:

> Home for the last time, out of the hospital, home because one
> of us would always be there. She sat in her chair, legs propped,
> never asleep; all night I listened to her breathing and gave the
> elixir every four hours. Unable to lie down; pressure sores, legs
> swollen, lungs filling up. [...] In the morning we watched
> *Tarzan* and then the visitors came. (16)

Having described the straight talking with which Corcoran treats the poems about his mother's death, I want to move on to discuss the poems about the poet's own medical experiences. Another private/ public prose poem in *Hotel Shadow* (2010) details such an episode. 'The Vaccination Queue' begins:

> I queued at the surgery for the flu vaccination. I was with the old, saw our ageing and I got it. We trailed out of the building and accepted our parts as extras in a British comedy. A queue is an opportunity to be orderly, anxious and complain in the service of humour. (66-7)

This humour is present in both the poem's subject and style: Corcoran handles the medical context with a smile. The 'ageing' folks gossip about the clinic interior: '– Look it says here, if you are breast feeding or trying to become pregnant, tell the nurse. – Well, I think you're safe then Edie.' The queue is comically human, the writing humane: 'Most of the women shouted at most of the men. – He can't hear me. Stand there, just wait. You're a bit deaf aren't you.' (67) Like the 'common poverty' discussed earlier, the vaccination poem tells us:

> Many were the respectable poor, who no longer exist in any political discourse. They wear cheap clothes; the men in pressed grey trousers and thin brown slip-ons; the women in sensible three quarter length coats and shapeless slacks. You queue up because it's free – and they have paid all their lives. So they act stiffly, like a posh hat on humility. I'm at home with them and try to be helpful. (67)

The straight tone is obvious; the mixing of medicine and economics self-evident; the private / public commonality is noted, but goes un-spoken in the queue. The poem then makes a humorous digression into an anecdote about a family doctor arriving on a horse for a home visit. He cracks a joke about Mrs Corcoran not killing her husband: 'I'd understand Mrs Corcoran but all the same, best not.' (67) Humour aside, once more we pick up on the birth/death, 'Next Wave' imagery as 'the succession of generations drops me in this queue.' (67) It is what helps the poet to 'stand here and shuffle forward' with his ageing fellow patients.

What comes next is a pertinent metaphor for the private/public borderline that defines these poems – 'a bright axis':

> I imagine every one of us standing here must be informed by such events – like a bright axis of personal identity intersecting the queue unseen and unheard. Our queue, snaking back through history via Beveridge, the Empire and beyond, is of course the English class system as vernacular drama. You know your place and how to behave, thank you. Nobody waiting for the vaccination pushed; one man faking confusion, cheated. The general disapproval unspoken hung in the air we all breathed. (67)

Though no experience is 'average' ('no death is average'), these subjects – health, poverty, generations, ageing – are the shared air 'we all breathe'. That seems to be particularly true of our experience of medicine, so it is perhaps inevitable that poems about social medicine will, at some point, become poems about personal medicine. Accordingly, the poem 'The Ingliss Touriste Patient' (from *Against Purity* in *New and Selected Poems*) documents a serious personal medical episode in Greece. The poem clearly plays off the title of Ondaatje's celebrated novel *The English Patient* (1992) and, unsurprisingly shares some of its concerns.[2] In 2003, Corcoran was hospitalised when, after a bout of suspected sunstroke, the local medical centre doctor suspected that he was having a heart attack. Corcoran was treated in hospital in Kalamata. The final diagnosis when he was back in the UK was acute labyrinthitis. The virus had also exacerbated a congenital heart condition (Corcoran had two brothers who were born and died before him as babies, both with heart complications). Whilst in the Kalamata hospital, Corcoran was tested and his brain scanned. The poem documents all this, beginning with the voice of his wife, Melanie, in a free-floating line: 'What do you mean too late? Is he in danger?' (42) that throws us into the poem *in media res*, as the poet's own consciousness floats between images and voices, both Melanie's and the doctor's:

> And I was afraid and thought I would die,
> lifting off the table, only the ceiling above me
> and the vertiginous air for your voice Melanie,

> – Yesterday you should bring him, you must
> be like sleep now, you must go to the hospital. (42)

The sensations of disorientation continue as the poet lies in hospital next to a small, unconscious Greek girl, Yorta. Her mother's voice ('Maria') drifts into the poet's mind: 'ella Yorta, ella ella, / wake up wake up my daughter, my child', but through a transposition of the letters from 'Yorta' to 'Aorta' to 'Iota', the poet even has time to pun that he is 'not caring one jot' (not one iota). 'There's something wrong with a letter, / a letter is unconscious, a letter is Maria's daughter / next to Aorta, mine, something is wrong with the invisible.' This sense of invisibility, of intangibility, floats over the whole poem. Experiences and language constantly shift, so that sensations become others; words transmute into others. Nothing is as it seems. As the poem repeats several fold: 'I was there and not there'. Even when the doctor instructs the patient to 'Stand up. / Close your eyes. / Stand feet together. / You have the hurt problem', in short, clear phrases, we are finally not sure of his meaning: does he mean 'you are hurt'? or is something lost in translation; 'you have a *heart* problem'? Is 'something wrong with a letter' again? Translation also rears its head as the poet attempts to anchor himself in this ever-shifting experience:

> And I was there and not there,
> wheeled off to brain scan land.
> Where is my wife? Will I come back here? Where is she please?
> Πού είναι η γυναίκα μου; Θα έρθει πίσω εδώ; Πού είναι
> παρακαλώ

to which a voice (the doctor's, or the patient's own?) replies:

> She's with the gypsies from the big camp
> sliding along the corridors, riding hips,
> I was back in the cardboard town by the airport,
> – where do they come from?
> – from here, they come from here.

Once again we find the personal experience of hospital pitched against the communal, just as Maria, the mother, feels she wants to bring Corcoran cold water to drink because, 'oh but we are all people, yes'.

It is at this point in the poem that the shifting waves of medicine, disorientation and hallucination admit that poet of the Mediterranean, Ezra Pound:

> I was there and not there:
> Pound in the olive grove raging,
> a ghost white man waving a broken branch
> in the perfect climate for the human nervous system;
> the olive tree blown green and white and
> the air like a lens for the Earth given a fair chance;
> Pound went down to the ship, Europa, the wreckage,
> raging, raging at the innocent ants of my harbour,
> its arms open to the various world.

This final phrase, 'the various world', echoes Louis MacNeice in 'Snow' ('The drunkenness of things being various'), while 'given a fair chance' may refer equally to 'the Earth', to the patient himself, or to Europe itself, since these lines about Pound are based on Pound's poem Canto 76 from the *Pisan Cantos*: 'As a lone ant from a broken ant-hill / from the wreckage of Europe, *ego scriptor.*'

Unsurprisingly, the poet's own mother also appears. All the poet's ghosts and loves (Melanie, Pound, mother, others) are here to 'clamour at the window'; they are always pressing in on his consciousness: 'I was there and not there with my wife and my mother' until, after a night of hallucinations ('My head was away and singing') the poet is discharged. 'I was ready'. Now Melanie can drive him home: 'so you kept driving and I lay down and the full moon / made its path across the water and I was there.' The poet patient/narrator has gone from being 'not there' to being 'there'; he has, for the moment, returned to the land of the living.

I began this essay with the concept of *apophenia*, a word that appears in *Words Through A Hole Where Once There Was A Chimpanzee's Face* (2011) and it is with this that I move to conclude. The *Chimpanzee* poems are a chapbook-length sequence of poems recording another serious personal medical episode. If the poet had returned from Kalamata in health, then the congenital heart problem behind his experiences later developed into something far more serious – paroxysmal atrial fibrillation. In September 2010, at home in Cheltenham, Corcoran experienced an ischemic stroke resulting from the condition – an embolism temporarily blocked the blood flow to the brain, closing down his centres of vision and short term memory. Recovery went on for months. The poems are divided into two parts, 'Going Down' and 'Coming Back', which equate to two Greek concepts: *katabasis* and *anabasis* respectively. 'Going Down' ends with the phrase 'this last word last katabasis' (no page numbers).

The meanings of *katabasis* (from Greek *kata* = downward, and *bainein* = to go) include: a descent downhill, the movement of the sinking sun, a military retreat (such as Xenophon's), a trip to the underworld (such as Orpheus in search of Eurydice, or Odysseus' journey to the underworld, Book 11, *The Odyssey*), or a journey from the interior to the coast. In poetics *katabasis* refers to a descending emphasis on a theme. *Katabasis* is, then, a descent in search of understanding or meaning, much as *apophenia* is a search for meaning in unconnected signs. *Anabasis*, on the other hand (from Greek *ana* = upward, and *bainein* = to go) is the ascent; the expedition from the coast into the interior (as in Odysseus' return to Ithaca from Troy) or, in poetics, a gradual ascending in emphasis.[3] The 'Going Down' section of the chapbook begins: 'Then I was falling and blind' [...] '*The descent beckons / as the ascent beckoned*'. The language of blindness and visual aberration characterise the sequence as much as the language of ascent/descent. As these early lines suggest, there is a climbing up before the sudden descent, just as there will be an *anabasis* later.

In an earlier poem – the penultimate poem of 'News of Aristomenes' (*Hotel Shadow*) – Corcoran first names these concepts, his character speaking of his own *kata / anabasis*:

> I've returned several times from where there is no singing,
> from Keadas, from Trophonius and at Leuctra, to Spartan frenzy;
> they will call me exegete of the katabasis, or some such,
> and each time there was never a singing like this one.
> [...]
> You have to go there and strike a dark bargain,
> lie down, hold barley cakes mixed with honey,
> go feet first into a mouth in the earth and shoot away
> as if caught in a river, a river of blackness covers your head.
>
> The return is difficult and never the same route as the descent.
>   (*Shadow* 57)

The lines seem to echo what would ironically happen to the poet himself within the year: illness (descent) and recovery (ascent). *Hotel Shadow* was published in October 2010 and so Aristomenes' lines were written *before* Corcoran's stroke, but *after* his previous heart problem. Other bouts of *katabasis* in the 'underground' of illness have found their way into Aristomenes' lines. Paradoxically, Corcoran himself becomes the 'exegete of his own katabasis' in the *Chimpanzee* poems and for all their intensity 'there was never a singing like this one'. In the poems, images of descent into the underworld are many (as in *The Odyssey*): 'hell', 'the insubstantial dead', 'the black river' and, in the second poem phrases such as 'when I was down there', 'the unnumbered dead / the blurred and breathless dead', 'the nations of the dead' and 'shadow'.

If this all seems quite dark, which it is, then Corcoran leavens his stanzas with characteristic wry humour. Early in the sequence we encounter the eponymous chimpanzee – a small black and white image in the margins of the text. The accompanying prose poem and verses here explain the chapbook's curious title: Lee Harwood sent Kelvin Corcoran a book – *The Wonder Book of Wonders* – which is 'in fairly good condition, except on page 88 someone has cut out the face of the chimpanzee. Hmm.' Corcoran then equates the 'male chimpanzee' (about whom some accompanying notes tell of his nest-building strategies in 'nature documentary mode') with his own alcoholic father. The collaging is distinctively a form of *apophenia*: a lived experience (Harwood's gift) moves into memory (Corcoran's father) into poetic analogy (the male chimp nest-builder). The faceless chimpanzee is also Corcoran himself, since the stroke left him with little control of his facial muscles and, hence, 'faceless'.

What follows is a set of prose and verse fragments dealing with the confusion of the stroke: 'I shouted – Tell that fucking man to stop fucking shouting. There was only me shouting; perfect', along with other details such as babbling 'random numbers', blindness, colour confusion, short term memory loss, blood clots on the brain, and the synaesthesia of 'Unexpected harsh sounds hurt and I see the noise'. Again, as in 'The Ingliss Touriste Patient', the dominant sensation is *floating*: 'faces floating over faces unseeing'. Corcoran includes both personal details ('I like to think of Lee sitting at the window of his flat in Brighton') and a medical register: 'The greatest risk of another stroke is during the four weeks following the first [...] The ABCD2 model also suggests the odds are with me', but, as always, he fuses the two into his poetry's lyric phrasing and figuration: 'Come on you anti-coagulants – take these chains from my heart and set me free.'

The theme of descent is re-presented in varying forms, presumably using *The Wonder Book of Wonders* as a source: 'A man in a weighted diving suit, / acetylene torch in hand makes wrecks fit to float', a sort of maritime surgeon fixing the wrecked hull of the body (or perhaps Pound's wrecked ship, the *Europa*?). The theme is extended with mention of Shelley's death by drowning, and humour about avoiding 'romantic sailor poets / death bed confessions / sea bed confessions / boats'. A series of quatrains follows, each beginning with a friend's name and a small vignette about their good humour and their gift of care and friendship: Peter (Riley) noting that 'the fibrillation department / [...] has pestered you quite enough'; John (Hall) 'returned from Finland / the lakes and the land and the lakes', and others. These are spare, intimate verses as the man tries to piece his own life back together again through the touchstones of friendships.

And of course through his love. The final poem in the 'Going Down' section begins with one of Corcoran's tender love poems to his wife, Melanie:

> Melanie what were you thinking
> when I was lying there blind?
> Did you fear I could leave you so easily
> or return a shade with nothing to say?

The stroke could so easily have left the patient with brain damage that would have robbed him of his language and therefore of his poetry. It is pertinent then that this poem goes on to recall

> Rain-soaked fields at rest in darkness,
> owls and foxes rooting out fresh words;
> hidden music sounding from the earth
> at each risen station of another world

in rhythmically confident lines, sounds and images that unify 'word' and 'world'; that bring fragments of experience together (*apophenia*), just as 'word' and 'world' must be brought back together again if we are to make any sense of things at all. These lines unify 'darkness' and 'earth' with the implied 'sunrise' of 'each risen station'. The whole scene is accompanied by the 'hidden music' that sounds directly from the earth. *Anabasis* is imminent.

The second half of the chapbook, 'And Coming Back', explores that *anabasis* in a sequence of sixteen poems. These are a mixture of verse (four quatrains to each) and two prose poems each of eight short stanzas. At a formal level at least, some order is being restored (measures of 16 dominate). But the leading principle is *apophenia*, by which Corcoran turns the condition into a place: 'I think I taught that girl, worked with that man / but no only in Apophenia, not in the world' (poem 1.3). These lines mark the difference between *apo*phenia and *epi*phany: in *apophenia*, the revelation is of patterns and meanings through random phenomena, in contrast to *epiphany*, in which the perception of real phenomena reveals some truth.[4] Apophenia as a place *and* a condition, describes both the visual and recollective aberrations of the stroke *and* the poetic technique.

Disorientation, in its literal sense of *disordered placement* is also characteristic. 'And Coming Back' begins with three women in coats on a street, 'red coat, black coat, something else coat' as they 'walk into town without a folded map' (poem 1.1). The patient/narrator has problems with identifying and naming colour, unlike the women who 'draw their colours from the literal'; there is no mismatch between 'what they see' and their memories, whereas for the patient/narrator what he sees and recalls is aberrant – he cannot make the pattern fit, or affords it bizarre signification. The sequence is characterised by recurring metonyms for 'orientation' and *anabasis/katabasis*: 'rising up' (1.1); 'walking upside down in the underworld' 'raising' and 'coming forth' (1.2); 'the ordinary ascent', descending' and 'stepping down' (1.4); 'the sun rises' and 'the miners of Kirkenes stepping down' (2.1) and many more instances. Other directional signifiers recur in: 'From here you turn left, then right at the lights' (1.3); 'the cardinal points' (1.4); 'pathfinder genius' and the naming of 'the Barents Sea' and the Norwegian explorer 'Nansen' (2.3), a figure who was also highly significant in the poetry of W.S. Graham. These fragments cohere to generate *apophenic* meanings – as readers we apprehend these meanings just as the patient/narrator undergoes the process of 'making the eyes to see' in this 'chapter of giving a man a memory' (1.2). This fusing of lived medical experience with writing process *and* reading experience is a perfect fusion of form and meaning. It is also deeply involving: we piece it together at the same time as the patient/narrator himself:

> Imagine these poems of the ordinary ascent,
> blinking sightless at the cardinal points;
> to make a series of journeys above ground,
> to know the names of holding up the sky. (1.4)

The last line echoes the author William Fiennes in his work of non-fiction *The Snow Geese*: 'Learning the names is a method of noticing.' Coincidentally both authors locate this writerly attentiveness within freezing, northern landscapes: Fiennes follows the return migration of the snow geese back to northern Canada (their own *anabasis*); Corcoran introduces 'the Arctic'. Significantly, the Arctic is not only colourless and disorienting, it is also as 'blank' as the patient/narrator's memory ('empty and endless for the mind to lodge at zero' [2.2]). It is open territory to be explored, hence the appearance of the explorer Nansen (via W.S. Graham). The North Pole is also, in terms of *anabasis*, 'upwards'. There are patterns to be made sense of there: 'the hexagonal abundance of whiteness dancing'. We know also from the many references to 'radio' in the rest of the poet's work – and from his techniques of discontinuous collaging – that he may find a way to link radio and the North Pole. The resolution is simple: in 1967 the Canadian pianist Glenn Gould recorded the radio documentary 'The Idea of North'. Gould is accordingly admitted to Corcoran's poems. The link is enough, but not *just* enough – it is extended into a set of richer patterns that become part of the process of 'coming back'. Corcoran was indeed listening to Glenn Gould's recordings of the *Goldberg Variations* (1741) whilst he was recovering, a fact embodied in the recurrence of motifs from J.S. Bach, including the *Variations*:

> And in the name of rhythmic continuity
> and the abstract necessity of those structures,
> I've taken my time to say these things to you;
> the contrapuntal requires such deliberateness. (2.4)

If Bach's *Variations* are one of the most significant examples of reworking a form (an aria with 30 variations), then Corcoran's sequence is similarly a 'contrapuntal' and 'deliberate' search for 'structure' and 'continuity' (2.4) from within the disorientations of his medical experience.

The final seven poems of 'And Coming Back' take us, unsurprisingly, to Greece and to Odysseus' *anabasis* from Troy to Ithaca; from the

Underworld back to the living. Poem 3.2 returns us to 'Arcadia and the fertile valley; / white on white, after such blindness / we sat in the courtyard of a Greek spring.' The patient/narrator is certainly 'coming back' now, as he sits reading '*The Book of Things* by Ilhan Berk' in the courtyard, whilst listening to the Algerian singer Souad Massi who 'opens her mouth to sing'. Corcoran also addresses the translator of İlhan Berk: 'George [Messo], this might be a way to talk: / stories, ambergris, a fat bee awake; / against history the morning dance' – and these things are certainly restorative: poetry, song, dance, story, the poet's personal history within the wider social and mythic contexts. Apophenia, the place, is becoming Arcadia, or Ataraxia, once again. It is both life-affirming and worth remarking upon: 'that we're here at all in the dancing trees, / standing on the green entangled ground' (3.3).

In these final poems the patterns 'come back' to, or re-approach, meaning. Corcoran's familiar figures find meaningful re-expression: Pound's *Europa* reappears in 'Yesterday a girl atop a white bull / went swimming past, Europa, the fool', and the father figure resurfaces: he is both Corcoran's own father ('I thought him dead but he's back') and, at the same time, Odysseus. The patient/narrator also *becomes* Odysseus in *anabasis*. Poem 4.1 begins with three significant words 'Telemetry, telekinesis, Telemachus'. 'Telemetry' is the use of automated, wireless data systems, as in the radio tracking of migratory (Odyssean?) wild animals (Fiennes' arctic snow geese?). As a way of mapping movement it is part of the lexis of dis/orientation in these poems. 'Telekinesis' is the parapsychologic idea that the mind can move, or at least influence, solid matter: for poetry, this might be a useful metaphor for the influential shaping powers of language. And finally 'Telemachus' – the son of Odysseus and Penelope. His name means 'far from the war' (he was absent, unlike his father, from the Trojan War), an etymology which lies behind the lines: 'Radio Troy in the Greek Administration Zone' and 'he sees himself in me, I'm far from fighting I said' (4.1). This speaks about both Greek myth as much as it does about Corcoran's own father/son relationship. As the poem notes: 'father son reunion spells big trouble in Ithaka'.

The paternal reunion is symbolic of various reunions: of the patient/ narrator with his mind, his memories, himself; of Odysseus with Penelope; of the poet with his own father. Poem 4.2 begins: 'Of course he's come back, I knew he would', which could equally be Penelope speaking of Odysseus; Kelvin's wife Melanie talking of him, or the poet himself worrying over his own father. Such pattern making with the mythic and the personal, with History and histories, with the public and the private, is one of Corcoran's significant contributions to the contemporary lyric. It is borne of the need to make significant, human meaning from bewildering, layered experiences:

> Facing death, love waits there in the deep,
> as the lights burn out and the wires melt
> the one word to bring to that moment,
> the only thing to hold onto at the dark door. (3.3)

The lines speak of connection in real physical terms – the 'thing to hold onto' – as well as through the pattern making propensities of the mind – it is as if *apo*pheny has become *epi*phany; real meaning in the material world. It is fitting then that 'And Coming Back' presents a penultimate poem with the affirmation of love from the wife's point of view. Like Joyce's modernist classic, *Ulysses*, in which Molly Bloom ends with her famous, affirmative monologue, Corcoran too nears the end of his sequence with the voice of Penelope / Molly / Melanie:

> I didn't think he would ever return,
> our lives apart unravelling, blue thread
> floating on the air, a lost word gone pelagic,
> but he's here, substantial, salty, like before. (4.3)

The woman's loving relief is palpable, just as her returned husband is palpable, 'substantial'. This is in contrast with the fear that 'he was become no man nowhere'. Here Corcoran plays on the Greek word *Outis*, a pseudonym for Odysseus, meaning 'Nobody'. When fighting the Cyclops, Odysseus says: 'Cyclops [...] My name is Nobody. Nobody I am called by mother, father, and by all my comrades' (line 366, Book 9). Again, this is myth, but this is personal: the wife fears that the stroke might erase her husband, as the poem in 'Going Down' suggested: 'Did you fear I could leave you so easily / or return a shade with nothing to say?' The Penelope / Melanie poem concludes in a tone of tender imploring:

> Every night I talked and talked to an absence,
> I've drawn him back, on and on I've said,

> to the rise and fall of the sea – I won't have this,
> come back, you must come back and speak to me (4.3)

and is as emotive as any of Corcoran's love poems for his wife – she prays for the man whose mind and memory are blanked-out as he wanders in the white-out of the 'North Pole', or the confusing terrain of Apophenia; he 'must come back'. And, as the structure of *katabasis/ anabasis* implies, and the poems bear out, he does return. The final poem is as personal as a poem spoken by Odysseus can be:

> I never thought I would get back here;
> the sea won't stop moving, the land now and then;
> but here I am, I hold my nerve, I make it happen.
>
> If there's an account to be given, no problem,
> I'll say what I did and did not do – straight;
> ships drawn up, burning towers, a woman,
> if there's a pattern to this it's only visible now.
> [...]
> They stare like I've returned from the dead – well. (4.4)

The straight talking is done. The public, the private, the mythic, the historical – their meaning in the pattern of the personal-public story is made.

NOTES

[1] See Wagner, Corinna. *Pathological Bodies: Medicine and Political Culture.* Berkeley: University of California Press. 2013.

[2] Both the novel and the poem are non-linear; both pitch a group of disparate characters, nationalities and languages into a personal medical context; both have love stories. In the novel, the injured airman László de Almásy owns a copy of Herodotus' *Histories*, a book with which Corcoran is quite familiar from his extended engagement with Greece. Furthermore, the 'Terpsichore' book of Herodotus' *Histories* (Terpsichore being the muse of dance and dramatic chorus, often portrayed holding a lyre) is layered beneath Corcoran's lines describing his sensations of disembodiment: 'My head was away and singing' (44).

[3] The Greek writer Xenophon (431–355 BC) wrote his *Anabasis* about the expedition of the Persian, Cyrus the Younger, against his brother, King Artaxerxes II, and the Greek historian Arrian (86–146 AD), wrote *Anabasis Alexandri* about Alexander the Great (336–323 BC).

[4] Both stand in contrast to *schizophrenic apophenia*, in which *delusional* phenomena are seen as revealing truths.

WORKS CITED

Fiennes, William. *The Snow Geese*. London: Picador. new edition. 2010.
Wagner, Corinna. *Pathological Bodies: Medicine and Political Culture*. Berkeley: University of California Press. 2013.

EKPHRASIS IN A CONVEX MIRROR:
DECAYING MONUMENTS AND BREATHING STATUARY IN KELVIN CORCORAN'S WRITING ABOUT ART

ZOË BRIGLEY THOMPSON

In 'Self-Portrait in a Convex Mirror,' the poet John Ashbery contemplates the longevity of art and considers what visual art conveys to a viewer about past artistic or public histories. Ashbery explains that 'Each person / Has one big theory to explain the universe,' but such a theory cannot 'tell the whole story' (*Self-Portrait* 81). This chapter admits Kelvin Corcoran's inheritance from poets like Ashbery that challenge teleological certainty. The analysis concludes, however, that Corcoran's ekphrasis is also inflected by English Romantic models, which challenge the permanence of art and its ability to preserve particular public legacies or personal histories.

The discussion to follow draws on James A. Heffernan's analyses of Romantic and postmodern ekphrasis in *Museum of Words*, which describes how 'the traditionally ekphrastic impulse to deliver in words the story signified by the pregnant moment of graphic art gives way to the desultory, inconclusive story of what the poet thinks and feels as he contemplates the painting' (182). Beginning with Homer, Heffernan describes how throughout Western history, the poet 'reactivates the struggle for mastery between the image and the word' and emphasizes that 'contention' (33, 39). Revolutionized by the rise of museums, twentieth century poetry is particularly inspired by 'the individuated work of art' hung on the gallery wall (Heffernan 138). This context produced 'the individual ekphrastic poem': Auden's 'Musée des Beaux Arts' for example, or William Carlos Williams' poems about Brueghel paintings (ibid). The poet becomes a self-conscious observer of art and art history, and in the context of postmodernism, poetry seeks to challenge the authority of images and words as well as mythologies of artistic identity. Heffernan uses Ashbery's 'Self-Portrait in a Convex Mirror' as 'a model for any postmodern poet seeking to represent a self that he or she knows can only be misrepresented or refracted by the very words that purport to advertise it' (174). In 'Self-Portrait in a Convex Mirror' (titled after the 1523/4 Parmigianino painting), the act of viewing this great work of art calls into question the assumed personality of the artist behind the work as well as the selfhood of the viewer under the influence of that work. According to Ashbery, the viewer becomes a character from an E.T.A. Hoffmann story 'deprived / Of a reflection' (73). The 'whole' of the viewer is replaced by the 'Otherness of the painter in his / Other room' (74). It remains unclear, however, whether that otherness is an echo of the artist's 'genuine' personality or a myth invented from the viewer's own assumptions about the artist and the artwork.

Like Ashbery, Corcoran contemplates in his ekphrastic poems the instability of the image and word, signifier and signified. In *Your Thinking Tracts or Nations*, a collaborative collection with artist/writer Alan Halsey, Corcoran eludes authorial conviction when writing about Halsey's art. In 'Picture Eight,' Corcoran responds to Halsey's drawing, considering his own absence from the picture:

> Alan I am out of the picture,
> if Coleridge had gone with Leake
> we'd have the world mapped;
> I am standing on the edge of the world.
>
> I am reduced to pure white bones.
> I am compact, immutable, absent. (27)

Corcoran, the poet writing about a work of art, is 'out of the picture.' Halsey's image features a drawing of a ship in a style that parodies prehistoric art; a rudimentary figure can be seen onboard, his arms raised in rage or victory and one hand is shaped like the head of an axe or scimitar. There is also a large fingerprint, a number of latitudes and longitudes, and words written in an old-fashioned script: some can be deciphered reading 'Image,' 'God,' 'Wonder,' 'Spiritual,' 'Heaven,' 'Eternity' and 'Lucifer.' The primitive figure rides the ocean mapping out these great abstract concepts; there is no uncertainty. Corcoran asserts, however, that the world is not mapped, and he references an incident from the life of the Romantic poet, Coleridge, during his time on Malta in 1804. When working as an under-secretary for Sir Alexander Ball, Coleridge was offered a mission with Captain Leake on a mission to the Black Sea to purchase corn; what such a mission represented, however, was Coleridge 'on the verge of building a career in the colonial service,' though finally such a mission never materialized

(Hough and Davis 34). Like Coleridge, Corcoran rejects the colonial mindset that seeks to map the world and instead stands 'on the edge.' The poet's identity decomposes to pure bone, and the words that he uses to describe himself are antithetical to the colonial project. He is 'compact' and self-contained while colonialism is sprawling and consuming; he is immutable and unchanging in contrast to the voracious growth of capitalist imperialists; he is absent, not domineering. Corcoran's writing about visual art works through postmodern questions about the authority of art and the stability of identity, but it also challenges legacies of British colonialism. The poet's identity crisis in 'Picture Eight' represents a rejection of teleological certainties propagated by certain imperialist visions of the world.

Corcoran's political ekphrasis is bound up with British models, and the reference to Coleridge is particularly suggestive. Coleridge was to write in 'Poesy or Art' that to set out to imitate nature was a doomed project: 'You set out with a supposed reality and are disappointed and disgusted with the deception,' but a better strategy might be to 'begin with an acknowledgement of total difference' (272). Coleridge is of course speaking about the relationship between poetry and the reality that it seeks to capture, but his comments might also apply to ekphrasis, and they are prescient in the context of postmodern ekphrasis which denies authenticity or genuineness in its quest to unravel a work of art.

Corcoran's association with the Romantics is cemented by a litany of references throughout his body of work, most of all to Coleridge, Shelley and Byron. Though his writing about art is more postmodern than Romantic, Corcoran does share some important strategies with Romantic poets, especially when it comes to questioning the permanence of art, of history and the legacies of art. In Heffernan's view, Shelley 'challenges the tenacity of power itself' in poems like 'Ozymandias,' 'by attacking an icon made to represent and perpetuate it' and 'undermining the assumption that visual art *can* perpetuate – or even unequivocally honor' (116). Heffernan finds a similar dynamic in Byron's ekphrastic passages that depict 'breathing statuary' (127). Weaving an inextricable alliance between love and death, Byron eroticises the deadness of statues, so they no longer represent 'the lover's desire to perpetuate the beauty of the beloved,' but instead display 'the price to be paid for the realization of that desire' (Heffernan 132). Both Romantic poets use ekphrasis to raise uncomfortable questions about the longevity or veracity of historic or personal legacies.

The analysis to follow explores Corcoran's unique blend of post-modern and Romantic ekphrasis. Such poems work on one level to undermine simplistic ideas about the relationship between the life of an artwork, its artist and the viewer who beholds that work. What makes his poems unique, however, is the political aspect that rejects crude or one-dimensional stories of historic or individual legacies. The first section of the analysis to follow discusses Corcoran's responses to art that interrogate British history and Western colonial legacies, analyzing further poems from *Your Thinking Tracts or Nations*. As in Shelley's 'Ozymandias,' Corcoran undermines any 'would-be embodiment of transcendental power,' so he can 'convert the face of power into an object of ridicule' and 'transform signifiers of absolute authority' into 'marks and signs of desperation' (Heffernan 117). The second section investigates Corcoran's poems about individual artistic legacies, focusing in particular on *Roger Hilton's Sugar*. Corcoran's poems about the post-war abstract artist, Roger Hilton (1911-1975), refuse typical sensational biographies of the artist and through mingling the voice of the poet and Hilton's monologues, Corcoran questions easy biographical summaries that seek to create meaning out of art through studying the personal life of the creator. Hilton's artworks and Corcoran's poems are the breathing statuary conjured by Byron, and, as in Byron, the poems 'radically revise[s] the traditional condition of [art] as the embodiment of life' (Heffernan 132). The ideal here is not that of Keats' 'Ode on a Grecian Urn,' the lovers '[f]or ever panting,' their ecstatic flirtation memorialized for perpetuity. Instead, Corcoran undermines the myth of Hilton – the erratic, sensual, alcoholic artist – emphasizing that though art 'radiates a life-like energy,' it is also 'perpetually fixed, and therefore perpetually lifeless'; it wears, in Heffernan's words, 'the face of fixation – the face of death' (132). The artist remains absent and unknowable, and Corcoran emphasizes that the otherness projected onto that other artist in another room is in fact the otherness within ourselves.

PORTRAIT OF A NATION

When Shelley writes of the statue of 'Ozymandias,' as a 'wreck' on the 'lone and level sands,' it is not to commemorate the subject's 'sneer of cold command' but to rejoice that though Ozymandias does survive, it is only as 'lifeless things' (294). Like Shelley, Corcoran's writing about art sometimes has a strong political aspect and Corcoran undermines despotic or dubious uses of power, especially abuses credited to British imperialism and Western capitalism. In the prose poem, 'Modern Wonders,' Corcoran invokes a real or imagined picture called 'Weighing the Earth', a title that recalls the experiment by British eighteenth-century scientist Henry Cavendish to measure gravity. Corcoran places the picture in the 'mind' of a '1950s scientist,' who is in turn a subject viewed by the reader: the poem begins 'We see' (*Next Wave* 12). The scientist imagines himself in a position of judgement 'crouched over handling mass against tiny golden weights,' but most intriguing is the 'companion in brown overalls' who 'has a magnet, it's lifting 46 tons, it is useful in industry and the home; but his face tells you it is not like weighing the Earth, it is like regret' (*Next Wave* 12). Cavendish's experiment represents the Enlightenment quest for knowledge which was a prelude to the embracing of empiricism, the rise of capitalism, Western colonialism and the Industrial Revolution. Such symbolism is positive in the mind of the 1950s scientist living in an era that was arguably the zenith of capitalism, but the regret in the scientist's companion subverts a magnificent portrait of the capitalist project. The experiment's importance is also undercut by the advertising-style motto, 'useful in industry and in the home.' Far from being celebrated in the picture as a glorious post-Enlightenment project, Corcoran shows that the experiment of 'weighing the earth' is a prelude to great folly.

The theme of historic legacies is taken up again in *Your Thinking Tracts or Nations*, Corcoran's collaboration with the artist, Alan Halsey, who provides a number of drawings that work as inspiration for Corcoran's poems. *Your Thinking Tracts or Nations* immediately places itself in the language of public discourse. Its title makes the nation equivalent with a tract, an indistinct area or space, rendering the idea of nationhood far more indistinct. A tract can also be a religious pamphlet or an anthem of scriptural verses which signals a didactic or spiritual aspect to the work presented. The prefix 'Your Thinking' is intriguing; it may be that an unspecified 'you' is 'thinking' about 'tracts or nations,' or perhaps the title animates those same 'tracts or nations' as 'thinking' entities with a life of their own. Either way, the approach to thinking about public legacies and histories destabilizes any simplistic conclusions.

This subversive feeling is anchored by Halsey's scratchy drawings – Corcoran calls it a 'stark and stubborn art' (*Tracts* 15). Halsey brings together parodic imagery from prehistoric, ancient Egyptian, and medieval artistic traditions, as well as maps, mathematical diagrams, scripted words and numbers. The pictures are presented in black and white rather than colour, though such reproductions concur with Corcoran's approach to notions of art and authenticity. Commenting on reproductions of art, Heffernan suggests that 'the gray glaze of a black-and-white reproduction stands about as far from the golden glow of the original as the original does from the self or soul it purports to represent' (173). Halsey and Corcoran reject a quest to create a sense of genuineness – that 'golden glow'. Corcoran addresses this idea directly in 'Picture Thirteen'. Addressing Halsey, he describes the process of writing these ekphrastic poems, admitting that he is 'scratching away' and 'feeling fairly fucked by it all' (*Tracts* 42). Far from being a window to the 'soul' of the artist or indeed the poet, Corcoran describes the poems as 'just scribble and dust that won't ignite; / it's about as deep as photocopy shine' (42). The 'golden glow' refuses to ignite, and, like Halsey's black and white reproductions, Corcoran's poems are removed from a sense of genuineness; they operate self-consciously at a distance from the artist and from the poet's own 'authentic' self.

Corcoran's approach to ekphrasis adopts a postmodern questioning which undercuts and destabilises the public histories and legacies in the visual iconographies employed by Halsey. In 'Picture 1' for example, Corcoran responds to Halsey's use of parodic images from particular artistic traditions. Halsey's first picture presents sparse drawings of Egyptian hieroglyphs and primitive depictions of fish and flowers, which are accompanied by more utilitarian numbers and arrows; and the scrawled word 'ASIA.' The cultural symbols of Egypt have been elevated in Western thinking as the prototypes for 'civilization' itself. Michael Rice explains in *Egypt's Legacy* that ancient Egyptian society 'imprinted a series of ideas about what a complex society should be' and such ideas 'became the dominant model' and influenced contemporary and future societies that would be both 'complex' and 'hierarchical' (xi). When Corcoran responds to the Egyptian symbolism and its legacies, it is not to celebrate Western 'civilization' but to hint at its transgression in Asia, to reveal how the West has violated the supposed cradle of its culture. Corcoran enters another continent when he describes 'Nilotic flowers at the door'; Egypt is 'the hot route to Asia' (*Tracts* 7). The phrase 'hot route' is pithy and evocative of something fresh, exciting and laden with opportunity. A hot route is also a particular play in American football, which is used to bypass a defensive blitz formation. Out of such an atmosphere of conquest, a figure emerges: 'Mr Tarred and Feathered stepping out unabashed' (7). The punishment of tarring and feathering originates in Europe and it tended to be a penalty for petty crimes such as theft (cf. Mellinkoff 156 n. 12). The subject of humiliation, however, is far from being ashamed, but steps out into Asia full of expectation. Echoing the earlier reference to game strategy, Mr. Tarred and Feathered has a 'groundplan'; 'his red channel' is 'behind him now,' a possible reference to the Suez Canal, the imperialist project that used Egyptian forced labour to link the Mediterranean and the Red Sea (*Tracts* 7). The attitude of Mr. Tarred and Feathered is utilitarian and capitalist. The 'burning bright beasts' of Asia are, in his mind, merely 'a trade memory of rumoured wealth' (7). Ultimately, in Halsey's use of ancient Egyptian symbolism, Corcoran sees not a celebration of Western culture, but a legacy of shame.

Shame inhabits Corcoran's vision of the West in his response to Halsey's third picture. In the illustration for 'Picture Three', the word London features prominently alongside a window, odd letters, abstract shapes and squiggles and a stick man carrying a flag. Corcoran describes London as 'the green capital of the singing world', the colour green having both fresh and putrid associations, while the sarcastic tone of 'the singing world' creates a sense of London's pomposity and obliviousness (11). Corcoran begins in seeming confidence with a strong assonantal rhyming couplet: 'When I arrived in London town / the monuments danced in a round' (11). Rather than celebrating London and its monuments, however, Corcoran departs from the finality and certainty of rhyme, adding that 'the theatre palaces were closed for a plague, / the far side of the river hung with shame' (11). The reference to a plague recalls the Great Plague of London in the seventeenth century, when filthy sanitary conditions led to an outbreak of bubonic plague. London is not a glorious city of achievements and progress here, but a metropolis divided by class and wealth, afflicted because of its lack of care for the poor and destitute.

If 'Picture Three' concentrates on British legacies, Corcoran's 'Picture Four' turns to Europe. Halsey's fourth illustration is dominated by a face lacking a mouth and with one eye blank. Other details include a rudimentary drawing of a four-legged animal, crude flowers, abstract shapes, and a map featuring numbered plots of ground. Corcoran begins his poem by associating the face with Europe, 'the unstable continent' (13). Europe is personified as female and Corcoran describes 'her great real burning / white rock and green shade' (13). The lack of punctuation in the phrase 'her great real burning' leaves uncertainty as to whether 'real' is being used as an adjective or a noun; is Corcoran ingenuously putting together two emphatic adjectives, or is it the 'real' itself which burns? The description of rock and shade recalls T.S. Eliot's 'The Waste Land' and the sinister invitation to view the 'shadow under this red rock, / (Come in under the shadow of this red rock)' (135). Eliot's shadow and rock have been interpreted as: an invitation to examine one's shadow self (cf. Maddrey 115); a negation of the relief promised to Isaiah in 32:1-2 (cf. Ackerley 30); a recreation of the sterility of life without love (cf. Miller 70); and as a sexually charged, erotic invocation (cf. Murphy 150). What is clear, however, is that Eliot is lamenting a lack of certainty or comfort for the modern subject in terms of identity, religion, love or sex. The legacy of Europe is not grand historical deeds, but an unsettling feeling of loss and insecurity. Consequently, Corcoran explains that 'If we look directly at her [Europe's] face / she is paler than this field' (*Tracts* 13). Just as the speaker of 'The Waste Land' finds that his eyes fail him when trying to perceive the hyacinth girl, so Europe is fading away, disappearing into nothingness.

In contrast to such uncertainty, Corcoran presents the words and deeds of European leaders who, in trying to build a legacy for Europe, create war and violence whilst extending the brutal philosophy of capitalist imperialism. Corcoran features Tony Blair – prime minister for Britain at the time the book was written – who 'explains what we must do / -best prig mode, though I couldn't speak / for the translation' (13). Blair's doublespeak brashly announced by megaphone is impossible to translate; communication between politicians and constituents is irrevocably broken. In response, the narrator loses the ability to speak, much as the speaker in 'The Waste Land' fails to speak to the hyacinth girl. In this case, however, the narrative is not romantic but political, and Blair is a poor and comical substitute for a romantic object of desire. Politics is significant again later in 'Picture Four' when Corcoran writes a kind of letter to Halsey on politicians and the subject of war, mentioning in particular the Yugoslav Wars of the 1990s. Identifying a more modern kind of imperialism, Corcoran notes that 'War is good and bad for business' and he imagines companies like Walter Bau and Ready Mixed Concrete 'at the borders, ready to run the wacky race' (14). The mission of restoring order in war-torn countries is more cartoonish than noble, and the reference to the Hanna-Barbera animation *Wacky Races* jars with the brutal reality of war.

As an antidote to the grand missions of Western imperialism, Corcoran conjures the mundane lives of former generations of ordinary people. Inspired by the numbered plots of land in Halsey's illustration, Corcoran describes an archaeological dig literally beneath the floors of a present day community:

> Excavated 42 tombs and a rubbish pit,
> males were buried with heads to the west
> females with heads to the east,
> children's burials ... seashells and small black counters,
> a game? the rubbish pit, pottery, signs of burning, a few bones.
> (15)

There is a mundane beauty and order in the uncovering of a former community. The most basic human needs are represented by the rubbish pit and tombs, the object of beauty that is the shell, the game counters and utensils for eating and cooking. The echoing rhythms of the lines about male and female burials signal simplicity of thinking and a harmonious mirroring of the sexes. The legacy of such ordinary lives is far more worthy than the imperialist schemes of grand Europe.

'Picture Six' anchors Corcoran's scorn for Western legacies, beginning with a letter to Jack Straw, the then British home secretary, who is described as a 'strawman' (20). Perhaps referring to the British Labour government's misguided support for the Iraq War, the 'straw man' suggests misinformation and misdirection. Corcoran seems to gesture to political misrepresentations about Iraq's supposed Weapons of Mass Destruction. The man also recalls Halsey's illustration where a primitive figure seeks to dominate the world. At the centre is a rudimentary sketch of a man with a bow and arrow and the word Terra is surrounded by semi-circles; there are a few more stick figures, a hand, letters and numbers, a tiny map of buildings and rudimentary four-legged animals. Corcoran's poem considers how human beings come to terms with the world around them and, in the epigraph for the poem, he quotes Barry Lopez writing about a sense of place in *Arctic Dreams*. Lopez describes the human mind as 'trying to find its place within the land, to discover a way to dispel its own sense of estrangement' (*Tracts* 20). Thinking through the implications of Lopez's statement, Kent C. Rydan suggests that 'for any place to be fully understood and appreciated,' one's goal must be to expand 'surface perceptions [...] by a grasp of the imaginative life and dreams which the landscape sparks and sustains' (232). Such an imaginative life can have the horror of nightmares; in his letter to Jack Straw, Corcoran describes 'the sun red off centre / over the dark utilitarian units' (*Tracts* 20). 'Picture Six' returns too to Eliot's image of the rock; the narrator is 'a rock in the Arctic ocean dreaming' and 'a painted rock' (21). The rock has been removed from Eliot's desert landscape and replanted in the scenery of Lopez's *Arctic Dreams*. The rock in the desert was estranged from contact, but the rocks in 'Picture Six' are surrounded by the ocean and are 'painted.' Beyond the desert, there are possibilities.

Like Lopez, Corcoran seeks to find another way of understanding place and culture, one that means going beyond 'surface perceptions,' as Rydan puts it (232). Corcoran looks for an alternative legacy for Britain and he turns back to Coleridge paraphrasing that poet's praise for laudanum (*Tracts* 21). Writing to his brother George in 1798, Coleridge explains: 'Laudanum gave me repose, not sleep; but you, I believe, know how divine that repose is, what a spot of enchantment, a green spot of fountains and flowers and trees in the very heart of a waste of sands' (qtd. Booth 42). By finding an alternative mode of perception, Coleridge escapes the sterile desert lamented by Eliot. Through poetry rather than laudanum, Corcoran conjures a vision of a different kind of England:

> one word undid me: riverside, to sit by a river
> in England – riverside, with others, to watch
> the river flow under trees in green shade –
> undid me here in this unfixed place.
> (*Tracts* 21)

The green shade of the white rock in 'Picture Four' is replaced by the idyllic shade of trees in a peaceful scene of tranquillity. Whether such a place is real or imagined as in Coleridge's drug-fuelled visions is questionable. The lines also eerily invoke, however, a source text for the red rock imagery of 'The Waste Land': Eliot's own poem 'The Death of Saint Narcissus' (cf. Eliot *Other* 2-3). Narcissus too is soothed by a river and he transforms from a tree to a fish to a ravished girl, but finally he is described as 'green' and the shadow of the rock is ultimately found in his own mouth. The comforting image of the English river is reassuring to the inhabitant of an 'unfixed place,' but the commonalities between Corcoran's and Eliot's imageries belie any idyllic notion of a peaceful, pastoral England. Ultimately, the legacy that Corcoran conjures for England and the West is not idyllic or civilized, but a 'bloody history' (22). The British are 'a tribe iron-shod, iron-bound,' a description which undermines notions of modern progress and recalls the industrial history of the West (22). Using Halsey's iconography of ancient symbols, maps and exchange or trade lines, Corcoran is able to mock the grand schemes and public legacies of Western imperialism, and to lament its terrible and irrevocable mistakes. What the poems suggest is that the West's attitude to the world has always been and still is summed up by the ultimatum: 'I – Want – You – Give – It – Or' (22). Corcoran's poems express an abiding longing for Western civilization to discover a more complex understanding of place and culture and the role of the individual within it. It is the desire for a culture not bounded by national sentiment, but resembling perhaps the nebulous tracts of the book's title.

PORTRAIT OF AN ARTIST

Your Thinking Tracts or Nations questions British histories and especially the symbolic significance of art objects which contribute to grand narratives about the progress of humankind and Western civilization. In 'My Life with Byron', Corcoran echoes Byron's passionate disapproval (in *Childe Harold* and *The Curse of Minerva*) of Thomas Bruce, seventh earl of Elgin, and his looting of the 'Elgin Marbles' in Athens. Unlike Byron, however, Corcoran identifies British imperialism as the source of the problem, not (as Byron suggests) Lord Elgin's Scottish background. In 'The Objects Were Not Paid For Or Got For A Fixed Price (Elgin),' the speaker scorns 'the triumph of Eng-a-lish classicism,' the mock accent on 'Eng-a-lish' deflating the seriousness of British traditions and legacies (*New and Selected* 77).

Although Corcoran is self-consciously postmodern in his representation of artists and their works, he has something in common with Byron in thinking about art as representing an authentic or genuine legacy from a deceased artist. Discussing Byron's treatment of sculpture in particular, Heffernan draws attention to the Fourth Canto of *Childe Harold's Pilgrimage* which includes ekphrastic passages on works of sculpture such as the Venus de Medici, the Dying Gaul, the

Laocoön and the Apollo Belvedere. In such passages, Byron initially revives a 'longstanding literary convention: the practice of discovering life and breath in statuary' (Heffernan 127). What makes Byron's ekphrasis unique, however, is not the act of making the statues live, but of '*participat*[ing] in the ever-changing life of his own narrative, in the restless moment of his own meditations' (129). Byron is aware of the sculptor too and he emphasizes that the sublimity of art derives 'from the power of mind which at once generates the work and is in turn signified by it' (129). For Byron, it is the desire of the artist that manifests itself in his or her work: their passions expressed for perpetuity. Yet it is hardly that simple, because, as Heffernan notes, if an artwork expresses 'the lover's desire to perpetuate the beauty of the beloved, it also reveals the price to be paid for the realization of that desire': being 'perpetually lifeless' (132). The artist is no Pygmalion, and the viewer of art can only remain frustrated when trying to resurrect a long-dead artist. Heffernan concludes that Byron views works of art as representing 'the kind of beauty that may be admired but nonetheless must be finally relinquished' (133).

Like Byron, Corcoran reveals some ambivalent feelings about the quest towards intimate knowledge of a work of art or the mindset of an artist. The section that now follows looks specifically at Corcoran's volume *Roger Hilton's Sugar*, which explores the life and work of the British poet-war artist, Roger Hilton. Like Byron, Corcoran's ekphrasis exists in 'the restless moment of his own meditations' moving between his own lines of thought, descriptive passages that seek to capture Hilton's art, and the unique monologue of Hilton himself (Heffernan 129). Hilton's 'power of mind' (to reuse Heffernan's phrase) is certainly palpable throughout the poems, yet as in his subversive treatment of Western nations, Corcoran's approach to the artist is complex and disconcerting. Rejecting the tendency of art critics to portray sensationalist or sentimental details from the artist's life, *Roger Hilton's Sugar* undermines any authentic knowledge in the relationship between the artist, artworks and the viewer. Corcoran's approach recalls Hilton's quoting of Rimbaud in his cover for the Studio International exhibition in 1976. Hilton invoked Rimbaud's poem '*O saisons, ô châteaux*' in which the poet questions what is understood from his words and describes them escaping and flying away (Hilton *Night* n.p.). Uncertainty about what poetry or art can capture is redolent in Corcoran's discussion of Hilton.

As an abstract artist, Hilton is perhaps an appropriate subject for a poet seeking to explore the limits and possibilities of expression. Charles Harrison explains that for abstract artists of Hilton's era, the point was 'to liberate painting from its subservience to the self-enchanted spectator, whose incurable tendency it was to look into paintings in search of congenial likenesses and reflections' (26). This is not to say that Hilton's paintings are not open to association, but, as Harrison puts it, they open up to speculation 'on their own terms' (26). Figures, especially of women, and landscapes have been identified in Hilton's art, but there is a greater purpose to his abstraction: to 'set in play in the spectator those processes of recognition and discrimination by which significant modalities in the natural world and in forms of human encounter are felt for and assessed' (27). Hilton challenges perception itself. Consequently, the few Corcoran poems that do present ekphrasis in the traditional sense, do not attempt to capture what the paintings represent, but offer a series of shifting impressions. For example, in 'The St Ives Section,' Corcoran describes an abstract shape as the sun 'written over with the ideogram of a lost language', or it might be 'a black cockerel, chest out, facing the day' (*Backward* 58). The first reading rehearses the view of critics like Harrison who describes Hilton as working 'at the point at which words will not do,' yet Harrison admits that Hilton also seeks to make the 'measure of what is meant' as 'an action directed towards another' and that this is what Hilton meant by 'truth' in painting (29-30). In reading Hilton's painting, Corcoran expresses the difficulty of representation, but the 'black cockerel' with all its fabled associations of pluckiness and defiance indicates the place where Corcoran's reading of Hilton meets the myth of the artist as an indomitable *provocateur.*

The title of the book refers to one of Hilton's notorious 'Night Letters,' missives written during Hilton's illness to his wife, Rose, which were usually of a humorous, irreverent or rude manner. One such letter featured in the newer edition of *Night Letters* (2009) features the words 'Fuck You WherE's My SUGER [sic]' written in vivid colours. In quoting this particular 'Night Letter,' Corcoran evokes what Adrian Lewis describes as 'colourful stories of [Hilton's] enlivening or outrageous behaviour, often associated with drinking or partying' (5). The title also indicates that *Roger Hilton's Sugar* engages with the end of Hilton's career when he was producing the 'late gouaches,' many of them being 'Night Letters'. Harrison notes the significance of Hilton's late works, describing the gouaches as 'humorous in a way that fine art is not generally supposed to be, vulgar in a fashion not generally allowed to high culture, delicate but also robust, generous but also acidulous' (30). When Corcoran does seek to capture Hilton's 'power of mind', it is always to pin down these qualities. Consequently, 'The Hilton Catalogue – A Selection' describes his paintings putting bawdy phallic puns about rope and snakes alongside personifications of women as water, valleys and harbours, and seemingly heartfelt laments: 'giddy up into / the dark country' (*Backward* 48). Corcoran's presentation of Hilton's paintings presents an imprint of the artist rather than a straightforward description of a work of art, and the abstraction of the imagery makes it an oblique portrait of Hilton rather than an obvious biography with smug certainty of intimacy.

Many studies of Hilton have embraced the myth of his outrageous and abrasive personality fuelled by alcoholism; for example, Andrew Lambirth's *Roger Hilton: The figured language of thought* intersperses critical commentary with anecdotes from Hilton's friends and family. Lewis admits, however, that such 'romantic myths' are problematic for 'the art historian in terms of how [they] can or should be used' (5). In writing about Roger Hilton, Corcoran challenges simplistic notions of the artist's legacy. The poems question whether one can move beyond personal and sensational readings of the artist's life. Just as Corcoran's poems about nationhood seek a more complex sense of place and culture, so his writing about Hilton moves towards a more intricate understanding of identity and especially artistic identity. Throughout *Roger Hilton's Sugar*, Corcoran maintains a sense of instability by mingling the narrator's poetic 'I' (presumably a persona of Corcoran) and the conjured voice of Hilton. This instability throws doubt on the authenticity of what is being said. Are they Hilton's dreams, thoughts, memories, or do they belong to the Corcoran persona? Who exactly is being portrayed by these poems? To what extent can the reader ever uncover genuine knowledge about the artist or the poet? Such questioning challenges straightforward biographical readings of Hilton and his legacy, which inevitably appear in gallery notes and the forewords of Hilton collections.

'Setting Out' shows Corcoran looking for Hilton in a landscape inhabited by the 'giant red women' of Hilton's figurative paintings (*Backward* 43). Corcoran mentions St Ives, the artistic centre with which Hilton was associated, but the description that follows could be imagined memories of Hilton or Corcoran's genuine remembrances:

> I sailed a painted boat fit for a boy
> against the whole white and crashing world
> – darling Bo, thank God you were born,
> when I was a boy there were horses in the field
> and I rode in a cart to cart me off in. (43)

This stanza could be Hilton speaking or Corcoran. The phrase about Bo *is* Hilton; the line is extracted from Hilton's *Night Letters* where Hilton is writing in praise of his son Bo. Thoughts about childhood are constructed around this quotation. The beginning of the stanza represents a regression to childhood; the act of sailing a boat is an absorbing distraction from the self-consciousness of adulthood. By the end, the speaker has turned to a biographical or imagined childhood, which invokes the bliss of one's first experience of other creatures – the horses. The final line strikes a bleaker note, however, echoing the English saying, 'It's not the cough that carries you off; it's the coffin they carry you off in.'

The memories become ever more personal, though whether they are actually personal to Hilton or Corcoran (or both) is unclear. The speaker imagines that his parents are once more alive, while he becomes a disembodied spirit in an 'anaesthetised sky' (43). His parents' 'faces [are] looking up like white words' (43). There is a sense of loss in describing the mother's and father's faces as ciphers: words written in white ink. Corcoran refuses to offer any comforting authenticity in his portrayal of Hilton; the parents are unknowable, indecipherable, and impenetrable. Any attempts to fathom the artist or Corcoran himself as a poet are doomed to frustration. Corcoran, however, cleverly offers a tantalizing glimpse of an emotional life, whilst also denying the pleasure of certainty.

What Corcoran offers in place of simplistic or sentimental biographies is a sense of Hilton's 'power of mind.' In 'The Language of Art Critics', it is not art critics speaking but a voice resembling Hilton's irreverent manner which is so familiar from his *Night Letters*. In allowing Hilton to speak in place of the critics, Corcoran offers a sardonic commentary on the contribution of critics to the perception of an artist's work. Hilton's voice defiantly self-defines, yet there is a note of sarcasm in the glib summing up of his work: 'My discontinuous line is sexual, intimate, savage, / your fantastic anatomy my vehicle' (44). Hilton's art is renowned for its sexual undertones, and the voice of Hilton poses and postures as a particular kind of artist. Questions remain, however, about how legitimate such a summary can be. As in 'Setting Out,' some faithful Hilton quotations are inserted. The second stanza begins 'As is your life, so is your line' (44) echoing Hilton's own words: 'As you live it changes the line you make [...] As your life is, so is your line. As you live it becomes more your line. The line says more.' (Hilton in Canney, *Introduction*, n.p.). The original quotation suggests that the artist's 'power of mind' inflects the art whether one likes it or not. But how does that idea sit with a poem that projects itself into Hilton's voice?

The third stanza might provide an answer returning as it does to the experience of sailing a boat and the supposed memory of horses and cart from 'Setting Out':

> My horses, carts, boats and flowers
> such earthly bodies in motion overlap,
> run into one another the quick sensation
> behind the big secret behind all thought.
> (*Backward* 44)

The doubleness of the speaking voice in 'Setting Out' is mirrored here in the images of 'overlap' and of meshing 'into one another.' The bodies of Hilton and Corcoran merge like bodies of water. Corcoran suggests that intimate knowledge of the artist might be found: 'the big secret behind all thought'; but he never elaborates on this suggestion. The poem tantalizes with potential discovery, yet Corcoran prizes 'the quick sensation' above the possibility of attaining certainty. This approach to artistic legacies elevates what Heffernan described as 'the restless moment of [one's] own meditations' (Heffernan 129).

Achieving an authentic portrait is difficult, and Corcoran makes an important point about the impossibility of knowing the artist through biographical readings of his work. This message is clear in 'The Hilton Biography – A Selection' which adopts Hilton's voice again. Corcoran's version of biography is declared as a 'selection,' immediately conveying an impression of its partial nature. The poem touches on key points in Hilton's life: his experience of a prisoner of war camp during World War Two; his alcoholism; the pettiness and abrasiveness of his personality in later life; his difficult relationship with his wife and children; and his trip to the South of France where he produced some of his last works before he died. Each of these moments is inflected, however, and made more complex. Hilton's World War Two experience is not pictured as heroic; Hilton declares, '[W]ho wants this fucking medal?' (*Backward* 45). Hilton's voice declares that he drinks not whiskey but '300 bottles of life p.a.' (45). The description is less clichéd than an obvious statement about Hilton's addiction, and it offers not so much an invitation to sombre judgement as an affirmation of Hilton's defiant attitude to his own drinking. The poem also captures Hilton's frustration with what Michael Canney described as 'the tyranny of everyday objects' such as 'pens that refused to write' (*Night Letters*, n.p.). Unexpectedly, however, Hilton also offers an uncharacteristic apology for his abrasive behaviour: 'Forgive me. I am a shit. It is all my fault' (45). Though there are some moments of self-doubt in *Night Letters*, Hilton's apology might be taken as a moment of fancy or a point in the poem where the voice crosses over to doubleness: the voice of Hilton and the voice of Corcoran intertwined. While never offering a simplistic biography, Corcoran's version of the artist's life does convey a 'power of mind' that imprints itself on Hilton's works. The poem ends with the weakened Hilton being wheeled along the seafront during his 1974 trip to Antibes; though immobilised, he still searches the horizon to 'see the god come raging from the water' (45). As Hilton concludes in *Night Letters*, it is better 'to go down with guns blazing and the ragged souls overhead' (n.p.).

Many of Corcoran's poems about Hilton inhabit the blunt, irreverent humour of *Night Letters*. In 'The Hilton Catalogue – A Selection', Hilton's voice gives partial glimpses of the desire and longing that informed his work, glibly unpacking the sexual symbolism of 'Captain Rope' and 'the blue spotted snake' (46-49). Near the end of the poem, however, Corcoran associates the powerful sexual currents described in Hilton's art with a sense of loss too. Hilton's voice describes 'My name lost' and 'no code to read' (49). While Corcoran's poems certainly seek to echo Hilton's 'power of mind' as an artist, he is also always aware of the impossibility of finding an authentic Hilton. Part two of 'From Botallack Out' takes the form of a question and answer session. Hilton's first answer draws attention to the fakery of the Hilton voice:

I thought when I was dead
I would not have to explain anything;
green branches shoot from my wrists
instruments of truth or nothing. (60)

While Hilton's voice represents a kind of ghostly return, it also recalls the impossibility of resurrecting Hilton. Corcoran's version of the artist, however, is based on the real man and calls upon Hilton's philosophy; the green branches recall Hilton's statement that 'The tendrils in the art vine are infinate [sic]' (*Night*, n.p.). Art, however, does not simply convey 'truth or nothing.' While Corcoran's version of Hilton conveys something of the artist's mind, Hilton's voice as a work of art has only the semblance of vitality much like Byron's 'breathing statuary.'

Apart from poems that inhabit Hilton's voice, Corcoran also presents some poems that inhabit the persona of the poet in the art gallery, but rather than producing what Heffernan describes as the 'individual ekphrastic poem' (138), Corcoran writes about frustrated attempts to see Hilton's paintings. Part one of 'Seeing Hilton' begins with a statement about the uniqueness of viewing a work of art: 'Nothing can replace the long, steady gaze, / face to face with the picture' (*Backward* 52). This experience, Corcoran suggests, might be a kind of personal interaction with the artist: the idea of a 'gaze' between the artist and viewer, of being 'face to face' in authentic understanding. What follows, however, is a series of failed attempts to view Hilton artworks. The Swindon Art Gallery and Museum is closed; the speaker goes to the 'wrong branch' of the Tate; and Bath Victoria Gallery does not answer his messages (52). The poem ends by repeating the opening line somewhat sarcastically, and the speaker is left with a post-card of Hilton's *Oi Yoi Yoi*. The reproduction cannot replicate the valid experience desired by the viewer, and that the postcard is specifically *Oi Yoi Yoi* is significant, because that particular work is usually read in relation to Hilton's biography. *Oi Yoi Yoi* is a figurative work featuring a female nude. When asked about the painting, Hilton told an anecdote about a quarrel with his wife, during which she was dancing naked shouting 'Oi Yoi Yoi.' The explanation of the painting is comforting and it undermines the abstract potential and plurality of meaning in Hilton's art. As in other poems, Corcoran signals a strong ambivalence about the desire to find an authentic unity with a work of art or its artist. The hopeless quest to see the paintings also raises questions about an artist's legacy, when it is virtually impossible to see those works of art because of mundane bureaucracy or human error. Even when the narrator does manage to see Hilton's paintings, the experience is far from being a straightforward exchange, far from the uncomplicated gaze mentioned at the beginning. In part six, the narrator finds a Hilton work in a gallery in Swansea and he imagines the wind sweeping through the town across the sea to Botallack in Cornwall, where Hilton had settled in 1965. Such a mystical reading of the experience, however, is undermined by the description of the Hilton painting as 'body over body over body, / each imperfect fit, a facsimile of layered truth' (56). Any obvious notion of truth cannot be found in Hilton's paintings. Instead, there is a facsimile of truth, an idea that undermines the purity of an individual work of art in an age of mechanical reproduction.

To discover a sense of authenticity or 'truth' in art or an artist's legacy was never the point of Corcoran's project, however. Writing about Hilton's death in 'Radio Hilton,' Corcoran recognizes the impossibility of resurrecting the artist, comparing the radio that announces Hilton's death to 'a thousand mile frontier closed down' (51). Something of Hilton's 'power of mind' can be conveyed, however. Initially maintaining the voice of the poet lamenting the artist's death, the narrator later describes his 'painting hands,' exhibiting that characteristic uncertainty over who is who, and destabilising any certainty about the identity of the speaker (51). Further on, Corcoran refers to one of Hilton's final 'Night Letters' which quotes Psalm 23.4: 'The radio that told me / … / was the rod and staff' (51). In Hilton's letter, under the psalm is the phallic spotted snake, and at the bottom of the page is a voluptuous, reclining female nude with the words: 'Adam and Eve and Pinchme went down to the river to bathe' (n.p.). The image of bathing appears in 'Radio Hilton' too, when a voice that might be Hilton or Corcoran asks 'shall we bathe again in that blue lick'? (51) Corcoran employs Hilton's themes of sexuality and death alongside an ambiguity of voice: how authentic is Hilton's speaking voice in the poem, and where do his voice and Corcoran's merge or cross over? The image of Hilton bathing in the river is a construction that glimpses a life, an emotional moment, but ultimately Hilton remains unreachable.

MONUMENTS AND MARBLES

Corcoran's writing about art can deconstruct monumental histories as represented by art objects with special significance in Western history, and it can undermine assumptions about any easy understanding of an artist's legacy. These two projects are separate, yet they share a few things in common. *Your Thinking Tracts or Nations* uses Halsey's drawings as a jumping-off point to destabilise glorification of British or Western history. Similarly, the art and legacy of Roger Hilton are used in *Roger Hilton's Sugar* to subvert simplistic notions of authenticity when it comes to understanding an artwork or meeting the 'power of mind' of the artist. Both collections display what Heffernan describes as 'a profound ambivalence toward the timelessness of visual art' and the idea that artworks can provide 'timeless perfection,' a moment of knowledge encapsulated and preserved in a straightforward and decorous manner (133). When Corcoran provides portraits of the West, it is only to emphasize the 'mock sublimity' of legacies in decay, while his reproductions of Hilton's legacy and work signal not just the enlivening aspect of art, but its 'petrifying effect' which can only offer 'a painted face' (133).

What is Romantic about Corcoran's discussion of art is the sense that the 'sublimity of the icon is checked by all that words do to undermine its authority, to reveal its material impermanence, or to expose its petrifying impact on the narratable flow of life' (134). In the context of postmodernism of course, such weaknesses can be applied to words too, so that in unravelling the problematic character of visual art, Corcoran also draws attention to his own predicament as a poet trying to capture the nature of things in words. Ultimately what one is left with in Corcoran's writing about art are glimpses of a possible 'truth', but most of all a sense of uncertainty about art or poetry as forms that commemorate human legacies. As John Ashbery puts it, art creates a 'Sense of something that can never be known,' and we continue to pursue that knowledge despite seeming naiveté and the fact that 'no one is listening' (*Self-Portrait* 77). Like Ashbery, Corcoran envisions art as a convex reflection of 'truth,' conveying a tantalizing glimpse of an authentic experience, but remaining unreachable, a goal to be quested for. He sums up the problem of art and poetry with the image of a mirror in 'Not The Sole Relations of Human Beings':

What place can poetry make?
Who lives there so mirrored?
Empty inside the glitterball
     (*New and Selected* 161).

Works Cited

Ackerley, C.J. *T.S. Eliot: 'The Love Song of J. Alfred Prufrock' and 'The Waste Land.'* Humanities E-Books, 2007. Web. 10 June 2013. <http://books.google.com/books?id=yLwlneqlacQC&dq=red+rock+ts+eliot&source=gbs_navlinks_s>

Ashbery, John. *Self-Portrait in a Convex Mirror.* New York: Penguin, 1976.

Booth, Martin. *Opium: A History.* New York: Thomas Dunne Books, 1996.

Coleridge, Samuel Taylor. 'On Poesy or Art.' *English Essays: From Sir Philip Sidney to Macauley.* Ed. Charles W. Eliot. New York: Collier and Son, 1910. 269-280.

Eliot, T.S. *The Waste Land: A Facsimile and Transcript of the Original Drafts including the Annotations of Ezra Pound.* Ed. Valerie Eliot. New York: Harcourt, 1971.

_____. *The Waste Land and Other Poems.* Ed. Helen Vendler. New York: Signet, 1998.

Harrison, Charles. 'Roger Hilton: The Obligation to Express.' *Roger Hilton.* London: The South Bank Centre, 1993. 16-32.

Heffernan, James A.W. *Museum of Words: The Poetics of Ekphrasis from Homer to Ashbery.* Chicago: University of Chicago Press, 2004.

Hilton, Roger. *Night Letters.* Newlyn Orion Galleries Limited, Penzance: 1980.

Hough, Barry and Howard Davis. *Coleridge's Law: A Study of Coleridge in Malta.* Cambridge: Open Book Publishers, 2010.

Lambirth, Andrew. *Roger Hilton: The figured language of thought.* London: Thames and Hudson, 2007.

Lewis, Adrian. *Roger Hilton.* Aldershot: Ashgate, 2003.

Keats, John. *Ode on a Grecian Urn, The Eve of Saint Agnes and Other Poems.* New York: Houghton Mifflin, 1901.

Maddrey, Joseph. *The Making of T.S. Eliot: A Study of the Literary Influences.* New York: McFarland, 2009.

Mellinkoff, Ruth. 'Riding Backwards: Theme of Humiliation and Symbol of Evil.' *Viator: Medieval and Renaissance Studies* 4: 153-176.

Miller, James E., Jr. *T.S. Eliot's Personal Waste Land: Exorcism of the Demons.* State College: Pennsylvania State University Press, 2010.

Murphy, Russell E. *Critical Companion to T.S. Eliot: A Literary Reference to his Life and Work.* Infobase. Web. 10 June 2013. <http://books.google.com/books?id=thqU29nSVgUC&dq=red+rock+ts+eliot&source=gbs_navlinks_s>

Rice, Michael. *Egypt's Legacy: The Archetypes of Western Civilization: 3000 to 30 BC.* London and New York: Routledge, 2003.

Rydan, Kent C. *Mapping the Invisible Landscape: Folklore, Writing and the Sense of Place.* Iowa City: University of Iowa Press, 1993.

Shelley, Percy Bysshe. *The Poetical Works of Percy Bysshe Shelley.* Vol. 2. London and New York: George Bell and Sons, 1892.

The Imperial Franchise Endlessly Renewed

Martin Anderson

> The world's great age begins anew,
> The golden years return,
> The earth doth like a snake renew
> Her winter weeds outworn:
> Heaven smiles and faiths and empires gleam
> Like wrecks of a dissolving dream.
> —P.B. Shelley, 'Hellas'

Empire figures prominently in Corcoran's poetry. Andrew Duncan describes what he calls Corcoran's 'primal object[s]' as 'effortlessly reach[ing] the plane of myth' (*Heresy* 149) and there probably are almost as many names of contemporary Western politicians in Corcoran's poems as of past emperors and empires. But it is the acquisition and coercive employment of Power through accumulation and monopoly of natural resources, and the consequences of this, which occupy Corcoran's attention. An attention which has in its sights the profound phenomenon which has bedevilled, and still bedevils, all human societies and which Colin Renfrew aptly iterates: 'Nothing in the development of human society appears more significant than the ascription of meaning and value to material goods and to commodities' (Renfrew 160).

Corcoran's 'The Empire Stores' (*New and Selected* 25-30) employs many of the motifs which constellate in his work around such a phenomenon. Section three opens with a tilt against consumerism 'unable to speak in a barcode dancing', a charge sustained through all of Corcoran's work. In this regard it's ironic how Alistair Noon's likening of aspects of Corcoran's poetry to Seamus Heaney's Bog poems in *North* ignores the way such poems often come perilously close to aestheticising violence by 'converting', through a certain visual and auditory sumptuousness, 'sensations into consumer goods' (Galeano *Days and Nights* 173):

> If we could write an archaeology of the soul,
> unable to speak in a barcode dancing,

the little birdies would sing for St. Valentine
with big light raining on a Vatican elsewhere.
('The Empire Stores', Part 3, *New and Selected* 27)

'If' – for those little birdies are the hopeful harbingers of that overriding concern which Corcoran shares with Shelley: for an ideal political and secular order as a solution to the perennial problems which beset us. A succeeding section of the poem conjures up, however, the contemporary Western media's pornography of violence: 'Anything but watching it live on t.v.' and 'the poverty of public discourse' which, in 'the present war', the invasion of Iraq, sustains it (28). The second stanza of section 3 invokes another prominent Corcoran motif:

But we came dark cloud boiling from white north
drawn by the smell of luxury goods;
the journey knocked narrative out of our poetry,
even pedants see it vanish as lives unravel. (27)

The initial conjunction underlines opposition to any utopian remit of the poet. Amongst its numerous guises in Corcoran's work, north represents that cardinal point of Atlantic mercantile kingdoms, those 'extreme metaphorical climates' of *Your Thinking Tracts or Nations*, from where 'Men in red jackets swallow shiny red beads / trading the nation by symbol and transparent greed' (*Lyric* 37) – such 'red' being for Corcoran a token, perhaps, of the belligerent Western imperial imagination: 'Too much blood has been shed for red' (Wyndham Lewis 90). These are places which 'Osama dreams of [...], burning' those 'towers of Manhattan', of a cold inhuman world of Poundian usury, 'an old bitch gone in the teeth' ('From The Hen Roost', *Shadow* 31). Such a north is situated at 'the edge of the European mind' where what predominates is 'rubble, empires of rubble' ('Reading *The Cantos*' 23). Or perhaps it should be the centre – of 'Europe the unstable continent / her great realm burning' (*Tracts* 13)? This north is as much a state of being as a place: 'Oh Oh I am north, a frozen mapp. Shrunk to / the core of my tiny house, under a sky of / ice-floes, tinkling.' ('The Catalogue of Answers', *Suzy* 40). In another guise North is also that place where Corcoran often finds himself in his poems, standing at 'the edge of the world', at the extremity of experience: this is the white world of the 'Inglish giant [which] brought forth the baby kapital'; the white world out of which Corcoran's 'Kurgan Nazis' step [pe] (*Tracts* 41). In this domain, the white world is both slayer and saviour of itself. For whilst it contains the seed of Nietzsche's 'Let us face ourselves. We are Hyperboreans' (Nietzsche 569) (the first written reference to Hyperborea is in Heroditus) and the proto-fascist Society of Thule (an ice-bound *urheimat*), it is also the region of the Fortunate Isles (which is also the land of the Hyperboreans) and of the Golden Race of Greek legend. Such isles would later contribute significantly to the iconography in Christian literature of the earthly paradise. If sometimes Corcoran's use of this imagery derived from the Golden Time and Golden Race of Greek legend seems, therefore, to be courting ambivalence it is because it is not felt that there is a need to distinguish Indo-European derivatives sharing an identical source: after all it is in the poem 'Hellas' where Shelley (a major inspiration for Corcoran's optimistic utopianism) invokes the image of the dissolution of empires, 'wrecks of a dissolving dream', and the revival of those Fortunate Isles of the Greeks and of the Golden Race: 'The world's great age begins anew / The Golden years return'. Within such a lineage (Hellenism was pioneered in Germany in the eighteenth century by Joham Joachim Winckelmann) the European Libertarian and the European Nazi are both pre-figured and do not stand distinguished.

'Luxury' and 'luxury goods' also figure prominently in Corcoran's poetry: 'But we came dark cloud boiling from far north / drawn by the smell of luxury goods' ('Empire Stores 3', *New and Selected* 27). 'Came', seemingly, accidentally:

> Kastalios said, where we go
> they are like us and unlike us,
> we will barter with them
> and keep safe in coastal waters.
> [...]
> We did nothing to make it happen,
> the big dolphin hit the deck;
> first fear, then radiance
> and after that the ship was not ours.
>
> Kastalios spoke out,
> we followed the bounding youth

> as if dancing, inland,
> we forgot our homes, our wives.
> ('Catalogue of Answers', *Suzy* 44)

These Argonauts of the unobtainable hooked by 'the market value of delusion' (*Tracts* 39) go 'crashing towards a bed of luxury where it all begins' ('From the Harbour' *New and Selected* 22): in their wake, 'Look. All the trees gone for ships // Ash Elm Boxwood Maple [...] / In the red book I am a small axe.' ('In the Red Book', *Suzy* 15). The axe also figures frequently in Corcoran's poetry, involved in the making of clearings during the pastoral stage of society, and later in securing timber for ships involved in trade and the imperial enterprise of opening markets. The attention to luxury goods in Corcoran's poetry is due to the fact that they accompany that important stage where the transformation of hunter-gatherers into the pastoralists and agriculturalists who will create surplus takes place: 'the hunter-gatherers stand like stone on the green path which has just become unfamiliar' ('From Where Song Comes', *Hotel Shadow* 11). The unfamiliarity resides not only in the speed with which 'subsistence became surplus' ('Catalogue of Answers', *Suzy* 45) and the fact that 'no sweet moderation shines in Port Albion / [...] they dream of wealth creation' ('from the Red and Yellow Book' , *TRandYB* 27), but in the inevitableness with which violence accompanies such wealth creation: 'To find the western path / I breakfasted swords [...] the fool with his finger on the trigger / [...] across the imperial world' (26). Ignorance of the nature of that transformation is used by Corcoran in 'The Empire Stores' to both castigate and rally his peers: 'The journey knocked narrative out of our poetry, / even pedants see it vanish as lives unravel' (*New and Selected* 27). Those poets who in the late 1980s Corcoran excoriated for not thinking 'hard enough', and who would 'prat about in art labs' (from *Qiryat Sepher* in *New and Selected* 170) are still, in 2004, 'sneak careerists' who need to 'wake up' ('Myriorama' 14) to the true nature of their history 'beneath the pretty page of a kind empire' ('The Empire Stores' 29) where the bromide 'displacing' (Porter *Guardian*)[1] is used instead of 'extermination', (Howells 103)[2] and of the world in general. 'Who wrote the history of truth telling [...] Ye boys of England [...] clean up the abattoirs and each chartered grave' and (earlier from the poem) 'make the ordinary language good or die' ('The Empire Stores' 28, 25). Poetry, Corcoran suggests here, is 'dying for want of intelligent talk' about just such a world. For it is from this

'journey' just referred to that the world which all poets now inhabit
emerged.

Corcoran describes the starting point of this journey in *Your
Thinking tracts or Nations* as if it exists in an apolitical space:

> I could draw a map of the place
> from memory, the striped animals,
> the handsome food running about,
> the small bay open like a mouth for trade.
>   (*Tracts* 22)

It is a kind of prelapsarian, pre-surplus value and pre-private property
state of uncorruptedness (cf 'the corruption absolute, normal' of
'Under the shadow of how it happened', from *TCL* in *New and Selected*
166): 'each winter I return there: / they are children in the garden'
('The Name Apollo', *Suzy* 33). Corcoran invokes this Garden of Plenty
this Earthly Paradise (a frequent motif, with variants) yet again in 'The
Empire Stores':

> To begin again, the girls coming and going
> set their feet in the meadow,
> in the red, the golden day, the invention of fair writing
> in the meadow by the sea.
>   (*New and Selected* 27)

The pastoralists and agriculturalists, the 'green invaders', of this journey
are the prototypes of later wealth creators and that surplus value (where
there is a surplus there is always a Power structure) so prized by 'call him
Blair, Bush, Sharon or Milošević / those who are wired to the world,
who cannot set ambition aside' ('From the Harbour' 23). This ambition
in 'The Empire Stores' envisages 'Caspian oil sucked across the Stans
to Karachi' (25). Yet in 'Catalogue of Answers' Corcoran identifies it
as a dual ambition: 'Let the yellow flower rise, let it radiate' (*Suzy* 40).
On the one hand it symbolises a non-utilitarian inspiration, one which
creates beauty out of such things as words and gardens: 'flowering green
/ my palm, this page' [...] 'there was no body no crime' (*New and
Selected* 149) and is emblematic of that Apollonian light of the tongue,
of poetic vision and the word as transfigured in 'a soft meadow split
asunder / in the centre, miracle of light' ('The Name Apollo', *New and*

Selected 98). On the other hand it is emblematic of that utility of the imagination which creates the 'powerhouse', or what in 'Catalogue of Answers' is referred to as the 'straight bearing' which is 'finally a powerline' producing the antagonism of mutual ambitions colliding like 'tectonic plates [...] against each other at the committee stage' ('Catalogue of Answers', *Suzy* 40) In this latter guise it accompanies the yearning for 'pasturage, good horses and green invasion /of the alphabet ascending' (*Tracts* 35) which came with the shift from foraging to pastoralism in that Neolithic revolution first proposed by Gordon Childes, and in the subsequent urban revolution of the Mesopotamian city states made possible by the production of surplus value: 'You Kurgan Nazis / you surveyors / you bones in the grave / with little beads for the kids' (*Tracts* 41). With these city states' 'blatant geometry of planning', the scene was set for trade circuits, bureaucratic regulation, a writing system for stocktaking and the inevitable soldiery to protect the trade routes along which came those materials from which luxury goods could be manufactured: such city states were also the precursors of later trading empires. Empires of countries some of which, having few natural resources (fortunes were made for example from exporting guano from South America to replenish European soils exhausted quite early in the modern era), subjugated countries which possessed natural capital in astonishing abundance. Such subjugating countries, whether National Socialist or Tory, were not averse to reducing the other of those countries to 'drifting smoke':

> What if I let the bloody history in?
> Imagine: when they came with the goods,
> a tribe iron-shod, iron-bound.
> How come they have the goods?
>
> I think in the centre of their minds
> danced an armed man, a-jig, a-jig,
> in that alpha beta of six sounds;
> I – Want – You – Give – It – Or.
>
>   *
>
> They left no marks in the snow
> but the host of the air in our blood,

> then all my own relations
> gone like the drifting smoke.
>> (*Tracts* 22)

The pathos of such a journey from hunter-gatherer to modern wealth creator Corcoran brilliantly parodies in *Your Thinking Tracts or Nations* with its arresting opening image of affluent vacationers floating like loot laden imperialists up river:

> We lived in the old house then
> held by deep fields down to the river,
> like silver snaking through the hills;
> hunter-gatherers would glide by on yachts,
> bargain for souvenirs, hunger for fluorescence;
> when they left we called it a movement in history,
> when they returned we called it the weekend.
>
> We lived in the old house then and everyone
> who danced and made music for the god
> wore masks, we got up on our toes in season;
> we did not think it was popularising
> not pushing back into darker fields:
> let the rubble tell you, put your face in that mask;
> my eyes sharpen when big night comes.
>
> We lived in the old house then, backed by mountains,
> you think we've gone, into the dry river bed, the hills;
> but you imagine the beads and not the thread
> as if we left a series of pictures but no words;
> then, when you rise along the dusty tract,
> on the next step up you see the blue surrounding sea
> and your mind is flooded with us.
>> (*Tracts* 36)

What is suggested here is the commonality of a psyche that is pre-industrial, an imagination that is pre-pastoral and most likely communalistic. An imagination not trivialised within a possessive individualist-self moulded by a consumer driven society such as Britain, where too many writers are still 'court historians swing[ing] on the rim of the imperium, / snorting stipends, vamping up the Empire News' and where 'the poverty of public discourse goes unsaid' ('The Empire Stores', *New and Selected* 30, 28). 'Bring my poets back to life' Corcoran inveighs in the same poem: poets such as 'Shelley and Ric and young MacSweeney'.

Barry MacSweeney is referred to twice in 'The Empire Stores'. His significance to Corcoran cannot be underestimated. In 'MacSweeney' he is represented as the repository of the apposite of that 'ambition' that the likes of Blair and Bush 'cannot [...] set aside'. For his is the 'yellow flower, ace of ambition / our cathedral and powerhouse' of the poet (*Tracts* 35). The poet is the traditional custodian of knowledge of the natural world as a mine of wealth of aesthetic and moral resource rather than as an entity to be plundered. Corcoran celebrates this in the figure of the poet MacSweeney:

> Here's a jar of honey for you;
> we stand the beehives in the fields of borage,
> the pollen's rich, the yields are high
> from the bright blue flowers you knew.
>
> Morning light spreads across the floor
> despite liars in public places,
> lapis miners get to work in Badashkan
> and wind lifts the ivy on the wall.
>
> I walked out into the street,
> we all moved together in a film;
> faces lit from below, easily engaged,
> and the blue autumn sky falling away;
>
> As if we said forever, buildings rise in air,
> life going in and out of them
> and that would be above ground,
> my girls growing up for instance.
>
> The valley of the assassins has been extended
> and escaped our rhetoric;
> I'll pour the honey in the ground,
> you rise up and spit the pearls in their faces.

The pollen's rich, the yields are high
from the bright blue flowers you knew.
(whole poem, *New and Selected* 34)

Honey is at the centre of this invocation – but it is not Grantchester honey! Rather, it is a product which, drawn from a fecund earth, serves as a foil to that natural world ravaged under the aegis of 'liars in public places' and as a foil to that strain in the culture of the West of *contemptus mundi* which such 'liars' propagate. Honey, in fact, is another motif present throughout Corcoran's work. Unsurprisingly so: the Osettes of the Caucasus, a region Corcoran's poems often circle with its suggestion of Indo-European linguistic and cultural origins, were descended from the Scythians and are said to have worshipped a bee goddess. Eaten and used to make mead as early as the 5th century BCE in the forest region of mid-Volga it was a major incentive for early Aryan speakers to control the region and also because bees-wax played a central role in the lost-cast method of metal casting used for weapons making. The challenge to the literary as well as to the political status quo in Corcoran's poem should not go unnoticed: 'I'll pour the honey in the ground, / you rise up and spit the pearls in their faces' echoes Pound's literary strategising with Eliot. Pound would heave a brick through the front window in a distracting feint whilst Eliot would nip round the back of the house and snatch the swag. A good enough reason to say 'the yields are high'! Yet those yields, as so often with Corcoran's motifs, are dual in nature. As part and parcel of the legendary ambrosia of the good life, a life of 'milk and honey', the longing for honey, 'I was drowned in a jar of honey' (*Tracts* 27) can all too easily transgress into an appetency for that luxury (honey becomes oil) which drives nations, as aggregations of individual appetites, into acts of overseas expropriation: 'furs, wax, honey and slaves' ('The Name Apollo', *Suzy* 33). In light of this Corcoran's pouring honey into the ground might be interpreted, therefore, as a symbolically subversive act undermining the pursuit of pleasure as an end in itself which seems to be the guiding principle (sic) upon which most modern Western consumer societies rest.

In *Your Thinking Tracts or Nations*, Corcoran laments MacSweeney's passing as the passing of the archetypal creative energy encapsulated in the glow of the yellow flower at night. That energy which the hunter-gatherers who 'glide by on yachts' hunger for the 'fluorescence' of. A self-transcending generative energy originally channelled into the activity of ritual, of 'dance and music for the god':

> Across fields silvery with democracy
> MacSweeney's borage blooms
> and poets die of frostbite, anger, bad luck.
>
> Black wing spread over them,
> frozen sky folded over them
> a picture of the world turned upside down.
>
> The light in their faces ignites,
> each pearl snapped off the endless thread;
> what life is left (is left) in words (?) ?
>
> What happened to those slow evenings?
> the easy music? Cold breath
> of ice caves took them.
>
> Across fields silvery with democracy
> where MacSweeney's borage blooms.
>   (*Tracts* 37)

The 'borage blooms'. So, perhaps, the 'endless thread' of a deeper communal and holistic imagination still resides within us, still haunts us? An imagination not cajoled by the glass beads and trinkets of invaders given over to the acquisition and extension of a coercing Power, whose 'beads' would later be transformed into the 'pearls' of a bourgeoisie which would become the engine of Western imperial enterprise and into whose faces Corcoran encourages MacSweeney to spit such tokens. If 'democracy has become a pawn to the dictates of globally volatile capital [...] a subsidiary of the stock exchange' (Grass *Guardian*) and if modern representative government so easily facilitates the organised violence of that 'finger on the trigger / across the imperial world', then does 'silvery with democracy' not carry a qualification, or even a health warning (why not 'slippery'?)

  Silver is yet another important motif in Corcoran's poetry, running like a bright seam through it:

> silver traced in white rock,
> there is one source – constant and the same –
> the conflict of interest is real enough,
> their mouths big and slack with wealth.
> ('Biography 3', *Shadow* 95)

In 'Inside Brittania', it represents, as with present day oil, the squandering of and squabbling over earth's natural resources:

> Hard work of all those years
> knotting hands and back
> twisted into fact
> [...]
> then, without panic, finally myth
> turning on the air
> the silver walls go down,
> (from *The Next Wave*, in *New and Selected* 148)

summed up in the line which follows and ends the poem in the frank language of pure self aggrandizement and gratification: 'I want it now I want it' (echoed by the colonialist's 'I –Want-You-Give-It-Or'). Metallurgy is of course, notwithstanding its importance to armaments, at the heart of any society at the stage of primitive accumulation:

> Change came hand to hand
> along new exchange routes
> dreaming a map of desire
> goods and beliefs unwrapped.
>
> Copper tin gold silver
> ('Sea Table', *For the Greek Spring* 61)

The knowledge of how to isolate metals by heating ore bearing rocks is an ancient one practised as long ago as 7000-5000 BCE by settlements of large groups of people. Corcoran problematises its contribution:

> The field of understanding, Pound said
> and how to extend it, imperial measure;
> tin from Spain, copper from Cyprus

with gold from Egypt as payment,
to run the arms race against Hittites.

The field of understanding, but not
an equation as yet resolved
as metallurgists did not say to the great Wanax
when, one bright and focused morning,
subsistence became surplus to feed experts.
('Catalogue of Answers', *Suzy* 45)

With its vast profits, silver rejuvenated, according to Engels, a moribund European feudal economy. Along with other expropriated New World, Asian and African resources such as gold and human flesh (life expectancy on a Caribbean sugar plantation was barely six years) it later made possible the investments necessary for Europe to finance its own industrial development – as it had earlier enabled Europeans to pay for luxury goods from the East which insisted on payment in gold or silver, Europe producing nothing they were interested in exchanging their products for. And later it made it possible for Europe, of course by less apparent neo-colonial devices, to sustain the underdevelopment of those once conquered countries and their deformed or ruined economies which had provided it with its 'external proletariat' (Galeano *Open Veins* 38). Under European colonial rule just one silver mine in South America, it has been estimated, was responsible over three centuries for the deaths of eight million miners (ibid 39). The projected life span of such a slave-miner has been estimated at no more than three or four months, roughly equivalent to that of someone working in Auschwitz's rubber manufacturing plant. (Stannard 89) Any 'attempt to devise a [...] non-economic explanation of imperialism is [...] unrealistic' (Hobsbaum 69). One would have hoped that the enthusiasm of present day Western academic historians of empire for *not* condemning it might have been tempered by Hobsbaum's further observation that emperors and empires are old but imperialism was quite new. The Western imagination, however, is still, by and large, an imperial and unpurged imagination; it still sends out its 'white boys on the road, zoot suits and patronage / a limited view of human nature / in a medium of implacable pessimism' ('The Empire Stores', *New and Selected* 26). A major strategy of its discourse, 'Do you think for one minute this dub dub over tracking / out of the ever living past très moderne?' (29) organised now around the selective indignation (Iran – but why not Gaza?) associated with the concept of 'human rights', not only 'lacks moral credibility' (Grass *Guardian* 2010), but has not changed much since 1550 when, in Valladolid, Bartolomé de las Casas, examining the negative representation by his countrymen of the cultures they were devastating, called it what it is: 'the estimate of brigands who wish to find an apology for their own atrocities'.

Such misrepresentations, vilifications, of the other, from 'Baron Politique, his titles / printed in gilt' ('You May Say To Yourself – Well How Did I Get Here?', *Suzy* 23) come in a long tradition of Western calumny: from the fifth century Greek's *Tyrant*, to the Victorian's *Despot*, to today's *Dictator.*

> When the Spartans came over the mountain
> and made us their slaves,
> self-appointed lords of the way it is
> with their global credit, pipelines
> and smart weapons in phalanx,
> our irrelevance came to an end.
>
> The hills at a certain hour turned mauve
> and these men emerged in our fields
> as if out of nowhere, clouds around their thighs,
> their mouths barking – Helot – Barbarian – Outdweller;
> they made Leuctra into an arms dump [...]
>
> Your picture of the world can be undone,
> stations off the air, iron ore shipped out;
> the sky as blue, the terraces of the sea rise and fall
> enough to break your heart each morning;
> we no longer walked the ground,
> the earth a shadow for another's empire.
> ('When the Spartans came over the mountains',
> from 'News of Aristomenes 4', *Shadow* 49)

It should come as no surprise, therefore, that here, 'on the collapsed ramparts of the golden west' where 'we have fallen into the hands of thieves / the barbarians who need barbarians / to make the bloody business spin' – barbarians who 'come screaming off the frozen steppes'

('Alexiares in Exile', *Backward* 86) like Corcoran's 'Kurgan Nazis' – that here, in the UK, we cannot get enough of books published about Hitler and the Nazis. But give us just a few dismantling the myth of a benign British empire and almost immediately everyone's hand shoots up and they shout 'Enough!' We can't tire of hearing about Nazi violence, but about British violence we will not speak. As if for centuries the inhabitants of those distant countries whose sovereignty we usurped had been merely content to lie down and let us roll over them, helping ourselves to their land, their womenfolk (serving the double duty of 'labour and of lust') (Heizer in Stannard 143) and their possessions, without so much as a murmur of dissent. Might it not very well be that the extension of the imperial franchise depends more than anything else upon, as well as a deeply lingering 19th Century Gospel of Progress which views non-European societies as composed of non-people fixed in an 'infant state [of] ignorance', (Robertson in Drinnon 242)[3] an unwillingness also to confront and examine that powerful Western fear of 'species pollution' lodged deeply within Judaeo-Christianity. Lodged deeply as far back as the Deuteronomic Code, where it is 'forbidden not only to yoke different animals to the same plough (Deut, 22:10) but even to sow different kinds of seeds in the same field (Lev. 19:19)' (Whyte in Dudley and Novak 15)[4]:

> Under the shadow of how it happened,
> ur-heimat in the racist mountains,
> the Magnetic I sails forth
> to name the bigger light
> seeking advantageous terms
> and a subject to predicate;
> all references to money are analogical
> as in, I can go on or clear out
> ideas that have no currency
> arresting the big adventure,
> a worn coin burns your hand,
> dead soldiers, scientists, poets,
> stack their faces in piles
> the corruption absolute, normal.
>
> > ('Under the shadow of how it happened',
> > from *TCL*, in *New and Selected* 166)

After all, as Raymond Williams observed: racism is 'a very powerful component in the ideology of imperialism' (Williams 93). And as Kastalios says in 'Catalogue of Answers', 'We did nothing to make it happen' – after the 'hit [...] first fear, then radiance, // and after that the ship was not ours' (*Suzy* 44) – as if a certain hard-wiredness to dominate exists in the Western psyche, sending its acquisitive 'Magnetic I' sailing forth upon all the oceans of the world seeking 'a subject to predicate'; converting, in that telling phrase, the entire world into a passive component in a hegemonic Indo-European, Hyperborean, sentence.

'Nobody thinks hard enough for poetry' Corcoran has said. And in this twenty first century Western land-of-luxury-goods where too many poets are

> marooned up stage mouthing air
> mighty history glares down
> that's our history, the cyclorama
> where everything is as it happens
> buried and shining in the streets
>> ('Nobody thinks hard enough...',
>> *Qiryat Sepher*, in *New and Selected* 170)

'Shining': like those hidden seams of silver running through other lands whose natural capital only made, and still makes, their inhabitants poor. Or like those 'shiny red beads' of men in the empire's red coats agog and aglitter with greed and the prospect of depredation. To see 'everything *as* it happens', here, in these glitzy financial citadels of *contemptus mundi* that are New York and London, rather than as it is misrepresented to us. To see everything as it *is* seems to be the irrefutable challenge that a poetry such as Corcoran's, compassionate, intelligent and informed, throws down not only to the writer but the reader: to 'If you speak like us say so'. A tall order today, indeed, for all of us buffeted as we are by the official debris of obfuscation, of denial and counter-denial, which circulates in this State of Organised Samsara. But within such a 'state' Corcoran places the potent symbols of contemporary imperial and coercive Power, Blair and Bush, against the moral alternative of the uncoercive archaic communalism of pre-pastoral man. The latter, glimpsed in its modern manifestation in the communitarianism of Shelley, and in the figure of Barry MacSweeney, is found, in contrast to such Power, not to be wanting.

It's only a sustained analogy
I've never been there of course,
I'm right here telling you

We live east of the Altai mountains
oasis cities in the steppeland,
we light our streets, pipe music all night

Imagine the postmark, the stamps,
our busy trade in visions,
outside is only arid and nomads

If you speak like us say so.
    ('Tocharian the I-E enclave', *Lyric* 17)

NOTES

[1] Professor Bernard Porter describes British settlers in North America as 'displacing [...] original inhabitants'.

[2] A word so unashamedly and ubiquitously in use in 19th Century America, and so representative of people's attitudes to Howells' 'red savages', that Robert Louis Stevenson in his *Across the Plains* remarked: 'I was ashamed for the thing we call civilisation.'

[3] The two-volume history by Robertson (a Scottish Calvinist minister who never set foot in America) was reprinted ten times between 1777 and 1803 and was the most widely read history in the new nation. His view of the aborigines, whilst providing a convenient justification for their removal or annihilation, projected a private fantasy which became a collective fact useful in contributing to the creation of a national identity: 'As the individual advances from the ignorance and imbecility of the infant state to vigour and maturity of understanding, something similar to this may be observed in the progress of the species.'

[4] How far Corcoran's extensive use of 'white' in his poetry, in relation to 'species pollution', suggests the contradictions it embodies is open to question.

WORKS CITED

Drinnon, Richard. *White Savage. The Case of John Dunn Hunter.* New York: Shocken Books, 1972.

Duncan, Andrew. *The Council of Heresy: A Primer of Poetry in a Balkanised Terrain.* Exeter: Shearsman. 2009.

Galeano, Eduardo. *Days and Nights of Love and War.* Delhi: Aaka, 2009.

Galeano, Eduardo. *Open Veins of Latin America.* London: Serpent's Tail, 2009.

Grass, Gunter. 'Interview'. *The Guardian.* 30/10/2010.

Grass, Gunter. 'The High Price of Freedom'. *The Guardian* 07/05/2005.

Heizer, Robert F. *They Were Only Diggers: A Collection of Articles from California Newspapers 1851-1866* in David Stannard, *American Holocaust.* New York: OUP, 1992.

Hobsbaum, Eric. *The Age of Empire 1875-1914.* London: Cardinal, 1987.

Howells, William Dean, 'A Sennight of the Centennial'. *The Atlantic Monthly*, 38, 1876.

Lewis, Wyndham. *Blasting and Bombardiering.* London: Calder and Boyars, 1967.

Nietzsche, Frederick. 'The Antichrist' in *The Portable Nietzsche.* New York: Viking, 1973.

Porter, Bernard. 'Point of View'. *The Guardian*, 02/02/2013.

Renfrew, Colin. *Prehistory. The Making of the Human Mind.* London: Phoenix, 2008.

Robertson, William. *The History of the Discovery and Settlement of America.* New York: Harper & Brothers, 1843.

Stannard, David. *American Holocaust.* New York: OUP, 1992.

Whyte, Hayden. 'The Wild Man Within', in Edward Dudley and Maximillian E. Novak (eds.), *The Wild Man Within. An Image in Western Thought from the Renaissance to Romanticism.* Pittsburgh: University of Pittsburgh Press, 1972.

Williams, Raymond. *Problems in Materialism and Culture.* London: Verso, 1980.

'In the Dream Village': Mapping Kelvin Corcoran's Prose Poems

Luke Kennard

'I have always been amazed at the way an ordinary observer lends so much more credence and attaches so much more importance to waking events than to those occurring in dreams. It is because man, when he ceases to sleep, is above all the plaything of his memory.'
André Breton, 'Manifesto of Surrealism' (244-5)

'It's a system – of valuation, habit, complex organic data, the weather and so on. Usually the choice is to track it backward, that is, most autobiographical impulse tends to follow this course. One can think of one's life as not worth remembering, in fact one can want to forget it – but if what has constituted it, the things 'of which it was made up,' as William Carlos Williams says, are dear to your memory and experience of them, then it may well be a record of them, a graph of their activity as 'your life,' is an act you would like to perform.'
Robert Creeley, *Was That a Real Poem & Other Essays* (51)

'If I stood up straight the line would be unimpeded.'
Kelvin Corcoran, *Melanie's Book*

The prose poem, multitudinous in its effects, styles, voices and rhetorical intention is synonymous, in the popular conception, with rebellion: it breaks the only rule (line-break) which we still hold sacred, so it goes, and must therefore be a clarion call; a Dadaist axe in the face of traditional form; 'at war with decorum' as the American critic Stephen Fredman has it. Poets have in fact employed it to various and contrasting ends, emerging from a variety of traditions, but some tenor of perceived radicalism is inevitable, *unifying*, even, and there is much to gain from an analysis of any poet (any poet aware enough to experiment with or master the form) who focuses on their prose poetry alone, or attempts a considered comparison between their *modus operandi* in verse and in prose poetry. Such a reading lends itself well to Corcoran's oeuvre because, while his use of the form is consistent from his first collection through to his most recent, the ends to which he employs it amount to a text book on its past applications and future possibilities. At times it functions as the 'fat battery' of the verse, the extra information which powers the oblique strategies.

> The family radio was smaller than the fat battery attached to it. We kept it in a tin; twanging Duane Eddy, the Shadows and assassinations echoed out of a metallic past.
> (*New and Selected* 112)

These short lines from *Melanie's Book*, juxtaposed with a detailed description of the salutation of Parnassos, are exemplary of the deep pleasures of Corcoran's style: the seemingly autobiographical, the political, economic and cultural history in the same breath (and the pop culture reference to Duane Eddy rubbing up against the next paragraph's high art criticism), the lyric touch in its well-turned, ambitious imagery ('metallic past'), a typical reification alongside the straightforward, concrete fact of the radio as a physical object.

It is also in *Melanie's Book* that we find the prose poem as dream text or interlude; the surrealist night to the rational day of the verse, where ambiguity is outdone by direct contradiction: 'In the dream I was driving down a narrow lane to an English village where I was born, or through a dangerous and disputed border country.' (*New and Selected* 121) This captures the uneasy parallel narratives of the dream state where an object or location can embody two natures or functions. We can think of Descartes' exemplum of *wax* here, which can exist in various completely different states and still be identifiable as wax. Indeed, we could extend this to poetry, which can exist in a variety of forms without losing its essential classification as a poem, where the prose poem could stand for wax in its molten form. The prose hardens into poetry; the militaristic vocabulary of the 'disputed border territory' also intimates that all is not well in the past we are to explore. A caveat that 'It does not come well arranged' is as much to do with the past traumas of the figures within the poems, which impedes and complicates their mental and physical journey, as it is a statement on the form. Why would we expect it to be well arranged?

I am following Andrew Duncan's line in interpreting Corcoran as a *dialectic poet* who 'shifts between layers of experience like a director cutting between different cameras. [...] Nothing is ever asserted, the positions never freeze, the balance of the poem shifts nimbly between opposing points of view.' (Duncan 150) To give a very brief philosophical gloss, the dialectic (as opposed to the rhetorical) seeks truth through comparison of contrasting perspectives and voices rather than appealing to the emotions or reason to persuade the interlocutor. In poetic terms, the dialectic seeks truth – with the reader – rather than believing itself to possess a truth which must then be impressed upon the reader. Duncan's working definition of the dialectic style is illuminating: it 'has the effect of not confirming the assumptions of the protagonists in the poetry – as virtually all other styles of writing do. We are immersed in the life-world of the characters until it seems normal.' (149). 'Assumptions' is the watch-word here, and how vital and necessary it is to navigate towards a literature that functions as more than propaganda for what its writer/protagonist holds to be self-evident. A poetry of shifting meaning and logic, the sacred and the profane, high and low comedy crossing wires with high and low seriousness, no fixed point but a shared journey. This is not dissimilar to the celebration of contradiction we find in the history of the prose poem.

Its variousness notwithstanding, a common factor among prose poems *per se* might be that the form cannot help but draw attention to itself, cannot help but comment on its own debatable status. It is, in appearance alone, a statement on form, a provocation and a doubt: can we really call this a poem? What is it that makes it so? It is therefore natural that the prose poem is frequently characterised by numerous postmodern tropes along the lines of the relationship between the writer and the reader, which relationship is challenged, worried, rebuilt towards various artistically necessary – if occasionally repetitive – ends. In the novel it is the kind of self-referentiality whereby the author enters their own text. Generally speaking the poet is already in the poem, so the authorial intervention (and some popular examples would include the narrator of Martin Amis' *Money* running into a rather shambling writer named Martin Amis, or the narrator of part three of Paul Auster's *New York Trilogy* interviewing a slightly pompous writer named Paul Auster) is replaced by the unlikely cameo. This can be a literary or historical figure, out of place, played for laughs, or for self-consciousness, as the text immediately becomes a construct on the introduction of a dead or clearly non-existent or otherwise unlikely character, an openly acknow-ledged construct between poet and reader. This is not a radical technique in itself, and of course there are degrees of success in its application – one thinks of Joseph Brodsky's *taking pot-shots at the deities*[1] – it could easily come off as lazily absurd or completely inane, and avoiding this is as dependent on the subtlety of execution as the underlying intention. The figure must serve some purpose beyond the joke of their being out of place; the writer must assign them a role or an archetype, such as the trickster figure epitomised by Ted Hughes' *Crow*.

This is the role the character of Descartes plays in Corcoran's first published prose poem from *Robin Hood in the Dark Ages* (1985). 'Descartes' is a poem in three parts beginning with a four paragraph prose poem. It opens with an archly off-hand announcement, 'Descartes came into the poem' and develops a tone of high nonsense, the narrative refracted through synaesthesia, collage and non-sequitur. The location is key: Corcoran is careful not to say 'Descartes entered my house'; the place this Descartes has infiltrated is the narrator's poem itself. (*New and Selected* 190-1)

This simulacrum of Descartes claims to have cycled from Stockholm, via Times Square, and shorn of direct speech we are invited to ascribe dialogue to the narrator or Descartes himself: 'It is as I thought, the valve worked loose outside Paris', muttered over the ruined bicycle or a synonym for madness, the valve being that which regulates, controls. Descartes is not interested in the small details of the poet's life: 'couldn't give a toss for rounded edges like playing cards, a Roman resting place; a holloway, two on the way to work…' A holloway is a sunken lane, a road which has dropped below the land on either side, but it isn't clear whether 'two on the way to work' refers to two separate holloways or a nascent alcohol problem. The rounded edges / playing cards make a pleasing, decorative analogy, (albeit for an object which is itself occluded) and the Roman resting place hints at historical allusion, all of which combines into an approach to poetry (rejected in this poem): a confessional piece hinging on a pleasing visual analogy and/or antique anecdote, well made and enjoyable (whatever the matter of the confession).

This is upended by the trickster figure of Descartes, a hologram of Descartes who cannot think (and therefore isn't); he makes an incongruous house-guest for the narrator in his contemporary domestic setting: 'He did not like his new job; the way the chairs, the hi-fi and the fire lean into each other.' The philosopher Descartes, in his *First Meditations*, asserts the primacy of thought over objects:

> I have convinced myself that there is nothing in the world —
> no sky, no earth, no minds, no bodies. Doesn't it follow that I
> don't exist? No, surely I must exist if it's me who is convinced
> of something. But there is a deceiver, supremely powerful
> and cunning whose aim is to see that I am always deceived.
> But surely I exist, if I am deceived. Let him deceive me all he
> can, he will never make it the case that I am nothing while I
> think that I am something. Thus having fully weighed every
> consideration, I must finally conclude that the statement 'I am,
> I exist' must be true whenever I state it or mentally consider it.[2]

His influence on the poem's narrator is a revolution: 'He changed my life, hat polish for a start and envy in the dark.' The latter could be dismissed as absurd juxtaposition, the quotidian (albeit a dated, preening example of the quotidian) with the emotional abstract, but in-keeping with the prose poem's habit of taking an imaginative leap from one word or image to create its next movement, the hysterical description of the 'it' in the paragraph which follows refers to the aforementioned envy as much as the thrown fruit:

> When he was tired, his mind elsewhere, tossing coconuts at
> the poet's lawn, anywhere but here, Descartes would sit and
> doze and fill the house with it. Brown, hairy, large. A fistful of
> encased piss milk, remember no memory, the mind elsewhere.
> The violated child, courage turn us now next the light through
> the leaves, this path can be traced to the Wiltshire border.
> (*New and Selected* 190)

The paragraph has a parataxis / stop-making-sense quality, swerving without warning from the classically surrealist misplaced object (the coconuts in the English garden) and the creaturely analogy (envy as something brown, hairy and large gradually filling the house), coming to stand in for the head which remembers no memory, to the cut-up sentence: the detuned radio of 'courage turn us now next the light through leaves, this path can be traced to the Wiltshire border' which follows 'The violated child'. This clause – an abuse of innocence – is too strong to be a mere element of a collage; there is no sense that we are in the complete amorality of surrealism where shocking or comedic effects are attained through the insensible juxtaposition of incongruous elements.

However oblique, it suggests rather the origin of a trauma followed by aphasia, a world without meaning: a literalisation of the effects of abuse as opposed to a representation. One of the pleasures of Corcoran's dialectic tendency is that it allows forays into the openly confessional and, while in a more pedestrian writer this would involve the intentional fallacy of taking the lyric 'I' for the autobiographical 'I', Corcoran's approach deftly steps around this. So fourteen years later in 'The Literal Poem About My Father' (from *When Suzy Was*, in *New and Selected* 91) we can trust that title or not; as a reader I choose to, but it doesn't matter – Corcoran is de-centred in his poems such that we ought to take it just as seriously if we believe it to be him or a character inverting the elegy. 'An alcoholic given to violence; / a thief; an abuser of his children; / an arsonist who was finally sectioned: each term I secure for clarity.' We may think here of Theodore Adorno's position on the impossibility of lyric poetry after Auschwitz: a well-wrought metaphor for an act of violence is, nonetheless, a well-wrought metaphor, an aesthetic device deployed to produce pleasure in the reader and the system of entertainment is of a piece with the system which committed the act of violence in the first place.[3] This is, of course, contingent on one taking the only plausible definition of entertainment, i.e. it should not exclude all but levity and harmless distraction: to be provoked into thought, to be troubled by the visceral quality of an arresting image, even to *use* the term 'arresting image', is to be entertained, is to take pleasure. What we find in Corcoran's 'Descartes' is what we find when an alternative to the lyric mode is sought, which is to say *difficulty*, the surface effects of an attempt to do right by the material.

In the prose poem's final paragraph the tone becomes conciliatory, addressed to a second person, turning away from the titular philosopher: 'No, he would not take a walk, but that dip down to the brook is the boundary of the two villages. Yes, you can go there, that's mine down by the brook. The horses of this complex geometry are curious as you go.' (*New and Selected* 190) The second and the third parts of the poem are transfigured into verse, the second person replaced by companionship, female and then male, a resolve to 'turn the hard U /

in love…' implied through the details of a life shared: 'Linda's paintings dry'. The unnamed partner in part 3 concludes the sequence 'well I'm glad / you're pleased by something, walking / out of a C19 novel and upstairs at speed'; even the implied peevishness is an element of familiarity and is used to spark off a further (pleasurable for the writer and the reader) analogy in the narrator's mind: he belongs to the moral certainty and providence and virtue of a bygone structure/form. This is not necessarily a criticism. Perhaps an allegory: not just the consolation of philosophy, but its potential to transform, the examined life, the life of the mind, as the second poem concludes after a lacuna in its final line: 'these are the forces of victory'.

If this is the prose poem as extended, multi-layered meditation, a canvas on which to paint more complex, wordy and oblique stuff than the verse, we find the complete opposite in Corcoran's collection of the following year, *The Red and Yellow Book*. Here the prose poem beginning 'I was with my mother when she died…' (*New and Selected* 180) concerns the poet's mother's death after a protracted illness. An elegy in prose poem form, it also openly refers to an alcoholic father who has to be removed from the hospital ('drunk and talking about euthanasia'). It is the explanatory journal entry which gives the taut and fractured verse in the collection its emotional context, a companion piece to the truncated notation of 'the last poem'. It is a prose interlude, with complete sentences and a linear memoir narrative, and yet the sentences have a powerful cadence. After a recollection of his mother holding the glass of ginger beer she has requested herself, a detail only hinted at in the previous poem, the paragraph concludes: 'In the teeth of death a human act', its metric stress polishing the beauty of the thought.

The final paragraph employs a refrain, but immediately undercuts it with heart-breaking timing:

'I was with my mother when – after so long it seemed hurried'

Grammatically perfect without a comma out of place, Corcoran frequently excludes full stops at the end of stanzas or lines where that expressed is transient or part of a continuum. The two concluding lines are a heartfelt epitaph ('a gentle woman of great strength / she raised five children in love') while also mirroring the envoi of a haibun, the seventeenth-century Japanese prosimetric form where a paragraph (or more) of prose poetry is followed by two lines of syllabic verse. They interrupt the poet's meditation on death with finality, and if the lines barely scratch the surface of a real life, with its contradictions and infinite uncertainty, they are no less true. Perhaps not 'the forces of victory' in 'Descartes', but something solid, a conclusive, respectful and fitting statement – the consolation of ritual (among which we can count poetic form).

1989's *TCL* sees Corcoran's most substantial and complex use of the prose poem form in 'The Strange Visitor' (*New and Selected* 156-7); it is also his sincerest statement of intent, a manifesto in the mode of a parable. On the surface this takes the distorted folk-tale or narrative approach of the prose poem, a habit we see from such disparate sources as Oscar Wilde's decadent parodies and Ivan Turgenev's inverted morality tales. There is a clear reference to Baudelaire's 'The Useless Glazier' in Corcoran's first paragraph, the strange visitor of the title being a kind of travelling salesman who produces 'From inside a voluminous coat [...] glistening sheets of gold, lapis lazuli, malachite and realgar.' (156). 'The Useless Glazier' is one of Baudelaire's best known uses of the form and concerns the narrator deliberately smashing the wares of a hapless glass salesman, admonishing him that his duty is to 'make life more beautiful' (Baudelaire 57), a manner of note-to-self given the window-like shape of the prose poem, not to mention its contained 'snap-shot' content and the irascibly, needlessly cruel behaviour of the poet within that (indeed, one of Baudelaire's other better known prose poems is called 'Windows' and concerns the pomposity of the observational author).

Unlike the archly storybook tone of Baudelaire's narrators, Corcoran's poem begins *in medias res*: 'Soon after a stranger called on him.' That we do not know what the preceding events are places us in the uncertain territory of the prose poem as opposed to the novel or flash-fiction. Where Baudelaire's protagonist lapses instantly into violence, Corcoran's does quite the opposite here, listening to and learning from the visitor in spite of the initial gaudiness of the display: 'With a whiff of the stage magician more used to entertaining the infants of bank managers and pornographers the stranger set the colours in a waterfall...' What follows is a delightful, lyrical description of delightful, lyrical art (poetry, prose poetry, prose, etc.):

> making a cave of his room; each twist revealing visions of small places, street maps and lives running on in the fold and flutter

of their semaphore. A suspicion of trickery, combined with a
knowledge of English poetry, formed in his mind.
(*New and Selected* 156)

We can note that in describing said gaudiness the young Corcoran
allows the political underpinning of his work at this time to emerge
with bracing directness: the work performed by the visitor is presented
as entertainment, the target audience is children, and not just any
children, but the scions of economic/sexual exploitation, insulated not
just from the world but from the very actions their parents commit
to propagate that world and the insulation it affords them. In fact,
a caveat: when Corcoran writes 'The visitor made him understand a
story' at the end of the piece's opening paragraph, this is not to say
that the visitor has taught the protagonist a lesson (nor even that he
intended to). There follows a story-within-a-story, as big a mainstay of
postmodernist literature as the authorial intervention, complete with
an indented margin to make it textually clear that we are now in an
allegory the protagonist has concocted to illustrate the lesson he has
derived from the salesman.

This indented allegory pushes the voice further into folk-tale: the
opening sentence, 'A man came to feel that he did not fit well in his
body' could almost begin with *There was once* (a less confident writer
would almost certainly have used this formulation), and its content
verges on the magic-realist: a dictionary that repeatedly spontaneously
combusts and requires damping down before it will function again.
While a composer of lightly surreal sheets of attractive metal might be
happy with this telegraphed unease and absurdist tangent, Corcoran
juxtaposes it with the bleakest of settings, the block of flats a 'fortress
of a civic hell'. If the cultural lives of the children of privilege are
disastrously limited, this is nothing compared to that of the exploited
workforce. The playfully strange image of the dictionary turns towards
a profound social injustice,

> After damping down and reconstruction the frazzled lexicon
> would assume a nasty utilitarian aspect, usually with a beige
> interior that promoted murder by squalid husbands in at-
> home clothes. They hung about in doorways and bemoaned
> the strictures of subjective political action. (156)

If the 'beige interior' of an emotion brings to mind earlier synaesthesias, that which it brings about is openly disturbing, the 'squalid husband's' acts of abuse (here taken to their logical conclusion) *are* acts of 'subjective political action', brutality the manifest destiny of a blighted, reduced education, gruelling menial labour and poverty. There is no means of escape as the language and meaning itself is continually destroyed (or spontaneously combusts) and rebuilt in a yet grimmer state. We conclude in a sincere lament: 'The ill-fitting man wanted to know what had happened to him, what had happened to his people', then we drop back to the meta-narrative as if waking from a nightmare. We leave the protagonist passively 'waiting for the story to end'. He opens the curtains; the strange visitor isn't referred to again, 'The gloom of another nineteenth century dawn advanced and a persistent novelist lodged narrowly in his mind began to shave the former experience.' The inner novelist represents the prose impulse, or the impulse to what Fredman calls 'prose sense', the creation of which here involves a *shaving* of the experience down to 19th century realism, a mode as bleakly utilitarian as the industrial revolution it depicts, the complete overthrow of Breton's 'beloved imagination', the divorce of thought from a subjugating, mechanised reality. I am not interpreting Corcoran as a Surrealist – far from it – but I would nonetheless argue that he achieves the resolution of the states of dream and reality which Breton calls for so passionately, 'the superior reality of certain forms of previously neglected associations' (Breton 248), which associations remain neglected almost a century later. The 19th Century has a metonymic function in Corcoran's work (recall the voice at the end of 'Descartes'), but also a literal: we ought to have moved on.

But which is the trickery? Are we, in a self-effacing switch (and the prose poem is certainly the preeminent form of self-deprecation, of failure[4]) to take the strange visitor's attractive sheets of metal for Surrealist prose poems, or are they the television screens, the reductive narratives of mass entertainment? The protagonist's 'knowledge of English poetry' suggests a reactionary orthodoxy to resist. A more direct insight can be gleaned from another window-shaped piece: an untitled prose poem in Corcoran's 1990 collection *The Next Wave*. Bordered by a bold rectangular outline, the prose poem concretely resembles the window of the domicile it describes: 'I live above the shop. I see things. I hold that tone as darkness comes from the lighted window.' Here words from a receipt and fragments of political conviction are placed alongside scraps of pulp dialogue and lyric poetry, on equal dialectic terms, as if the reader were flicking through channels:

> Your ref. none/amount £22.50. These people are rich because others are poor. I think the sky is a cage without music. Inside a character says – take your hand off my gun you little fool
> (*New and Selected* 151)

The text of the poem itself is caged by its black border – suggesting a receipt, the oblong sheets of metal from 'The Strange Visitor', or the self-contained studio flat? – wherein the collaged lines invite us to appreciate their own ambiguity. 'I live above the shop. I see things' could be a flat statement of fact, but could equally be a hubristic declaration of perspective; the narrator sees things because he is outside of or above economic matters.[5] What follows becomes either an ironic comment on his own conviction (the things he sees aren't actually up to much – a transaction, a television show) or an illustration of his ability to see connections where others can't. The final mirror sentences of the poem are equally conversational, even casual, in tone: he watches the sunlight on the grey and brown rooftops and comments, 'I saw a picture like that once. It was called the invention of writing.' Images and carvings entitled or concerning the Invention of Writing customarily refer to ancient Sumerian tablets of cuneiform text (pictograms visually representing that which they stand for) dating back to 3000 BC and earlier. Their purpose was trade and commerce, economic record keeping; this is the purpose of writing, this is why it was invented and, the narrator 'above the shop' suggests, little has changed. The oblong border makes the prose poem a slab of cuneiform, and we are to read it as we would a priceless tablet thousands of years old, i.e. we do not treat it as the shopping list it literally is, we decipher it for its wider implications for the culture.

This metonymic use of 'language origin' symbolism can be traced throughout Corcoran's work, contemporaneous and of a piece with his use of myth and history. An untitled prose poem in *Lyric Lyric* begins with the poet at work, thinking: 'I could write through the table...' and the act of engraving is juxtaposed with the landscape the poet stays next to: 'Look at the sea, its immense rolling indifference, I love it.' (*New and Selected* 132) That love, declared as casually as one might pronounce upon a good meal, is also a kind of awe, encompassing fear

– via the observer's own mortality – as well as joy. That the register is incongruous with the sentiment – *we're all going to die; don't you love it?* – only makes the scene more immediate and authentic. It represents the moment of inspiration and creation and takes us to that moment rather than distilling it for its effect: a poetry of scrupulous honesty. Likewise, the interjections in this prose poem are literal interruptions: '—Are you alright down there Linda? Is the baby alright?' which act as a foil to the philosophy as well as the literal presence of the next generation. The last lines turn the poet's house into his tomb: 'Everything inside is mine, it took me years... All that stolen time, never to be returned. Then whoosh, the centre dysfunctions, an accident or failed organ. Everything gone. Look at the sea.' Here the poet is the home-maker: even in making a home we are curators, collecting and arranging symbols, trying to reify the impression we leave on the world.

To interpret the details as aleatory and the links or interruptions as arbitrary would be to overlook the intricacy and deliberation of the dialectic technique and to miss out on its fertile, infinitely readable possibilities. Duncan's analogy of a filmmaker is particularly apposite here: 'The composition is in frames, internally consistent and even plain; which are juxtaposed with frames of different axioms, different knowledge status, different silent rules' (Duncan 147). Silent rules which, even if we cannot articulate their axioms or means, we sense through their ends. The American authority on the prose poem, Stephen Fredman, refers to this sense as 'not-understanding',

> a positive experience available to translators, writers, readers, or anyone involved in a complex hermeneutic activity. Not-understanding of this sort is a pleasurable, relaxed, receptive state (what Ashbery calls the delicious sensation of drowning) in which a feeling of strangeness or mystery hints that certain ineffable thoughts or connections may be possible... The state of not-understanding is available any time we trust in a meaning beyond our present understanding, and it manifests as an aura around language. (Fredman 108)

Which latter is a figure of speech – it doesn't literally manifest at all – to evoke, as far as it is possible, the sense of magic or mystery one gets from a poem, or prose poem, working on them. Trust is central to this relationship and it's the quality I find hardest to instil in my own students.

The moment a poem tries to do more than directly communicate an entertaining moral drawn from the poet's experience, their collective tendency is to dismiss the author as a charlatan, obfuscating their lack of substance behind textual disruption. Words like 'pretentious' or 'random' are reached for as a defence mechanism and any notion of trust is pre-emptively withheld. *This is a fundamental lack of humility*, I shout, bashing my lectern. *You are directly participating in our country's cultural deforestation.* To return to Duncan, the two types of frame are combined 'so that both tilt sideways to reveal something much deeper, partially refuting both of them, and itself mysterious, to be uncovered in glimpses and by leaps of reason.' (147) As in our reckoning with any mystery, it is inevitable that we will get things wrong, leap in the dark, misinterpret the glimpses, but then this is poetry, not a cryptic crossword.

The reader's act of deciphering / positive not-understanding reoccurs with clarity in *When Suzy Was* (1999), a collection which sees Corcoran's most consistent use of the prose poem form throughout. 'The Book of Answers' recalls a literary-critical conversation with 'Lee' (Harwood). Here Corcoran uses the form to write plainly about not-understanding – 'reification as a type of behaviour in the moment of the poem.' (*New and Selected* 88) If reification – to treat an abstract concept as if it were concrete – is the worst vice of undergraduate poetry, it is also the highest ideal of the finest. This is a skeleton key to all of Corcoran's prose poems: that 'moment' is what he invites us as readers to participate in; this, after Adorno, is what makes poetry possible in the 21st century. The elements of travelogue poem 'The Roadside Shrine' (100) appear 'As if by arrangement', but what we are invited to read into is their equality. The 'plastic coke bottle' of oil to refuel the shrines lamp is as remarkable a detail as the Orthodox icons within the shrine which itself is likened to a broken television or 'a crane operated lucky dip machine.' These analogies resonate with their visual accuracy as well as their gently irreverent subtext. In the third and final poem of the sequence Corcoran gives us a deep insight into the purpose of icon painting ('to open a window in the sky') gleaned from Timothy Ware's book on the Orthodox Church (102). The purpose of religious devotional art is contrasted with the utilitarian road sign, the pure entertainment of the carnival game – but this is further juxtaposed with the history of the design of the coke bottle; just as the icons are cheap reproductions in tacky frames, the face of Christ reminding the poet of Robert Powell, who played Christ in Zeffirelli's mini-series; the coke bottle itself is 'a corruption of Samuelson's 1916 classic; / the figure dull and thickened out.' The comment on industrialised production, simulacrum and original speaks for itself. The images of both are faded by the sun, which gives the oil the effect of being permanently alight without burning down. But 'neither effect is proof of anything / but the great Spring day rising on Parnassos.' (102)

If that which is observed proves nothing, the notation takes on the aspect of a list, an objective record of events. American poet Michael Davidson took this to the extreme in his prose poems of the 1980s which comprise unadorned lists: 'At one point the idea of a list was a sort of ultimate autistic construct, because it would create the illusion of a random series that would relate immediately to my life.' But in trying to strip the minutiae of his life down to the barest details, Davidson discovered that he couldn't resist the narrative impulse, as if it were hard-wired into language itself,

> I began to realise that I wanted to tell stories; I wanted to describe events. And the problem, of course, occurred in the first few words: as I began to describe the event I was faced with my own language staring me back in the face. I simply couldn't describe. I found myself involved in the forms of mediation that were constantly coming up in front of me.
> (cited in Fredman 148)

The poet as mediator, go-between for the Oracle. A form of magical thinking we are instantly warned against in the same collection through Corcoran's prose poem, 'God is Not A Ventriloquist'. It begins with a formally characteristic self-referential move:

> I'd thought to make this book a version of the oracular process, to find out what is always there in the making of the poem; ambiguity, bounding like Koretas' goats across the high meadows of language in the Spring of the god's returning.
> (*New and Selected* 97)

Koretas is the name of a goatherd in a story by Diodorus (1st century BC). Koretas noticed that his goats began to bleat strangely when they approached a fissure in the land, which becomes the legendary 'vapour emitting chasm' whose vapours intoxicated the oracle at Delphi into becoming the mouthpiece of the gods. The goats' bounding becomes the bounding of creatures possessed (with language and its inherent ambiguity).[6] We can look back to Bashō here, whose collections of prose and haiku continually comment on their own success and failure, encompassing Bashō's own plans for the book in question: 'I'd thought to make this...' Corcoran goes further, reifying that self-consciousness as the central force, the impulse to create indivisible from that which is created: 'I see the ritual, in all its versions, as a blueprint for introspection at the centre of the world – the thought of it.' (97) That blueprint for introspection builds language. Corcoran invites us to 'imagine the enquiry as the unearthing of the poem', so that reading his work becomes a collaborative process, an excavation. In like manner, the prose poem can be seen as the marble block from which the poem is carved, an endeavour in which the reader participates. And perhaps in the best contemporary poetry, form – where we find form – is only the sinecure which creates the illusion of a finished sculpture. 'At what point, and by whom, the meaning was fixed is unclear.' As in Creeley's valuation, 'one can think of one's life as not worth remembering', or one can accept that this is all we have. Fragments shored against... To see through everything is to see nothing. Look at the sea.

NOTES

[1] The British poet Charles Bennett recalls Joseph Brodsky critiquing a poem in which the writer was mocking and contemporising an ancient myth. 'It was something along the lines of: *It is easy and simple to denigrate – but the really imaginative thing to do is re-celebrate* – the real trick is to re-energise the myth and make it powerful [and terrifying] in contemporary terms.' (Bennett, in correspondence).

[2] See Descartes, *Meditation II: On the Nature of the Human Mind, Which Is Better Known Than the Body.*

[3] Corcoran writes about Adorno in *Qiryat Sepher*, his collection of 1988 (Qiryat Sepher means 'city of the letter' and has to do with the origins of the Phoenician alphabet) in a poem called 'Adorno', which concerns a modern street scene, scantily clad young women, a vandalised statue, 'sassy pavements melt libidinous summer / terminal shop of slashed prices but no jobs.'

[4] In the sense that we laugh at the clown who deliberately sabotages his own act, having entered into an agreement with him that we will believe he means to perform the act sincerely.

[5] If the lines feel familiar they echo dialogue from a somewhat more ambitious television series than the one harvested for scraps within the poem. In the David Lynch series *Twin Peaks* the character Mike (or the one-armed-man) who exists halfway between the spirit- and the real-world talks of his time spent with ambiguous creatures who trade, quite literally, in human misery and suffering. 'We lived among the people. I think you say convenience store. We lived above it. I mean it like it is. Like it sounds.' This ethereal speech is later literalised by Lynch in a scene from the feature film *Twin Peaks: Fire Walk With Me*.

[6] See 'The Chasm at Delphi: A Modern Perspective' by Kristin M Heineman.

Works Cited

Baudelaire, Charles. *The Poems in Prose*. trans. Francis Scarfe. London: Anvil Press. 2002

Creeley, Robert. *Was That a Real Poem & Other Essays*. San Fransisco: Four Seasons Foundation. 1979

Danchev, Alex. *100 Artists' Manifestos*. London: Penguin. 2011

Davidson, Michael. in Fredman, Stephen. *Poet's Prose: The Crisis in American Verse*. Cambridge: Cambridge University Press. 1990

Descartes, Rene. *Meditations on First Philosophy*. Indianapolis: Hackett. 1993

Duncan, Andrew. *The Council of Heresy: A Primer of Poetry in a Balkanised Terrain*. Exeter: Shearsman. 2009.

Fredman, Stephen. *Poet's Prose: The Crisis in American Verse*. Cambridge: Cambridge University Press. 1990

Heineman, Kristin Marie. 'The chasm at Delphi: A modern perspective'. Refereed paper from the *31st Conference of the Australasian Society for Classical Studies*. Perth, WA. 2010.

Personal Reflection – 'This Interior Light'

Alicia Stubbersfield

Kelvin Corcoran is one of the rare poets who appeals to those on opposing sides of the debate on poetics. We see his capacity for intensely humane and personal reflection in his description of his father when he

> came off his bike, cracked his head, staggered home delirious and collapsed through the door. She tried to lift him up, saw the blood, shrieked and dropped him smack down on the flagstones. Later, the doctor, discretely dismounted, asked if she'd tried to kill him – I'd understand Mrs Corcoran but all the same, best not.
>
> (*Hotel Shadow* 67)

This extract from the prose poem *Hearing Mishearing Doug Oliver* is as direct and personal as anything Sharon Olds might write – and more infused with a welcome black humour. Contrast that with his capacity to conjure the reality of place while he draws on myth and literature in *My Journey to Euripides*,

> I went south in the oven of summer
> around the bare finger of land for Matepan,
> those days the sea filled my mind
> and Laconia filled my mouth.
>
> (*Backward* 77)

The opening of this stanza is reminiscent of *The Waste Land* but, as with all of Kelvin's poetry, the learning is worn lightly and we respond to the sparse clarity of the language which creates heat and emptiness. The form is quite different from the quotation from *Hearing Mishearing Doug Oliver* but no less evocative.

Kelvin has plenty of what my family refers to as *the Irish genes* – which means, for us, a tendency towards dissolute behaviour and sentimentality. He manages that perfect trick of taking us right up to the edge of the sentimental so that we are deeply moved, not just by his many evocative love poems but also by a poem such as 'MacSweeney'

(*New and Selected* 34), which honours the memory and work of the poet Barry MacSweeney, who died tragically young in 2000. The poem opens with the conventional enough 'Here's a jar of honey for you;' but moves through references to the blue of borage, inferred blue of 'the lapis miners', the 'pearls' of MacSweeney's poem 'Pearl' (but also giving us wisdom, semen, even, perhaps, the mixed blessing of Steinbeck's *The Pearl*) and back to the 'bright blue flowers you knew'. The intensity of the blue conjures not only the music of the Blues, Lawrence's *Bavarian Gentians*, our reaction to MacSweeney's poetry (and to Kelvin's as well). And, the pure blue of Greece is there too.

When I first met him he was Deputy Head at a large Cheltenham comprehensive school and, despite his responsible job, he managed to exude an air of recklessness. No-one was quite sure what he might do next and there were certain members of the English Department who thought he was capable of almost anything and treated him warily. A reputation he liked to court! He and I enjoyed being the delinquent subculture in meetings, devising games to keep ourselves entertained, such as competing to name the most stumps in literature: Candy in *Of Mice and Men* started off the list. I think Kelvin won.

His students loved him and still do. When he was ill I told a student from the school who was then studying Creative Writing with me. Immediately he contacted all the other people who had been in the sixth-form group Kelvin taught and they rallied round. The genuine worry about their former teacher and the desire to contact him was a delight, and a testimony to the relationship Kelvin had with his students. The sixth form loved the challenge of his classes, the academic rigour and the way he gave them no quarter: essays had to be handed in on time and discussion was expected to be informed. After listening to the sixth-form group Kelvin and I shared comparing Hamlet's *To be or not to be* soliloquy with Adam's speech after the Fall from *Paradise Lost*, a group of Inspectors said they had never heard anything so erudite at that level. These comprehensive-school students knew he wanted them to succeed, but it wasn't just the ambitious and successful who benefited from Kelvin's teaching. He often was given the most difficult classes who thrived because they had fun as well as being nurtured into making the most of their talents. Kelvin once said to me that they had no idea how close his own experience had been to the difficult lives they were living, 'Each night we breathed a drunk's mythology.' ('The Literal Poem About My Father', *New and Selected* 91). There aren't many teachers who choose to remember their own experiences and empathise with those troublesome students who give everyone a hard time. They tended not to give Kelvin a hard time, however, as he has that ability to be kind, sympathetic, fun and strict. Characteristics which add up to respect.

Respect is a maligned word in contemporary culture. Overused and not usually earned. I felt really lucky when I arrived in the same department as Kelvin, not just because of the unlikely situation that I would find myself in an English department with another poet, but because I became friends with a brilliant poet and a brilliant teacher. Someone who earned respect.

That also much-maligned word, love, suffuses his work. Love for people and places. His love for Melanie is celebrated, as is her love for him, in the poem 'A Season Below Ground',

> I think this interior light travels with us,
> your face looking forward as the music wanders
> the dark enfolding road we leave behind.
> (*Hotel Shadow* 64)

The down-to-earth reference to the car's 'interior light' allows us to engage with this personal, optimistic and yet yearningly romantic image and is typical of Kelvin.

His daughters are surrounded by his love, and are often mentioned in the poems, sometimes almost as an aside 'My girls growing up for instance.' ('MacSweeney' *New and Selected* 34). His friends bask in it. An email from 'Kelvino' will be witty, entertaining and loving – he is able to gather us up and make us feel better. He loves music and loves to share music with friends, whether at home or at gigs. That sharing might mean hurtling along the motorway at a hundred miles an hour, Kelvin driving while rummaging about for the absolutely essential CD you MUST hear RIGHT at that moment. You, white-knuckled in the passenger seat, as he explains that it's ok because if the car rolls it'll be fine because of how it's constructed. I remember coming back with Lee Harwood from a reading in Abergavenny and Kelvin driving through Welsh rain, along winding Welsh lanes in the absolute and, frankly terrifying, dark.

Kelvin's evocation of Greece is both personal and mythical. His lovely sequence 'Madeleine's Letter to Bunting' (*Hotel Shadow* 78-

82) gives us so much of what I'm talking about: the creation of a personal and mythical Greece, a political context, personal experience and the marvellous addressing of a daughter by a father 'Madeleine, my unabashed girl'. The short sequence describes Kelvin receiving Madeleine's poem when he can 'see the red hibiscus in the darkness' so that we are already inhabiting an exotic and almost mythical world as much 'in amazement' as he is. We accompany the poet while he gardens, and recalls how he 'planted songlines, a lemon tree, shrubs' – the abstract and evocative 'songlines' juxtaposed with the prosaic 'shrubs'. He comically climbs a eucalyptus and 'grasped the springy boughs in my useless arms.' The sequence is linear in that it is divided into Day 1 to Day 7 but the content ranges backwards and forwards – a Cubist view of a week with reality 'Five cats and a dog came to be fed' next to 'Dionysus has been sighted // all along this coast..' and 'We could launch the ship of lights ...and sail south... candid islands of lyric and rock and sky...', infused with Kelvin's thoughts about his daughter, Madeleine, whom he addresses, placing her with the French feminists as she already has 'the trick of writing from the body.'

The celebratory nature of all these elements is Kelvin. Kelvin the poet, teacher, partner, father and friend. It has been hard to write these 'personal reflections' for two reasons: firstly it's difficult to make it clear that he's still very much alive when 'reflecting' and secondly because re-reading poems and re-reading the dedication *Alicia Come Back* in my copy of *Backward Turning Sea,* after I had started work in Liverpool, makes me cry. In a good way, of course. In that way that the best writing and the best friendship moves us, because we are challenged and comforted, discomforted and recognised in equal measure. I admire Kelvin's poetry enormously because of his ability to be both erudite and personal, 'Only poetry can do this / from an island invaded / by the world...' ('Biography 2', *Hotel Shadow* 91) – his poetry is 'invaded by the world' and rooted in it, while expanding outwards to take in the literary, the mythic and all that our imaginations can draw from. I admire the man for the same reasons. In his presence you are simultaneously rooted in reality and inhabiting an absurd and imagined world. And also because I can rely on him to let me know which band I should be listening to next, then tell me something inappropriate to make me laugh.

FROM *GLENN GOULD AND EVERYTHING*

KELVIN CORCORAN

Along Commercial Street at homing time,
the air sits a certain way in November light;
at the dance school door she said to her daughter
– Oh well you've remembered that then?

– Yes I did, it would be good, don't you think?
and the words hover on the air eternal;
above the grey circuit of the tilting world,
raise my flag here, unfurled with the turning leaves.

The music clattered down the stairs and out the door,
she released her mother's hand and stepped up to tap.

*

He plays Byrd's Sixth Pavan and Galliard
and the winter trees seem to move accordingly,
spare transparent leaves of unremembered green
propose a season of satellites and backlit thought.

There's nothing to see here, just the earth turning
through an interval sustained, though I think I hear
the king shall reign for ever and ever, sense soon
returns and Byrd's bass line like the world breathing.

Sunlight steps up from the floor at the window
and I see everything come in and begin again.

*

We're so inland I think my eyes change colour
sea shanties go unrecorded in the local cults,
only the sky whispers maritime, cathedral blue
for the circling beasts over fields of mud.

After a low in the South West approaches
the country shrinks and the money migrates,
you can imagine the spineless tribe in charge,
telling lies about the poor and their care.

The weather is not a sign of the human condition
but attention to it is one way to let everything in.

                    *

        From Year Zero to play the piano
        he sat on the chair his father made,
        eyes level with the keys suspended
        his hands like birds descending.

        Guerrero's technique and the folding chair
        hovering 14 inches off the ground, no brakes;
        his hands rise and fall and run thinking
        to climb the black and white ladder of sound.

                    *

At night the dead knock on the words,
they come in from the street and line up
with their black mouths open, they tap tap,
on the empty heart of the poetry of the world.

The struts and curves wear and break, case obscured
the breath leaks out of them across the table.

A dark inheritance, that tap tap, then nothing,
a voice about the house barely heard
the other side of the wall, at the next door,
all purpose fails in the senseless dust it stirs.

                    *

        Glenn place the fingers of your right hand
        over the fingers of the left, good, now, tap tap.

Can you feel the exact pressure required?
Tap tap: that clarity calibrates the singing world.

*

He sets out to work with object in mind,
the shadow ace in layers, slight at this hour;
one sound answers another in calm geometry
and the landscape's there, with or without us.

At this point Apollo takes flight again
and the idea of music invades the world.

It says what we think we have we don't have;
the thought of a voice singing behind the door
discloses at last the shape of it all,
before we spoke against the wordless surface.

*

Is that ghost singing behind the music?
A faint responder in the great profusion,
from Lake Simcoe across the whole world
humming the safe passage in deep ocean.

Subject to the advance of a cerebral embolism
cell by cell the brain closes, a raging fire
he knew and let go of knowing in one move,
walked across the room and opened the door.

The sky pours backwards in bloody darkness,
the living medium of all that music gone;
and if the hand is part of the mind
it rose up and stopped and he let go.

*

There are those voices which travel
along the airways above the street,

one to another making the marvel
out of the slow evolution of speech.

Who placed these words in my mouth?
What shall we eat when we get home?
Turn around three times, hold steady
and tune the truth to everything.

Open the door, a second door of light
lies on the steps we climb to the lit world.

*

By train from Berlin to Leipzig on time
sky and flat fields, the first green of Spring,
there must be a name for this exact colour
a stand of birch surrounds the shining water.

Through Südkreuz and Wittenberg
listening to Glenn Gould turn the crank
of Herr Bach's magical banjo;
how would he have travelled here?

Wig flapping bird-like on a horse,
aboard a coach or roaring in a sidecar?
The horse runs on and the heart will not stop,
the music pours out miraculous.

*

Three birds at distance aligned
lifting in a south west sky
examine the quality of experience,
then two, then the light running.

Layered vision in place where late
the low grey curtain falls.

Contrapunctus the faithless choir,
sparrows blackbirds risk their arm,
flit the garden as the weather beats out
bare hymns of us men and women.

> *

> That the world may be an orderly pleasure
> rendered so by the architect of sound
> even the spaces and intervals charged.

> Singing the Goldberg to the waking birds
> Herr Bach and Glenn take their morning walk
> arm in arm around the St Thomas Kirche.

> In the moment of human invention
> a language immaculate and unambiguous
> fills the innocent streets of Leipzig.

> *

The chart's littered with symbols,
an asset floated here, a sell-out there;
expect a low front from the west,
starry signs for a prince views a food bank.

There once was a mythology of weather
but meteorology ruined it,
let brute cause out of the bag in the sky
and we had to be taught humility again.

Schematic rain rains on the just and unjust alike
distributed unevenly, an unkind music in the air.

> *

> 30th Street Studio Manhattan
> Dear Mr Gould Dear Mr Davis
> deep in the wood panel

resonance under a kind of
blue and Goldberg sky.

The child plays one note only
leans in to listen diminuendo
away from home a dark wood
the world a closing silence
and again one note, listen.

'Producing everything from one thing.'
In the heart of knowing, not knowing,
architectonic passing sound we are
music in the mind compresent;
everything from one thing, for delight.

                    *

Along Commercial Street at homing time
he plays Byrd's Sixth Pavan and Galliard,
we're so inland my eyes change colour
from playing the piano since Year Zero.

At night the dead knock on the words,
place the fingers of your right hand
over the left to free the object in mind,
that ghost singing behind the music.

There are those voices which travel
on time by train from Berlin to Leipzig,
three birds at distance aligned.

That the world may be an orderly pleasure
the chart's littered with its symbols,
everything from one thing for delight.

ACKNOWLEDGEMENTS

Some of the poems published here from *Glenn Gould and Everything* have been previously published in *Painted, Spoken* magazine; thanks to Richard Price.

The editor would like to gratefully thank the essayists in this book for providing so freely of their time. I would also like to express my deep thanks to Kelvin for his patience, cooperation and above all his thoughtful and energetic collaboration in the making of this book. My acknowledgements are due to the University of Exeter for providing the time and resources to develop and complete this work. In particular, thanks are due to the HASS Strategy for a small grant in the Medical Humanities, which has allowed me to research the medical essay herein, along with other forthcoming works on medicine and poetry.

Notes on Contributors

Martin Anderson is a visiting Professorial Lecturer in English and Comparative Literature at the University of the Philippines, Diliman. His books include *Snow: Selected Poems 1981-2011*, *The Hoplite Journals* and *The Lower Reaches* (all from Shearsman Books).

Zoë Brigley Thompson has published two collections of poetry, *The Secret* (2007) and *Conquest* (2012), both from Bloodaxe Books, and both Poetry Book Society Recommendations. She is the editor of a collection of essays, *Feminism, Literature and Rape Narratives* (Routledge 2010).

Andy Brown is a Senior Lecturer at Exeter University. His latest book was *The Fool and the Physician* (Salt Publishing). A new collection, *Exurbia*, is forthcoming from Worple Press. He is co-editing *A Body of Work: poetry and medical writing* for Bloomsbury. www.andybrownpoetry.blogspot.co.uk

Ian Davidson's recent publications are *Partly in Riga* (Shearsman Books 2010), *Radical Spaces of Poetry* (Palgrave 2010) and *Into Thick Hair* (Wild Honey 2010). He is Professor of Modern and Contemporary Literature at Northumbria University.

John Hall is a poet, a Professor of Performance Writing, and an essayist. *Keepsache*, a second *Selected Poems*, appeared in 2013 (etruscan books), as did a two-volume collection of essays (Shearsman Books). www.johnhallpoet.org.uk

Lee Harwood's recent books are *Collected Poems* (2004), *Selected Poems* (2008) and a series of interviews with Kelvin Corcoran, *Not the Full Story* (2008)— all from Shearsman Books. A new collection of poems, *The Orchid Boat*, is forthcoming from Enitharmon.

David Herd is Professor of Modern Literature at the University of Kent. His most recent collection of poetry, *All Just*, was published by Carcanet Press in 2012.

Luke Kennard is the author of four collections of poetry and a novella. His latest collection is *A Lost Expression* (Salt Publishing 2012). He lectures at the University of Birmingham.

Kat Peddie is reading for her PhD at the University of Kent. She has published in various magazines and reviewed for *The Shearsman Review* and the *Journal of British and Irish Innovative Poetry*. She co-edits ZONE magazine. www.zonepoetrymagazine.com

Peter Riley lives in retirement in Hebden Bridge, having been a teacher, bookseller, and a few other things. He is the author of fifteen books of poetry, and some of prose concerning travel and music. His most recent book is *The Glacial Stairway* (Carcanet Press 2011).

Jos Smith is a researcher and writer with a focussed interest in contemporary literature of landscape and place. He is currently a postdoctoral research fellow of the British Academy, at Exeter University, writing a history of the environmental arts charity, Common Ground.

Simon Smith's fifth full-length collection of poems is *11781 W. Sunset Boulevard* (Shearsman Books 2014). In 2009 he was awarded a Hawthornden Fellowship. He works as a Senior Lecturer in Creative Writing at the University of Kent.

Alicia Stubbersfield lectures in Creative Writing at Liverpool John Moores University. Her fourth collection of poetry *The Yellow Table* (Pindrop Press) was published in 2013.

Scott Thurston lectures in English and Creative Writing at Salford University. His latest book is *Reverses Heart's Reassembly* (Veer Books 2011). He co-edits the *Journal of British and Irish Innovative Poetry* and co-organises *The Other Room* reading series in Manchester.

Publications by Kelvin Corcoran

Robin Hood in the Dark Ages (1985). London: Permanent Press, foreword
    Tom Raworth.
The Red and Yellow Book (1986). London: Textures.
Qiryat Sepher (1988). Newcastle: Galloping Dog.
TCL (1989). Durham: Pig Press, afterword Lee Harwood.
The Next Wave (1990). London: North and South, afterword George Evans.
'Remember Remember' (1991). Cambridge: Poetical Histories.
Lyric Lyric (1993) London: Reality Street, afterword Rosmarie Waldrop.
'Saturday Night in the Bardo' (1996) Sheffield: West House Books.
Melanie's Book (1996). Sheffield: West House Books, afterword Iain Sinclair.
'The Name Apollo' (1997). Sheffield: West House Books.
When Suzy Was (1999). Kentisbeare: Shearsman Books, afterword Roy Fisher.
Your Thinking Tracts or Nations (2001). Sheffield: West House Books.
New and Selected Poems (2004). Exeter: Shearsman Books.
'Helen Mania' (2004). Cambridge: Poetical Histories 61.
Roger Hilton's Sugar (2005). Nottingham: Leafe Press.
'Xenophanes of Colophon' (2007). Sheffield: West House Books.
Backward Turning Sea (2008). Exeter: Shearsman Books.
What Hit Them (2008). Hunstanton: Oystercatcher.
Lee Harwood: Not the Full Story – Six Interviews (2008). Exeter: Shearsman.
'On The Xenophone Label' (2009). Sheffield: Longbarrow Press.
'Madeleine's Letter to Bunting' (2009). Sheffield: Longbarrow Press.
Hotel Shadow (2010). Exeter: Shearsman Books.
Words Through A Hole Where Once There Was A Chimpanzee's Face (2011).
    Sheffield: Longbarrow Press.
For the Greek Spring (2013). Bristol: Shearsman Books.

Inclusion in Anthologies
the new british poetry (1988). Gillian Allnutt, Fred D'Aguiar, Ken Edwards,
    Eric Mottram (eds.). London: Paladin.
Assemblage (1990). Paul Currah (ed.) Essex: Essex University.
Floating Capital: New Poets From London (1991). Adrian Clarke and Robert
    Sheppard (eds.) Connecticut: Potes and Poets Press.
Cambridge Conference of Contemporary Poetry (1991/1996). Cambridge.
Poets on Writing (1992). Denise Riley (ed). London: Macmillan.
Prospect Into Breath: Interviews With North and South Writers (1992). Peterjon
    Skelt (ed). Twickenham and Wakefield: North and South.
Exact Change Yearbook (1995) Manchester: Carcanet/Exact Change.
Conductors of Chaos (1996). London: Picador.
Danse Macabre (1997). David Annwn (ed.) Sheffield: West House Books.
Sneak's Noise: Poems for R.F. Langley (1998). Cambridge: Poetical Histories.

Other: British and Irish Poetry Since 1970 (1999) Richard Caddel and Peter Quartermain (eds.). Connecticut: Wesleyan University Press.

April Eye: Poems for Peter Riley (2000). Peter Hughes (ed.) Cambridge: Infernal Methods.

A Meeting for Douglas Oliver (2002). Peter Riley and Wendy Mulford (eds.) Cambridge: Infernal Methods/Street Editions/Poetical Histories.

Onsets (2004). Nate Dorward (ed.) Willowdale, Ont.: The Gig.

For Tom and Val (2004). Bill Corbett (ed.) Boston: Pressed Wafer.

Don't Start Me Talking: Interviews with Contemporary Poets (2006). Tim Allen and Andrew Duncan (eds.) Cambridge: Salt Publishing.

The Reality Street Book of the Sonnet (2008). Jeff Hilson (ed.) London: Reality Street Editions.

Websites

Archive of the Now	http://www.archiveofthenow.org
Ahahdada Books	http://www.ahadadabooks.com
Leafe Press/Litter	http://www.leafepress.com
Great Works	http://www.greatworks.org.uk
Shearsman Books	http://www.shearsman.com/pages/books/authors/corcoranA.html
Jacket	http://jacketmagazine.com
Longbarrow Press	http://longbarrowpress.com

www.ingramcontent.com/pod-product-compliance
Lightning Source LLC
Chambersburg PA
CBHW060347030726
47497CB00003B/632